THE MYSTERY OF THE KINGDOM OF GOD ON EARTH

OGHENETHOJA UMUTEME

THE MYSTERY OF THE KINGDOM OF GOD ON EARTH

MEMOIRS

Cirencester

Published by Memoirs

MEMOIRS
PUBLISHING

Memoirs Books
1A The Wool Market, Cirencester, Gloucestershire, GL7 2PR
info@memoirsbooks.co.uk | www.memoirspublishing.com

The Mystery of the Kingdom of God on earth (c)Oghenethoja Umuteme,
First published in England, 2014

ISBN 978-1-909874-69-5

Unless otherwise indicated, Bible quotations are taken from the King James Version. Scripture quotations marked with ESV, are taken from The Holy Bible, English Standard Version® (ESV®)_Copyright © 2001 by Crossway, a publishing ministry of Good News Publishers. All rights reserved.

All rights reserved. No part of this book shall be reproduced or transmitted in any form or by any means, electronic or mechanical, including photocopying, recording, or any information storage and retrieval system, without permission in writing from the copyright owner.

Address all enquiries to the publisher; Restoration Media House Limited
+234-8101700665, +2348076190064,
Email: rmhltd.info@gmail.com

Although the author and publisher have made every effort to ensure that the information in this book was correct when going to press, we do not assume and hereby disclaim any liability to any party for any loss, damage, or disruption caused by errors or omissions, whether such errors or omissions result from negligence, accident, or any other cause.
The views expressed in this book are purely the author's.

Printed in England

SPIRITUAL CAUTION

If you have not received the Holy Spirit, and desire the deep things of the Spirit, you will not understand this book – therefore it is needless to continue from here. But you can right that now by asking for the Lord to give you the Spirit that would enable you to understand all that is revealed here. I encourage you to be steadfast in your service and worship of the Lord throughout the period you will read and study this book. This is not a book you should read intermittently. It is a book that is highly recommended during a fasting and praying period, so that the Kingdom will reveal itself to you. Shalom!

DEDICATION

Kadosh, Kadosh, Kadosh

Yeshua, Ha Mashiach, HaKadosh

Adonai Maccaddeshem

Eloah, HaKadosh Maccaddeshem

Hakadosh, barukh hu

Ha Mashiach Yeshua, HaPalat

Ha Hoshea

Yeshua –

Ha go El

Ha Moshel

Moshia Ha Olam

Ha Amen

Hadavar Elohim

Chokhmat – Elohim

CONTENTS

	Prologue	
Chapter 1	The Origin of Kingdoms	Page 1
Chapter 2	The Promise of a Kingdom	Page 41
Chapter 3	The Kingdom Wars	Page 106
Chapter 4	The Kingdom of God on Earth	Page 174
Chapter 5	The Purpose of the Kingdom	Page 206
Chapter 6	Building Kingdom Relationships	Page 221
Chapter 7	Operations of the Kingdom	Page 242
Chapter 8	Prosperity in the Kingdom	Page 273
Chapter 9	Developing Kingdom Character	Page 300
Chapter 10	Allegiance to the Kingdom	Page 320
Chapter 11	The visit of the King of kings	Page 334
Chapter 12	Enlarging the Kingdom	Page 357
Chapter 13	Losing the Kingdom	Page 405
Chapter 14	Countdown to Judgement Day	Page 422
	Epilogue	Page 489

PROLOGUE

Some time in 2006, a young man walked into my office and gazed at me. He asked, 'who are you? I saw you this night, ministering in our church to such a large crowd, that when my Bishop came in, after he had been delayed by a flight schedule, no one was willing to let him speak as we were all engrossed with your teaching.' A woman came with her husband, one early morning – looking at me as though she was afraid, and I could hear her husband whispering to her – 'tell him what you saw.' When she finally opened up, she said, 'I saw you ministering to a crowd, and I heard a voice saying that this is what you have been called to do.'

I smiled and thank them. Revelations upon revelations – many see me in their night visions helping them out of their predicaments. Many saw me teaching them the word of God. The Lord was revealing what He has planted into me to those who have the eyes to see, and were closed to me. A woman came and said – 'I saw you this night and all the pastors were gathered around you and you were teaching them.' Yet, another would come, saying – 'this night I saw you giving communion to angels, and someone standing by your side whose face no one could look into.' I was driving with my wife one morning, and we came to a police checkpoint – the police looked at me and asked, 'who are you?' and I answered 'a citizen of this country, and I am an engineer with an oil and gas firm.' He shook his head and said, 'you are a servant of God', then said I should drive on. My wife looked at me and said – 'you are hiding, you had better answer so that we would have peace, things haven't been easy for some time now.'

Incidents happened dramatically, and I was really afraid to answer the call because of what I felt people would say, especially those who knew my past worldly life. I was involved in car accidents and I would come out unhurt. I was on my own walking down a road one afternoon when I was knocked down by a motorbike and in that dying state, I asked God to strengthen me, and I received strength – I stood up and was taken to the hospital. There were several other instances of being rushed to the hospital for ailments that were difficult for me to understand, until I knew all these were a forceful means to make me answer the call of God.

In a dream some time on the 20th of August 2007, I heard a voice – 'I come quickly to apportion unto every man the reward of their service.' Then, as I gazed into the sky in that dream I saw a hand from heaven with a sickle stretched out of the clouds towards the earth. I was frightened because I know that a sickle is an agricultural implement used for harvesting, and especially, when I see what is happening in the house of God today – Revelation 14:14-16. This implies that the Lord is ready for the harvest of His faithful Saints and the righteous out of this crooked world. At about 9am on the 5th of August 2013, I heard a voice, 'Get prepared for the harvest.'

In yet another dream in early 2008, I saw myself moving from one home to the other, pleading with parents to send their children to be enrolled freely in the Lord's school of ministry, where they would be trained and learn about the ways of the Kingdom of God. This was a call to train labourers for the work of mission. This was necessary, going by the events that are happening these days where we have more God haters than those who sincerely love Him. There is already a high level of immorality, crime, pastors preaching and teaching falsehood, etc.

These incidents kept me thinking for days. Then in another dream around August 2008, I saw a very tall, isolated multi-storey building by a sea coast, in a serene and beautiful environment, yet the residents were living in darkness, and a voice said – 'give them light.' I searched everywhere for a source of power within the neighbourhood, but I couldn't find any. It was when I pondered over this that I heard the word – 'You are the Pastors' Pastor.' This also frightened me because I had no qualification to pastor anybody yet, and not to talk of becoming one who would pastor other pastors.

In yet another revelation, I was given a piece of galvanized steel rod, about a foot long, to bend. I tried to no avail, and could not bend it – then I heard, 'my statutes couldn't be bent by any human wisdom.' This was a call to teach sound doctrine, just as the Lord will speak to Saul - Acts 9:5: *... it is hard for thee to kick against the pricks.* Yet I had no clue of what the Lord wanted from me. And later I started seeing servants of

God from all over the world appearing to me in a dream and some would drop their phone numbers for me to call them whenever I needed them. Some would come to me for counselling. There was a day, I just came from the office, and I decided to lie on my bed, just then I saw myself caught up into the clouds. It was so real that I felt the cold of the cloud rushing across my body. I was floating, conscious, yet afraid an airplane would crush me. While there, I heard myself calling out to some servants of God, as if in search for their whereabouts. When I had returned back to my bed, I heard a voice – 'what did you see?' Frightened, I said, 'nothing,' and the voice said – 'your eyes are not yet opened, surrounding you were a multitude of Angels, who ensured that you were returned safely to earth. I am leaving you now, but will come back in March 2012.' Then I was left alone. I wondered what was happening to me. Then, again, on the 3rd of December 2011, I saw myself in a courtroom. People were being judged – all the youths that came into the courtroom were sentenced to eternal darkness. As I stood in amazement, looking at the golden lights that filled the room, the judge, whose face I could not look into, bent His head down as many people were being sent into the darkness. Later I was told to leave because I was not supposed to be there, and I found myself landing in a hall with plenty of lights. Then I woke up to the physical.

Where were all these leading me? Now I understand. This book will explain why later.

It all started some 2000 years ago, when the power and the wisdom of God left the throne of God in heaven to minister to the hearts of men; teaching them the ways of the Kingdom of God in heaven, and filling their hearts with the songs of the Angels of God in heaven, and ever since then, the presence of God is here on Earth. This is the premise of which I write this book.

Prior to my answering this call of God, the Lord had revealed to me in several dreams, as recounted earlier, that people are under demonic manipulation. I heard a voice sometime in March 2014 – 'I hate the manipulation and hypnotization of souls.' This implies that in our prayers we often end up sending manipulating and hypnotizing spirits to seduce souls of unsuspecting people, so that they can give us what we demand from them. God loves free will giving.

It was in a night vision, on the 26th of May 2012, that

I heard a voice echoing from a very far distance, and gradually the voice drew nearer and nearer, with the same words repeatedly until I woke up in fright: *Who will go before me like Moses and Elijah did, to tell this generation their sins so that they would repent?* Was I going the same way as others that the Lord was now looking for someone else to do His work? I wondered about this several times, until the 23rd day in November 2013, when I knelt down and prayed that the Lord should use me, and give me the same anointing upon Moses and Elijah that made them to confront evil practices in the land.

This book, however, was difficult for me to title, but as I wrote the last chapters, it dawned on me that I was writing a very long essay on the subject of the Kingdom of God on earth, hence the book's title: *The Mystery of the Kingdom of God on Earth.* The facts in this book are justified and have been proven to be ideal references for all those who want to trace their way back to the Lord, with several Bible verses, both from the New Testament as well as the Old Testament scriptures. The Rhema revelations were also given a special place.

What does this book contain? Well let's start off by saying that it lays down what man's duty is to God here on earth. If that were the case, would it now be as voluminous as this? Well, people understand things in different ways, and for spiritual discourse that has to do with the faith and conscience of the people, one has to lay down the points as morally and spiritually convincingly as possible. As one reads with an open heart, one will come to understand what the Kingdom of God means to Him and the writers of the Bible, and one may also begin to see the lapses in what we hear and do read, as the practice of the Christian faith. In the course of my observation, I have come to see that while many servants of God wish to win souls into their massive cathedrals, they have in most cases affected the plausibility of the people's belief in God. Those who grew up in homes of want and deprivation have held the preaching of wealth for wealth seekers. Others, who have had spiritual attacks while growing up in the hands of witches and wizards, have taken to spiritual warfare as the ensign of the Kingdom of God. Many who studied and have acquired various higher degrees have, like the Chaldeans and magicians of old, tried to win the hearts of their fellow elite, and as such have twisted the scriptures to woo them into their church, and, of course, also paddled their boat into the deep sea, for a bigger catch. Ironically enough, these bigger catches would not want to be ordered to repent every Sunday, so they have to become pastors too who would oversee their own branches, where they have their types, and then they would pervert the word of the Lord. They too got away with their hearts' desire as servants of God quickly granted them their disguised request, and they with their cohorts are now offering polluted bread on the altar of the Lord. Some see the need for marketers, who would sell their ill-informed books, or who would become the immediate market for their books, and so took to the streets to gather those who have decided that they would only serve the Lord when He bent to their standard, and have wooed them into their churches, in their unrepentant form, bending scripture standards to allow them to stay as their congregation members. These are used as seductive agents to get rich and promising society aristocrats to donate their money to support their purportedly claimed 'work of God.' And in these churches sexual immorality is on the increase. Still others see the church as taking their tithes and offerings, and as such they have decided to own churches where they would preach the gospel with poor or no spiritual understanding, and many unsuspecting worshippers have also been led astray by their act. Still all we see in many circles are people who have made up their mind to cry louder and louder, in their over-popularised all night wait on the Lord, alas! if one day, the Lord would meet them at the point of their needs - they have the doctrine of NRNS - No Retreat No Surrender - or PUSH - Pray Until Something Happens. And many of these prayers have been answered by the devil. A word of advice from the Bible says – 2 Timothy 2:4,5: *No man that warreth entangleth himself with the affairs of this life; that he may please him who hath chosen him to be a soldier. And if a man also strive for masteries, yet is he not crowned, except he strive lawfully.* How many have missed the crowning of the Lord already?

Oh! How I remembered the word of the Lord as He looked at the oppressed children of Israel by these categories of people – and their state was that of a wandering herd of sheep without a shepherd. What then did Jesus preach and died for?

The Bible says that the disciples continued in their own doctrine and way of life after the death of Jesus, implying that in the land of Israel, there existed already multiple kingdoms in the days of the Apostles – that of the devil, Judaism with Pharisees and Sadducees, and the Kingdom of God as preached by Jesus, also referred to as the Kingdom of Light. So we would then classify the Kingdoms into that of light and that of darkness. The Kingdom of Light on earth started with a handful, 120 members. Peter was their head, or the king, appointed by the King of kings. Sooner, the precious blood of Jesus would buy more kingdoms and territories, and more kings would arise to oversee these kingdoms on behalf of the King of kings.

Many have wondered that if Jesus then be the 'King of kings,' who are those referred to as kings? Some claimed it talked of an unparalleled kingship compared to the kings of the world, but that wouldn't really fit in, because Christ didn't come to be ranked with an earthly king. This statement in Revelation 19:16 refers to those He has called, and to whom he has handed over part of His large estate worldwide, who hitherto were idle, and He called them to serve in His vineyard.

Throughout this book, the servant of God is seen as the king who is enthroned by God through Jesus, to oversee a portion of the estates belonging to Jesus in a command – *Occupy till I come*. An occupant shouldn't make a mess of the estate before the rightful owner comes. This well said, the title of king bestowed here on the servant of God, who now oversees a kingdom, in the many kingdoms of God here on earth, is done to help us drive home the fact that we live in a kingdom, and therefore should live a life of royalty.

How did I come to this fact? Well it was in the month of March 2013, while supervising the commissioning of a pipeline project on an engineering site. I was inside a Toyota Hilux driving to another location with other colleagues, when I heard a voice – 'You are a king, and your wife is the queen. All I need from you is to raise my children with royal cultures and characters that I will teach you.' After that, I was in the church one Sunday morning when all of a sudden, I saw a pulpit made of wood and sprayed with gold, sitting on the altar. Several revelations have followed since then, making me know that we are indeed in a kingdom. Implying further that the lives we live often may really not showcase what the Lord wants from us.

Some time ago, a standard rule of engagement was

opened in the book of Ezekiel from chapter number 40 through 46. And especially, Ezekiel 44:7,9 says: *In that ye have brought into my sanctuary strangers, uncircumcised in heart, and uncircumcised in flesh, to be in my sanctuary, to pollute it, even my house, when ye offer my bread, the fat and the blood, and they have broken my covenant because of all your abominations. Thus saith the Lord God; No stranger, uncircumcised in heart, nor uncircumcised in flesh, shall enter into my sanctuary, of any stranger that is among the children of Israel.* I was led into this portion of the Bible on the 24th of April 2014, while the church was having a one-week fasting and praying session. Those who must work with the king, the servant of God, so that the King of kings will be pleased, are clearly explained above. To put in another context, to explain this explicitly, we would look into the words of Psalm 78:5-7: *For he established a testimony in Jacob, and appointed a law in Israel, which he commanded our fathers, that they should make them known to their children: That the generation to come might know them, even the children which should be born; who should arise and declare them to their children: That they might set their hope in God, and not forget the works of God, but keep his commandments.* What we just read explains the terms of a covenant with God, which we are all into; the reason we are called the children of God, whom He has rescued with His precious blood upon Mount Golgotha.

The key elements of the terms of the agreement are:

- God has given us a testimony in Jacob, through whose lineage Jesus came - Isaiah 27:6: *He shall cause them that come of Jacob to take root: Israel shall blossom and bud, and fill the face of the world with fruit.*

- But to establish this testimony in our lives, a law is given and we are expected to obey these laws. These laws explain the rules of engagement, whenever we are ready to reason with Him - Isaiah 1:18: *Come now, and let us reason together, saith the Lord: though your sins be as scarlet, they shall be as white as snow; though they be red like crimson, they shall be as wool.* Of what use will there be a session to reason if there was no existing rule of engagement? Of what importance is sin and the need of forgiveness if there was no agreed set of rules that governs a relationship? So the context of discussion is clear.

- To ensure the Lord's arm of protection and provision extends to our children, we ought to also make them obey the terms of the 'deliverance' agreement we had with God the day we declared for His kingdom and He extended His banner of love over us, which I refer to later in this book as the *Immanuel Cloud* of His presence. This way, God can establish our lineage as a people unto Him. Here is what the Lord said of Abraham – Genesis 18:19: *For I know him, that he will command his children and his household after him, and they shall keep the way of the Lord, to do justice and judgment; that the Lord may bring upon Abraham that which he hath spoken of him.* Severally parents, especially in some nations of the world, no longer have the right to force their children to follow the Lord. This is one war the devil has waged against the Kingdom of God. But we have a consolation in Proverbs 22:6-7: *Train up a child in the way he should go: and when he is old, he will not depart from it. The rich ruleth over the poor, and the borrower is servant to the lender.* If we train our children with the right wisdom to seek the Lord, so that they would not be ruled over by the world, then the Arm of the Lord will not depart from them. Verse 7 says - *The rich ruleth over the poor, and the borrower is servant to the lender* – and this explains what takes the heart of men from

God; the chase after wealth – lending and borrowing, and oppression. Is this the world we want our children to grow up in? This is why we are in this discussion; to set a standard for our children and us, so that we can do away with the worries of this world, and live a life that showcases the beauty of the glory of God every day of our lives.

- The last part of that Psalm 78:5-7 says that our children will replicate whatever they have learnt of the Lord unto their own children so that there will be continuity of relationship with the hosts of heaven. Is this what we have done? If we did this, then this world wouldn't be in the mess it is right now – today all we see is extortion and deceit. And in their greed they will exploit you with false words - 2 Peter 2:3.

What then will the Kingdom of God do for us as a people? To explain this, one would have to pick up a piece of learning from John 5:14: *Afterward Jesus findeth him in the temple, and said unto him, Behold, thou art made whole: sin no more, lest a worse thing come unto thee.* Was the Lord trying to crack a joke with the newly healed? No, I really don't think so. The man was in his pre-condition of sickness and deprivation because of sin.

If this sinks into our understanding, then the fact is made clear that whoever lives in sin is cast out of the Kingdom of God, until such a person does away with the pride of living in sin, and seeks the Lord. What many have done is that, instead of coming to seek the Lord and pleading for His mercy and repenting wholeheartedly until they have the sincere feeling in their heart that they have mended their ways and have connected their spirits back to God, they would come to God with all manner of demands and requests, and it will seem as though they are giving God an ultimatum. We shouldn't forget that earlier in John 5:2-4 the Bible says - *Now there is at Jerusalem by the sheep market a pool, which is called in the Hebrew tongue Bethesda, having five porches. In these lay a great multitude of impotent folk, of blind, halt, withered, waiting for the moving of the water. For an angel went down at a certain season into the pool, and troubled the water: whosoever then first after the troubling of the water stepped in was made whole of whatsoever disease he had.* These were cast out from their homes and the temple, and were made to hopefully wait for the Arm of God to steer the water. Which would mean that the moment the angel turned the water, the Kingdom of God was felt, and the first to get in would receive the effect of the Shekinah – the Glory of God, and thus would be healed. However, the Shekinah existed momentarily and fades with time, because the Angel only bore the *'Immanuel cloud'* like a mantle wore around the Angel, to help him to actualise his mission. When Jesus arrived at the scene with the *Shekinah,* the man was healed, and this would admit him back into his home and the temple. To this end, Jesus revealed that the reason for his being 'cast out' was sin. So we would really do well to remain in the Kingdom of God to experience His Shekinah if we can adapt to the tenets that sets the Kingdom in place. It is about us stepping into the pool. The pool here could represent the Kingdom of God here on earth. Many where around the pool, yet it is the one that stepped inside that experienced the Shekinah and was made whole at that instant. Even when Jesus came there, it wasn't all that were healed. This is the reason why the ritual of water baptism involves a stepping inside.

I also see the Kingdom of God as a call to restore - Isaiah 54:3: *…and make the desolate cities to be inhabited.* How can this be when many are yet to understand the culture of heaven, and live by it? The Lord bears us in

His womb when we yield to Him (Isaiah 46:3), so that we can be born-again (John 3:3) into the world of the spirits, because God is a spirit (John 4:24). This first birth will qualify us to see the Kingdom of God, though then, we are still like children (Galatians 4:1-2), being fed with milk (Hebrews 5:11). As we grow in the wisdom and doctrine of the Kingdom under the guardian of Holy Spirit, we become born of water and the spirit, and we are admitted into the Kingdom (John 3:5), where we are fed with spiritual meat (Hebrews 5:14). These require that the Kingdom should be administer by a leader appointed by the Lord, who is a custodian of the spiritual milk and meat released for the upkeep of the Kingdom, and who would be used by the Lord as His physical means of communication for those who are still babies in spiritual things, and then to help those maturing to know what to do when the need arises (1 Samuel 3:3-10). We would recall that as Samuel grew in the Lord, he with time set up a process of leadership in the Kingdom – 1 Samuel 10:25: *Then Samuel told the people the manner of the Kingdom, and wrote it in a book, and laid it up before the Lord.* In another portion of the Bible, the Lord explained the duty of His servants - Matthew 13:52: *Then said he unto them, Therefore every scribe which is instructed unto the Kingdom of heaven is like unto a man that is an householder, which bringeth forth out of his treasure things new and old.* The servant of God is custodian of hidden secrets, both new and old, and these he will use to administer the Kingdom handed over to Him. He is a scribe employed by the Lord, to document spiritual information as revealed to him from the realm of glory above, whenever he ascends in the spirit to discuss Kingdom matters. Ezekiel ascended unto the realm of God some years ago, before the birth of Jesus as recorded in Ezekiel 37:1-14, and he learnt that to establish the Kingdom, the dry bones must receive life, and it was the duty of the servant of God to do in accordance with the instructions of God. And the result of this would be - *And I will put my Spirit within you, and you shall live, and I will place you in your own land* – Ezekiel 37:14. Two conditions stated here establish us as heirs of His Kingdom; the indwelling of the Spirit of God, and His placing us in His Kingdom. This is what He did to Adam at the beginning – He breathed into him the breath of life, Adam became a living soul, and God took him into the garden He had specially made. This garden was the first Kingdom of God on earth and because it did not have the presence of the Holy Spirit, man couldn't sustain the Kingdom – there was yet no voice speaking to man, thus, 'this is the way, walk in it' – Isaiah 30:21.

We will now see what kingdom characters we should apply in our day-to-day lives.

How should we make our request and how should we communicate in the Kingdom? Jesus is the Prince of Peace, and if we accept this as His person, then we will learn from Proverbs 25:15: *By long forbearing is a prince persuaded, and a soft tongue breaketh the bone.* Meaning that our prayers should not be as though we are having a quarrel with the Lord. The rule of communication is hinged on having good persuasive skills, in our prayers and in our requests unto the Lord. The text *'a soft tongue breaketh the bone,'* simply means that when we speak softly and tenderly into His ears, He will temper justice with mercy, and allow us to have our righteous desire.

How should we praise in the Kingdom? We will also get a clue from Psalm 47:6-7: *Sing praises to God, sing praises: sing praises unto our King, sing praises. For God is the King of all the earth: sing ye praises with understanding.* We are commanded to keep on praising

Him, but with understanding. Why? Verse 8 of Psalm 47, says - *God reigneth over the heathen: God sitteth upon the throne of his holiness.* He is Holy, and requires those that must worship Him to do so with this understanding, that He abhors ungodliness. Is this what the servants of God are dying for? Have many not perverted the precepts of the Lord to please men and serve tables?

To be able to serve, everyone claiming to be called by God must function only after receiving the mantle.

We would take learning from the Book of Revelation, chapters one through three – The servants of God are the stars in the hand of the Lord. The churches are the candlesticks. When the servants of God become corrupt and can no longer reflect His lights, they are cast out of His hand, and out of His sight. As Jesus walks in the midst of the candlelight representing the churches, anyone that is not bringing forth good light will not receive His attention. He expects His servant to put such a candle in order. Anyone who wants to hold His hand must first touch any of the stars in His hand. Anyone coming into His vineyard must get information from those already working there. This is how dedication comes.

To this end, knowing the sensitivity of the job of a

pastor, anyone who administers a church without receiving a mantle from the Lord is leading people to eternal destruction.

In a Kingdom, the Lord teaches His children the ways of His Kingdom - Micah 4:2: *And many nations shall come, and say, Come, and let us go up to the mountain of the Lord, and to the house of the God of Jacob; and he will teach us.* So by extension, the pastor of a flock of sheep feeds the children of God with divine wisdom from the throne of God. Often servants of God receive visions and would reveal them in books or in teaching sessions.

We can understand this from the words of our Lord, Jesus Christ in Luke 13: 18-20:

Then said he, unto what is the Kingdom of God like? and whereunto shall I resemble it? It is like a grain of mustard seed, which a man took, and cast into his garden; and it grew, and waxed a great tree; and the fowls of the air lodged in the branches of it.

And again he said, whereunto shall I liken the Kingdom of God? It is like leaven, which a woman took and hid in three measures of meal, till the whole was leavened.

It is clear from verse 19 above that the Kingdom of

God is set by God Himself, who anoints His servants, establishes them with the knowledge of His Kingdom in heaven, plants them and waters them to grow to the extent that they become great in the sight of men, with the signs and wonders of God manifesting in their lives to the extent that everyone would sing the praise of their exploits by glorifying God – Matthew 5:16.

The birds perching and singing, as referred to in Luke 13:19 above, would tell of the comforts that these servants of God would bring to His children as they live by the Kingdom's values daily.

In verse 20 we also see that God also raises His servants, training them until they are perfect, and then He would plant them in the midst of others so that they can replicate what they have been taught until everyone receives the Kingdom values of heaven and begin to act and live by these. This also aligns with Daniels interpretation of Nebuchadnezzar's dream in Daniel 4:19-22.

Let us also see Matthew 13:44: *Again, the Kingdom of heaven is like unto treasure hid in a field; the which when a man hath found, he hideth, and for joy thereof goeth and selleth all that he hath, and buyeth that field.* An illustration that would fit in here is that the Lord looked into the heart of Saul, later St. Paul, and saw the energy in him to exterminate believers, and He arrested him to work for Him and for the growth of the Kingdom of God. The treasure in the field could also represent the pasture for the grazing of sheep. And this would fit no other image than the sheep of Christ grazing in a commission that He sets up. The treasure in the field is the zealousness in the heart of the labourers in God's vineyard and at the heart of these are God's servants. The ability of the sheep to graze successfully depends on the availability of green pasture (Psalm 23:2). This is the available wisdom of God in His Kingdom which He teaches His servants and would want them to also feed His sheep likewise (Jeremiah 3:15).

Another verse of the Bible that opens the mystery of the Kingdom of God is Matthew 13:45-46: *Again, the Kingdom of heaven is like unto a merchant man, seeking goodly pearls: Who, when he had found one pearl of great price, went and sold all that he had, and bought it.*

Now let's compare this verse with Matthew 25:29: *For unto every one that hath shall be given, and he shall have abundance: but from him that hath not shall be taken away even that which he hath.* We also see that these verses are talking about the church of Christ. Now these churches are given specific instructions and tasks, which we refer to as the 'Anointing Character' or "calling' upon the servant of God' as was the case of St. Peter and St. Paul, and may also be seen in Jesus' rebuke of the servants of God in the book of Revelation 2 and Revelation 3. In Ezekiel 34, God also had a case against these sets of people, who are supposed to act as kings over the Kingdoms of His large Kingdom, ensuring that heavenly values are transferred into the hearts of men.

We would also see from Matthew 13:47-48: *Again, the Kingdom of heaven is like unto a net, that was cast into the sea, and gathered of every kind: Which, when it was full, they drew to shore, and sat down, and gathered the good into vessels, but cast the bad away.*

This verse is the premise upon which many servants of God have allowed all manner of persons to come into the house of God without the intention of repenting, believing that at the end, the Lord would harvest those good ones. The problem is that when you have more of these mixed together with genuine repentant believers there would be multiplication of evil communications, which would then corrupt the hearts of those desiring to make heaven. As with the tares, they would definitely struggle with available nutrients in soil, leading to stunted growth of both the grains of value and the tares. If this would be, then the servant of God has a lot to do to ensure that the word and the character of the Kingdom is continuously emphasised, and not to let the fear of losing members of the Kingdom affect the truth in their teaching of the truth.

In all, we would see that when we belong to a church in which God has raised His servant to minster to us we will see the above manifestation of the presence and the hand of God in the commission. So, instead of people forming fellowships because they don't want to be submissive to servants of God, we should repent and stop these heresies that are blacklisting many of us before God.

As you read this book, ask yourself if you ever belong to a Kingdom commissioned by God. The evidence is easy to know as explained in Luke 13:18-21, re-quoted below for the purpose of emphasis:

Then said he, unto what is the Kingdom of God like? And whereunto shall I resemble it? It is like a grain of mustard seed, which a man took, and cast into his garden; and it grew, and waxed a great tree; and the fowls of the air lodged in the branches of it. And again he said, whereunto shall I liken the Kingdom of God? It is like leaven, which a woman took and hid in three measures of meal, till the whole was leavened.

This book is based on a series of revelations I had. In a larger sense, it is full of mystery and may be difficult to comprehend at the first go. In 2008, I was in a dream with a crown upon me yet living in a hut. Where is it heard that a king lives in a hut? Well that was how I saw myself in that dream. And I asked the Lord, why am I in a hut with this crown? and He said, the more work you do in my vineyard the more I will enlarge your kingdom. In other words, God wants me to invest the anointing I receive in His name, representing the mark of the Order of Melchizedek on my forehead. And as I act the word of God daily, I also understand that if I live by the character of God (John 1:1) I would see the Kingdom of God being enlarged as more people come to respond to the message He has given to me by the day.

Many have always wondered what the Kingdom of God is all about. Now we know. The Lord says in Luke 21:31-32: *So likewise ye, when ye see these things come to pass, know ye that the* **Kingdom of God is nigh at hand**.

Verily I say unto you, This generation shall not pass away, till all be fulfilled. This implies that we are all in the Kingdom already. Since that day of the Pentecost, when the Holy Spirit was released, that was when the Kingdom of God came and dwelt in our midst. This Kingdom, which is the shadow of the new heaven and earth that the Lord will finally institute, where we would be in immortal form, is to create an opportunity for us to be united with God in the Spirit. It is my desire to present this book as simply as possible, yet enable the reader to have a thorough understanding of the Christian faith we profess.

I have presented here, with the heart of a storyteller, an exploration of God's Kingdom on earth - what it is and what it represents. And also to make the world know that we are not noise makers as many have termed Christians to be, as a result of their nights of praying and crying, but we are kingdom receptors and our cry is to plead before God to have mercy upon the unrepentant souls. This is how we would invest our resources in the winning of souls. Hereto, we would say that the nights of prayers we undergo are because we care that so many lost souls would be heading to eternal destruction and as such we are holding the hand of God, so to speak, from destroying them yet.

As you read this book, you will also begin to have spiritual insights into the purpose of the life humans live here on earth, and how we could reorient our lives to showcase the values of God in heaven, here on earth. Shalom!

Oghenethoja Umuteme
Founding President/Senior Pastor,
Royal Diamonds International Church
(Christ Movement International Ministries)
Port Harcourt, Nigeria

CHAPTER ONE

THE ORIGIN OF KINGDOMS

The first Kingdom was started by God in heaven (Genesis 1:1, Isaiah 66:1), then for Him to be able to visit earth, he had to establish another kingdom that suited His personality. This new kingdom was handed over to man to oversee, until man lost it when he could not live by the culture that sets that kingdom in place. We would see how God started the beautification process that would turn the earth into a place of His footstool in the first chapter of the Bible. And this would be seen in the desire of God as espoused by Jesus in Matthew 6:10: *Thy kingdom come, Thy will be done in earth, as it is in heaven.*

CHAPTER ONE

And since then it has been the desire of God to build a new kingdom, or what we would call a human colony, after His heart. After the downfall of man, He would have commenced the building of a new kingdom that would bear His name with Abel, but his cold murder rendered that possibility futile. Since the onset of sin, which launched a mass attack on the destiny of mankind, it has been the desire of God to have a generation that would bear His name for the purpose of having heavenly values fully transferred to Earth, and then this Earth would be holy and would merit being His footstool. We would see that in 2 Chronicles 7:14, God made us to know that some people are called by His name. These are the ones who adhere to the rules of the Kingdom, which God was transferring to Earth. So the values of the Kingdom from 2 Chronicles 7:14 are seen to include humility, dependence on God's wisdom through prayer and fasting, and seeking righteousness through repentance.

Sin pushes God far away from mankind, it surely does! And because the Earth is filled with sin, it has become more of a refuse dump with sin, smelling like human excreta everywhere. God cannot walk the face of the Earth anymore until the Earth is turned into the Kingdom of God, with the values of Heaven, so that we would worship and serve Him as the Angels do in heaven, through kingly obeisance. This is why Jesus says in Luke 22:18: *For I say unto you, I will not drink of the fruit of the vine, until the Kingdom of God shall come.* We are the fruits upon the branches of the vine referred to here (John 15:1), and we cannot bring glory to His name until we imbibe the principle of the Kingdom of God in our hearts, and live them in our daily lives (Matthew 5:16). This is why the Lord is raising servants, now called men of God, to become kings who would manage small kingdoms, known as the church, where these values are taught until the Lord returns, in a heavenly instruction – *'occupy till I come.'* And this will be the standard test for anyone who would make it into the new Earth. This is why Jesus is the King of kings and Lord of Lords, meaning that anyone God had called to be His servant, acting as a royal priest, in His holy tabernacles worldwide, is a king and a Lord, ordained after the Order of Melchizedek. So that as these colonies exist on Earth, teaching the Kingdom values of God, as the Angels do in heaven, with hierarchy, the mind and thoughts of God's children will become filled with royal values, and they would once again be united as one big royal family. The duties of the servant of God are seen as one who teaches God's children Kingdom values. This is the licence to living in the new earth. The Bible says in Proverbs 14:2: *He that walketh in his uprightness feareth the Lord.* How can we walk in uprightness?

This is why the Bible says also, in Proverbs 9:10: *The fear of the Lord is the beginning of wisdom: and the knowledge of the holy is understanding.* In this wonderful thought-provoking verse we would see the Kingdom values displayed –

- ✓ The **Fear** of the Lord
- ✓ The **Wisdom** of the Lord
- ✓ The **Knowledge** of the Holy, and
- ✓ **Understanding** the way of the Lord.

These are what make up the values of heavenly royal life. The Fear of the Lord is the singular reason why we are admonished to *maintain good works* unto the name of the Lord (Titus 3:8). What are the good works referred to here? These are the works of all adherents in the Kingdom and the reason for maintaining these good works is so that the Lord can draw us unto Himself at the end of the day – Titus 3:7: *That being justified by his grace, we should be made heirs according to the hope of **eternal life.*** What then is grace, and how does grace come? The Holy Spirit is the bearer of grace, and we receive it input unto us when we receive the Holy Spirit. We have grace without our personal labour; it was given to us as a result of the loving kindness of God towards us all – Titus 3:4-5: *But after that the kindness and love of God our Saviour toward man appeared, Not by works of righteousness which we have done, but according to his mercy he saved us, by the washing of regeneration, and renewing of the Holy Ghost.*

We can get some clues about the good works we are required to maintain, as adherents of the heavenly Kingdom of God by doing the opposite of what is contained in the book of Titus 3:3: *For we ourselves also were sometimes foolish, disobedient, deceived, serving divers lusts and pleasures, living in malice and envy, hateful, and hating one another.* Implying that what we need to pray for now that we have been admitted into the school of Kingdom values of the Lord includes – against the spirit of foolishness, disobedience (rebellion), desire of the things of the world such as travelling to many places to have 'fun', living in malice and envy, hateful in spirit and hating one another. Jesus condemned these negative characteristics too in Mark 7:21-23: *For from within, out of the heart of men, proceed evil thoughts, adulteries, fornications, murders, Thefts, covetousness, wickedness, deceit, lasciviousness, an evil eye, blasphemy, pride, foolishness: All these evil things come from within, and **defile the man**.* The last underlined statement says – *defile the man.* And this shows that the purpose of the Kingdom of God is to 'purify the defiled man.' And this is only possible when the Holy Spirit tutors us.

This is further expatiated in Isaiah 11:2-3: *And the spirit of the Lord shall rest upon him, the spirit of wisdom and understanding, the spirit of counsel and might, the spirit of knowledge and of the fear of the Lord; And shall make him of quick understanding in the fear of the Lord: and he shall not judge after the sight of his eyes.* So we would see that in the Kingdom of God, the Spirit of the Lord is the 'Kingdom values' Bearer or Custodian or focal point.' This well said, let's break down this further into a line process of progressive importance:

CHAPTER ONE

Stage 1 – The Spirit of the Lord rests on all those who wholeheartedly seek the Lord

Stage 2 – The Spirit of the Lord comes with the full manifestation of the presence of the Lord, resulting in every Kingdom adherent who has received the Spirit of the Lord, which is the Spirit of leadership, to be filled with the Spirit of Wisdom, Understanding, Counsel, Might, Knowledge and the Fear of the Lord.

Stage 3 – At this point, the adherent responds quicker with answers to situations that beat human imagination because he/she now live with a voice of intelligence that guides him/her – Isaiah 30:21. He would not judge after the sight, but with spiritual understanding.

This explains the fact that all Kingdom adherents operate with what I will call 'Spiritual Intelligence' (SI). This is why I frown over people who are yet to discover the truth in the God they serve, that today, believers are afraid of the devil, and have been the object of manipulation by unsuspecting spiritualists.

The desire of every child of God would be to learn how to live in a kingdom, which is called a church, overseen by a king, who we call a servant of God, so that they will learn the ways of the King of kings, as this is the quality required of them before they can live in the coming new Earth. Hence Prophet Micah reveals - *He will teach us his ways, so that we may walk in his paths* – Micah 4:2.

This is also the reason why in every home, the man is the head, and assisted by the wife, the children are supposed to be taught how to respect elders in society. Many of us want God to change people, but the Lord said Abraham shall lead his children after Him, and the Bible also says that the elders should live by example and that the older women should teach the younger ones (Titus 2). So it is our responsibility to teach the values of the Kingdom of God, so that from the day of birth, the child is taken through the path of life that glorifies the creator, until such a time when no one need to teach anybody about the ways of God again - Jeremiah 31:31-34. This should be the earnest expectation of every servant of God as we teach the knowledge and understanding of God - Jeremiah 3:15.

This explains why the servants of God needed to be respected as people bearing the burden of the Lord, and as custodians of the tradition of the Kingdom, so that they will divulge the secrets one by one unto us. People should volunteer to minister unto them, helping them in provision of whatever they need, and these ones must be ready to take instructions from him (Acts 19:22). To be frank with my reader – there are secrets and there are secrets. Many can never get into the print, or across the pulpit. The Holy Spirit reveals Jesus more and more to His servants - *for he shall receive of mine, and shall shew it unto you (John 16:14).* Many of what the Holy Spirit showed to them would eventually become guided secrets. If you look closely into what we just read, there is something key there – *receive of mine;* meaning to explain what the Lord requires of us, and to make know to us, and to show us the pattern of life accepted in heaven. And these would become the sermons, in most cases, that are preached on Sundays – though sometimes these are highly coded and meant for those who have grown the ladder of spiritual maturity in Christ (Matthew 13:13, 1 Corinthians 3:1, Hebrews 5:12-14). You only get these secrets through your personal relationship with the servant of God. All the trainings and teachings a servant of God gives to his adherents are meant to test their understanding of spiritual secrets, through the use of the shadows of the original as illustrations – once it is confirmed, in most cases through the dreams you reveal to him, which he confirms, because in most cases, he sets these dreams in place, to ascertain if you see clearly. This must happen under an environment of righteousness, holiness and the zeal for the burden he bears. He will then from time to time, as he adjudges faithfully, begin to speak to you as one matured in the things of the Spirit. From that moment onward also, the Spiritual realm would begin to see you as one of theirs through his recommendation, and would with time, after testing your loyalty, reveal information to you. Until Moses recommended Joshua, God didn't speak with him – Joshua 1. Before Joshua's recommendation, he had been a minister to Moses – Exodus 24:13: *And Moses rose up, and his minister Joshua: and Moses went up into the mount of God.* And at the heart of this service to him is your gift, and taking care of him – Proverbs 18:16: *A man's gift maketh room for him, and bringeth him before great men.* Greatness is hidden in secrets. Once you get these secrets, your days of struggle will be over. How do you think Joshua operated after the death of Moses? Why do you think God had to lead Paul to Ananias (Acts 9:17), and then Paul would, who was a mere Pharisee, could boast in the Lord, as one endowed with spiritual gifts – Romans 1:11: *For I long to see you, that I may impart unto you some spiritual gift, to the end ye may be established.* Spiritual gifts are established in spiritual secrets.

Something surprised me when I got to Romans 1:12: *That is, that I may be comforted together with you by the mutual faith both of you and me.* We would notice that Paul withdrew his promise in the verse 11 we earlier read. This shouldn't be a surprise because the letter was addressed to the Romans, who naturally would not want to be Lord over, which is how they would perceive his statement as though he was more favoured with spiritual gifts than they are - and looking at Rome today being the seat of Papacy and all the politico-religious happenings in the Roman Catholic Church, one will understand Paul's predicament. Yet Paul indeed had some spiritual gifts and information to share as a result of his spiritual journeys. A fact so clear would be what was contained in his parchments, which he told Timothy to come to him with. What was in these parchments that made him qualify them with the word *especially*? - 2 Timothy 4:13: *... when thou comest, bring with thee, and the books,* **but**

especially the parchments. Just like Paul, many servants of God are also unable to reveal what they had learnt as a result of their spiritual encounters because many may see it as him Lording over them, especially when they also claim out of pride that they indeed hear God speak too, just as Aaron and Miriam challenged the authority of Moses over them. We would see that Moses ended up handing over to Joshua, who was loyal to him. What many have not asked is why most servants of God would hand over to a very close relative, friend, spouse or children before they die? Why would the Lord reveal the book of revelation, with such a depth of spirituality to the one He handed over His mother? - John 19:26-27: *When Jesus therefore saw his mother, and the disciple standing by, whom he loved, he saith unto his mother, Woman, behold thy son! Then saith he to the disciple, Behold thy mother! And from that hour that disciple took her unto his own home.*

Why would this disciple be a centre focus in John 21:20 - *Then Peter, turning about, seeth the disciple whom Jesus loved following?* Why was this disciple a concern to Peter? It is because John was suspected of holding some spiritual secrets, and of course Christ confirmed their fears when He said - John 21:22: *Jesus saith unto him, If I will that he tarry till I come, what is that to thee? follow thou me.* And their action in verse 23 only underlines this fact more - *Then went this saying abroad among the brethren, that that disciple should not die ...* I always advise that we get close to God's servants to receive these spiritual impartations.

The closer you get to the servant of God, the more you hear these secrets, a good reason not to miss any gathering where he is present and will minister. It is these secrets that establish servants of God, and distinguish them. At the depth of the heart of the servant of God are the treasures of his encounter with the immortal realm. In explaining the presence of the immortal in our midst which is being perfected daily by the Holy Spirit, who brings down the Shekinah, Saint Paul puts it across this way – 2 Timothy 1:10: *But is now made manifest by the appearing of our Saviour Jesus Christ, who hath abolished death, and hath brought life and immortality to light through the gospel.* Servants of God have a character that distinguishes them – *wise as serpents, and harmless as doves* – Matthew 10:16. One thing people must not do is to pretend and lie before a servant of God. Let me say this – they know more than you can imagine. Many can read your thoughts from afar. You must apply caution in dealing with them. They have the power to bring down a whole city or nation with the words of their mouths – Luke 9:54-55: *And when his disciples James and John saw this, they said, Lord, wilt thou that we command fire to come down from heaven, and consume them, even as Elias did? But he turned, and rebuked them, and said,* **Ye know not what manner of spirit ye are of.** At the early part of their ministry, they often use the power they have received to destroy because of immaturity and to resist oppression – 2 Kings 2:24: *And he turned back, and looked on them, and cursed them in the name of the Lord. And there came forth two she bears out of the wood, and tare forty and two children of them.* And another instance will be seen in Acts 5:9: *Then Peter said unto her, How is it that ye have agreed together to tempt the Spirit of the Lord? behold, the feet of them which have buried thy husband are at the door, and shall carry thee out. Then fell she down straightway at his feet, and yielded up the ghost: and the young men came in, and found her dead, and, carrying her forth, buried her by her husband.* But as they mature in Christ, they learn to forgive, and become kind with bowels of mercy, becoming as perfect as the God that called them to serve– Matthew 5:48. This does not mean that they should be served and worshipped – be mindful of this, else you jeopardise the opportunity of his redemption at the end, and you too won't get to heaven either. All the glory and honour must be unto the Lord. **Provide** for their needs when it is in your power to do so, it is an act of righteousness – **Emulate** their good works in Christ – **Assist** them as they bear the burden of the Lord – **Respect** them as custodians of the secret things of the Lord. This forms the Provide, Emulate, Respect and Assist (PEAR) responsibilities of all kingdom adherents.

Failure of this PEAR responsibility towards God's servants was decried by Jeremiah in the book of Lamentations 4:16, 5:12:*The anger of the Lord hath divided them; he will no more regard them: they respected not the persons of the priests, they favoured not the elders. Princes are hanged up by their hand: the faces of elders were not honoured.*

The children of Israel had neglected God and His kingdom teachings right from the tabernacle of God, even in their home. If we don't respect our pastors, those whom God has call to lead and teach us, then we might be lacking a treasure in God's kingdom. This is why God hates rebellion. Those who have Kingdom values in their hearts don't rebel. Only those who rebel are those who bring down a kingdom. Willingness and obedience are needed to live in a kingdom, and then enjoy its fruitfulness. The word of God says in Isaiah 50:10: *Who is among you that feareth the LORD, that obeyeth the voice of his servant...* A servant of God has an earthly human life to live on earth and so requires physical things to stay alive physically, and these should be provided by the Kingdom adherents - Romans 15:27. We would often measure our submission to the cause he bears for the Lord with how he responds to your call of distress – spiritually and physically. I would advise that all adherents should walk his or her way into the heart of God's servant up to the point where he can give you his private line to call him anytime. Remember he has been given to you as a gift from the Lord. No wise person will throw away his/her gift, especially when God gives it to him/her. They may be difficult sometimes – don't forget the story of the woman and the unjust judge, with perseverance, he will attend to you – Luke 18:2-8. The servant of God is the first gift the Lord gives to you. Here is an example of the call of a servant of God – Isaiah 42:6: *I the Lord have called thee in righteousness, and will hold thine hand, and will keep thee, and* **give thee for a covenant of the people, for a light of the Gentiles**. From this verse you see that he is given to the people as a covenant of the Lord. And, again, here is Paul's exposition on this issue – 1 Corinthians 3:21-22: *Therefore let no man glory in men. For all things are yours; Whether Paul, or Apollos, or Cephasor the world, or life, or death, or things present, or things to come; all are yours;* these are the gifts of the Lord to us, hence we are not to glory in them but to glory in the Lord, and to thank Him for giving them to us. If we learn to take care of all that God has given to us, we will experience life abundantly.

Now let's see what we must take care of from what we just read:

- **Servants of God**, represented by *Paul, Apollos, Cephas*.
- **The world**, which we must make a better place by harnessing all that the Lord has kept in it – the rivers, plants, animals, the air, etc, for the good of mankind.

- **Life** – we give life by giving others the hope to live and also receive life from the testimonies of hope of others. We are to take good care of the life God has given to us by watching the things we eat and drink, what we bring into contact with our body, etc.

- **Death** – we must be mindful of the fact that one day we will depart this earth, and as such plan ahead of time for the event – making sure that the Lord would accept us as His when we leave the earth rather than be cast into outer darkness.

- **Things present** – the gospel of truth, which is preached to us, and which we ought to preach to others.

- **Things to come** – The coming of the Lord; an event we must consistently pray to be part of.

Our service to the Lord should therefore be aimed at the Now, and the Future. Many Believers are so mindful of the future that they forget the input of the Now. What we do now have a way of affecting our future, so also, how we carry out the works of the Lord in His Kingdom on earth, have a way of affecting our hope of eternal life. We all have things to take care of for the Lord, and we must act profitably in this wise. All these show that we are indeed a peculiar and chosen people with special tasks to fulfil in a Kingdom of the order of heaven.

Noah was a servant of God, who bore the voice and the burden of the Lord – the burden of righteousness. He walked the face of the earth to warn people about the danger that would soon visit the earth, but he was scorned and rejected. God then used Noah and his wife, their children and wives, to build a new kingdom, and that colony brought forth the world we see today. Thereafter, as people increased in size and numbers, there was need for separation and territorial control, and with it, territorial challenges. The means to surmounting these challenges and sustaining the territorial boundaries from external control and influence in a judicially managed pattern and order was needed. An instance would be seen in Genesis 10:5, 32: *By these were the isles of the Gentiles divided in their lands; every one after his tongue, after their families, in their nations. These are the families of the sons of Noah, after their generations, in their nations: and by these were the nations divided in the earth after the flood.*

We would see a display of this territorial control by nations that lived upon the surface of the Earth as the

Israelites sent words to kings whom they would eventually pass through their lands – Numbers 21:21-22: *And Israel sent messengers unto Sihon king of the Amorites, saying, Let me pass through thy land: we will not turn into the fields, or into the vineyards; we will not drink of the waters of the well: but we will go along by the king's high way, until we be past thy borders.*

Does this send a message as to why Jesus had to make mention of the gates of hell – Matthew 16:18? The Bible recorded that God destroyed thirty-one kings - Joshua 12:24, to enable the children of Israel to have a safe trip into their inheritance. Now let's see the climax of this evil territorial control as espoused by Jesus in Luke 21:10: *Nation shall rise against nation, and kingdom against kingdom.*

More kingdoms have grown with the multiplication of man on the face of the earth. And gradually, the Kingdom values of God are been polluted by the desires of man, engrossed with the claim of superiority and survival. To have a better understanding of what we are discussing, it would also suffice to read Genesis 10:8-10:*And Cush begat Nimrod: he began to be a mighty one in the earth.*

CHAPTER ONE

He was a mighty hunter before the LORD: wherefore it is said, Even as Nimrod the mighty hunter before the LORD. And the beginning of his kingdom was Babel, and Erech, and Accad, and Calneh, in the land of Shinar.

Who was behind this great kingdom? The Bible says he was named Nimrod, the son of Cush, a grandson of Ham, the son of Noah.

Humans, under the supervision and forceful control of this great hunter, in the manner of his hunting aggression, led the first set of those who wanted to stamp their names on the face of the Earth – Genesis 11:2-4:*And it came to pass, as they journeyed from the east, that they found a plain in the land of Shinar; and they dwelt there. And they said one to another, Go to, let us make brick, and burn them thoroughly. And they had brick for stone, and slime had they for mortar. And they said, Go to, let us build us a city and a tower, whose top may reach unto heaven; and* **let us make us a name**...

God saw the imagination of their hearts and sent down confusion to enable them to separate again into smaller units that also grew to become diverse kingdoms thereafter. God was gradually losing the world to man's desire and ego. Man wanted to live in a kingdom, and so kingdoms upon kingdoms – they multiplied. They grew! Man's ingenuity could not be compared with anything else but self-esteem and determination, and heaven lost the control of man. The reason for this is not far-fetched. Adam existed in a kingdom – The Kingdom of God with the presence of the tree of life in that garden – Genesis 3:22, Revelation 2:7. He must have narrated the story to his children, who then wanted to replicate the authority Adam had lost to his ignorance and foolishness, while he was yet a king with power over the creations of God. This desire of humans was not overlooked by God, as he eventually gave Israel a king after their long demand –1 Samuel 8:7. The coming of Christ established a better covenant and a heavenly presence here on earth by taking over the Kingdoms of this world, and handing them over to those he appoints to oversee these kingdoms as kings – Take note of the phrase, *'kingdoms of our Lord'* in that for there to be kingdoms of this world, there must be kings on earth, who would represent the Lord – Revelation 11:15: … *The kingdoms of this world are become the Kingdoms of our Lord, and of his Christ; and he shall reign for ever and ever.* The presence of these kings over these kingdoms establishes the reign of Christ over them. And again, these kings are the servants of God. They maintain territorial controls, and them with the Angels, set the Kingdom standards, as pleasing unto the Lord (see this clue in Revelation 2 and 3, and Exodus 23:20).

In His teaching, Jesus gave us a clue to what man's problem is, the reason behind our disregard for the things of God, in Luke 19:21: *For I feared you, because you are an austere man: you take up that you layed not down, and reap that you did not sow* – many don't want to invest what God has endowed them with, to serve Him. This is the main reason for man's separation from God. This also was the character of the devil in heaven when he challenged the authority of God and wanted to build a throne higher than that of God, as revealed in Isaiah 14:13. Later in a separate chapter we shall discuss the devil and his kingdom so that we would see how we could avoid his cunning tactics and live for God. Many still see God as a wicked man who demands too much from man. This is a very wrong perception of the King of kings. The earth and all that it contains belong to God. The moment man knows this the earlier mankind would yield to the authorities put in place to unite them back to God,

CHAPTER ONE

As the years grew so also the separation between God and man grew. All manner of imaginings to give man joy and praise, and not an iota of thinking about the values of the Kingdom of God, manifested in the heart of man. Adam had passed on the stories in Eden, but with the years, these stories became fables, then allegories, and then mere tales of misfortune. There was no yardstick to measure this separation of man from God and with time the cord of life grew thinner and man's kingdoms developed to care only for man's insatiable quest for sustainability and brew of evil.

This was when organised kingdoms were established everywhere man's foot was found and man's relationship with God dwindled the more into the appreciation of gods, because man couldn't seek the face of God anymore as a result of sins. Wars between kingdoms and within it grew to a level God could not accept as a result of human struggles for material things. Man yielded to the devil, serving him with their thoughts. So when God was set to clean up the mess on Earth, the main focus is seen in Jesus' advice – Matthew 6:24-26: *No man can serve two masters: for either he will hate the one, and love the other; or else he will hold to the one, and despise the other. Ye cannot serve God and mammon. Therefore I say unto you, Take no thought for your life, what ye shall eat, or what ye shall drink; nor yet for your body, what ye shall put on. Is not the life more than meat, and the body than raiment?*

Behold the fowls of the air: for they sow not, neither do they reap, nor gather into barns; yet your heavenly Father feedeth them. Are ye not much better than they?

What was this message intended to yield? I tell you that many would stand in amazement, others would be furious because of the effect this message would have on their business, and yet many would want Him dead as they would lose their customers, those whom they have used their spiritual tyranny to oppress at the temple. Most of Jesus' messages were delivered at the heart the city's business centre – and the seacoast – Matthew 4:25: *And there followed him great multitudes of people from Galilee, and from Decapolis, and from Jerusalem, and from Judaea, and from beyond Jordan.* Let's see what is so unique about Galilee, Decapolis, Jerusalem and Judea, where He drew these great multitudes mentioned above, and through these we would have a clue as to what the Kingdom of God came to correct:

CHAPTER ONE

■ **Galilee:** Jesus walked this land with great works. According to a note in the Easton Bible Dictionary: 'It is noteworthy that of his thirty-two beautiful parables, no less than nineteen were spoken in Galilee. And it is no less remarkable that of his entire thirty-three great miracles, twenty-five were wrought in this province.' The 'sermon on the mount' (Matthew 5) was preached in Galilee. The first miracle of water to wine was performed in Galilee. His Transfiguration happened in Galilee. His first disciples were call in Galilee. Here He preached His first message – *repent for the Kingdom of God is at hand.* If we dig further into the origins of Kingdoms we would see why Galilee was such a pivot for the Lord's will for mankind. Here is what prophet Isaiah remarked of this place – Isaiah 9:1-2: *…in Galilee of the nations. The people that walked in darkness have seen a great light: they that dwell in the land of the shadow of death, upon them hath the light shined.* These people were walking in darkness. There was not an inch of the presence of the Lord in their midst. So Jesus started by announcing the Kingdom of Light to them. Surely this message would attract the kind of attention it deserved, and to crown it all, the Lord espoused what this new Kingdom of His was going to do for them in Matthew 5. Further He also had discourses on 'The Bread of Life,' on 'Purity and Sanctity,' on 'Forgiveness,' and on 'Humility.' Why was Galilee living in darkness and dwelling in the land of the shadow of death as espoused by Isaiah? Here are the facts:

- It is a city situated on the coast of the sea, with an influx of traders and business-minded individuals.

- There would certainly be a high level of corruption resulting from buying and selling of goods and services, immorality, power tussles and idolatry as those who want money also worship idols – hence the mention of mammon, etc. In Nigeria for instance, a Galilee type of city would be Lagos or Port Harcourt, and these two cities also boast of the influx of pastors, prophets, magicians, sorcerers, harlots, politicians, etc.

- So we would say from the understanding of what Galilee represented in Jesus' ministry that he preached against the practices of wealth seeking – Matthew 16:26: *For what is a man profited, if he shall gain the whole world, and lose his own soul?*

CHAPTER ONE

Now we move on to the next place where a great multitude also followed Him.

- **Decapolis**: Where is Decapolis? Of what importance is their way of life to helping us understand what the Kingdom of God represents? Our clue would be that of a man who lived in this land and was possessed of demons – the popular legion story. The pathetic story of his bondage, and that of the whole city by inference would be seen here – Mark 5:5: *And always, night and day, he was in the mountains, and in the tombs, crying, and cutting himself with stones.* Then Jesus said to the evil spirit in him – Mark 5:8: … *Come out of the man, thou unclean spirit.* The place was a home of swine – Mark 5:11: *Now there was there nigh unto the mountains a great herd of swine feeding.* Swine are related to spiritual uncleanliness – Matthew 7:6: … *neither cast ye your pearls before swine …* And to support this fact, the legion of demons which possessed the man, begged Jesus to cast them into the swine –Mark 5:12: *And all the devils besought him, saying, Send us into the swine, that we may enter into them.* The devil does not desire what is Holy. And in the Old Testament, God detests swine. If going by the Old Testament standard this city is unclean, we have a basis for a restructuring. So in continuation of the institution of the Kingdom of God in Decapolis so as to get rid of the works of the devil which had mutilated the city, Jesus commanded the newly freed man to announce the Kingdom because the people had told Him to depart from their city, but this would not stop the intention of Jesus to establish the Kingdom of God in their midst – Mark 5:19-20: *Howbeit Jesus suffered him not, but saith unto him, Go home to thy friends, and tell them how great things the Lord hath done for thee, and hath had compassion on thee. And he departed, and began to publish in Decapolis how great things Jesus had done for him: and all men did marvel.*

From here we would see that the Kingdom of God is here to transform and to make us presentable as it happened to the man – Mark 5:15: *And they come to Jesus, and see him that was possessed with the devil, and had the legion, sitting, and clothed, and in his right mind...* Our encounter with the Lord will free us from the manipulation of the devil, and we will be with our *right mind.* In many parts of the world we still have people who are not in their right frame of mind, and are being tossed up and down by the devil – these people need to be set free by the preaching of the gospel of truth. We now go to the next city:

CHAPTER ONE

- **Jerusalem:** The Lord lamented over this city, and the disciples wished that Jesus should restore the city and bring back the Kingdom of Israel. What manner of sin enveloped this city and caused the *Immanuel cloud* to depart from it? Here is the verdict of the Lord concerning this great city that once enjoyed the presence of God - Matthew 23:37-39: *O Jerusalem, Jerusalem, thou that killest the prophets, and stonest them which are sent unto thee, how often would I have gathered thy children together, even as a hen gathereth her chickens under her wings, and ye would not! Behold, your house is left unto you desolate. For I say unto you, Ye shall not see me henceforth, till ye shall say, Blessed is he that cometh in the name of the Lord.* This city admonishes the devil rather than God, and hates anything that concerns God. The inhabitants do not appreciate the servants of God, and as such they are left at the tormenting hand of the enemy. In Nigeria for instance, the Niger Delta states or the South-South geopolitical zone and the Eastern states or the South-East geopolitical zone hardly value the servants of God the Lord has raised for them. They are seen flirting after those raised in other areas at the detriment of the revelations of the Lord present in their midst. Many of those they relied on, because they are not from these lands, have also come to defile, and make desolate, the people and the land, and carted away their wealth in building bigger cathedrals and other establishments in their home lands, just as the Babylonians did to Jerusalem. World politics also has to rear its ugly head in the church. The Lord in Mark 5:19 didn't look for another to proclaim His good news in Decapolis, but one of them, and they listened to his testimony. And I have thought, this is the man the disciples tried to stop when they saw him using the name of the Lord to heal, and when they reported this, Jesus quarrelled with them not to have done what they did. If every town, city and nation will not behave like Jerusalem, but will instead accept whomever the Lord has raised for them, there will be peace and progress.

- **Judea:** Where is Judea? What makes Judea a place of interest to the Lord, as one desiring the preaching and the institution of the new Kingdom values and principles? We would see as we go into the Bible. The Baby Jesus was protected by His parents from Herod, who ruled over this land – Matthew 2:22: *But when he heard that Archelaus did reign in Judaea in the room of his father Herod, he was afraid to go thither:*

notwithstanding, being warned of God in a dream, he turned aside into the parts of Galilee. Why would God warn against Judea? It is because it was under the rule of a tyrant, who has established the Kingdom of the devil in the land – with multiple idolatry worship, corruption and immorality. Prior to this time, Judea was a land people visited to worship the Lord, because the house of the Lord was there – Ezra 5:8: *We went into the province of Judea, to the house of the great God, which is builded with great stones, and timber is laid in the walls, and this work goeth fast on, and prospereth in their hands.* Then the people sinned against God, and the Shekinah left them and the enemy hunted their land and carted away the precious things in the temple, and made them slaves in Babylon – Ezra 5:12: *But after that our fathers had provoked the God of heaven unto wrath, he gave them into the hand of Nebuchadnezzar the king of Babylon, the Chaldean, who destroyed this house, and carried the people away into Babylon.* Soon after this happened, the land was filled with strangers who polluted the land and the treasure of the Lord, which hitherto distinguished them as the people of God upon the face of the earth. Then idolatry multiplied, and with it came immorality. Judea became a stronghold also of the Lord's ministry, showing that evil was losing its hold on God's children – Acts 11:1,29: *Now the apostles and the brethren that were in Judaea …And the disciples, every man according to his ability, determined to send relief unto the brethren that dwelt in Judea.* And this would mean that idolatry, corruption and immorality were on the decrease. Is this what is experienced today? This is evidence that the Kingdom of God has invaded a locality – when evil begins to disappear from the land. When we started our ministry, the land was filled with all manner of sin – idolatry, whoredom, immorality, prophets and pastors of the devil with their agents all over the place and robbing people of their hard-earned money etc. But today, they have all disappeared one after the other. There was a day when in a dream I saw someone I didn't know padlock the church door. When I woke up from that dream, I told my wife that we were moving into the then uncompleted building to start worship and let me see the devil that will stop us from doing the work of God. While we were there, these devil-incarnated prophets and pastors would send their agents to the church, and from there would lure many to their gatherings, where they would demand money from them to perform magic for them, and these unsuspecting people were deceived, because they had no knowledge of the works of the devil. The land was once filled with many prophetesses who were actually harlots, used by the devil to fight the Kingdom of God. And I heard the voice of the Lord one morning – 'they want to set up an Altar of the Mermaid Spirit in the church.' I was angry and one Sunday I warned that anyone who was an agent of this heinous crime against the work of God would be exposed. And in another service around November 2013, I was in the altar when I heard a voice – 'don't you know what to do?' Obviously I didn't know what to do, and I replied thus. Then the voice said, 'call every mother out to the altar, and let them lay a curse on everyone used by the devil to pull down the work of God in this altar.' I did, and the women came out and swore with the kind of zeal that still beats my imagination. After that event, peace returned to the church, and one after the other, all the perpetrators of rebellion left the church, and now the church is seeing growth and love. The last mentioned in that Matthew 4:25 is – beyond Jordan, so we would just treat this, to know what practices of evil attracted the Lord there.

CHAPTER ONE

▪ **Jordan and beyond:** Jordan is located where we have the river Jordan, which became a historic point where John baptised people unto repentance. Now the fact that this place was used as a place for baptism posed a question as to what manner of people had or still inhabits the land. In the book of Genesis 10:13 we read: *And Lot lifted up his eyes, and beheld all the plain of Jordan, that it was well watered every where, before the Lord destroyed Sodom and Gomorrah, even as the garden of the Lord, like the land of Egypt, as thou comest unto Zoar.* Good! The land was inhabited by Sodom and Gomorrah. We are told that these inhabitants were wicked and sinners in Genesis 13:13: *But the men of Sodom were wicked and sinners before the Lord exceedingly.* After God destroyed the early inhabitants (Genesis 19), Jordan also became a land full of pride – Zechariah 11:3: *… for the pride of Jordan is spoiled.* So God wouldn't have chosen a more ideal land than the land were a heinous sin against His person was practised, where He would unite all men back to Him through the baptism of Jesus there.

So, we would see the reason for His mention of 'Mammon' at the onset of His message to them. The spirit of Mammon was eating deep into Galilee, Decapolis,

CHAPTER ONE

Jerusalem, Judea and Jordan and beyond into the land of the Moabites. Two powers operate in our church today - Christ and Mammon. Many servants of God would allot time to preach Christ, maybe once in a month, and use two Sundays to preach Mammon, then use one Sunday to preach about tithing and sowing seed into their own lives. The moment servants of God started preaching mammon, the world turned upside down - church attendance increased in their thousands, immorality entered into the house of God, and peace took to its heel. The Bible says of the reason for the establishment of the Kingdom of God on earth - 2 Corinthians 10:3-5: *For though we walk in the flesh, we do not war after the flesh: (For the weapons of our warfare are not carnal, but mighty through God to the pulling down of strong holds;) Casting down imaginations, and every high thing that exalteth itself against the knowledge of God, and bringing into captivity every thought to the obedience of Christ.* What are these high things that exalted itself against the knowledge of God, and bringing into captivity every thought? Nothing else but the love of the world.

The worship of Mammon was the reason for all the sins that were committed against God. Even now, more money, and more money, is what is preached, and the more preachers raise altars for mammon, the more people lose their grip on the values of the Kingdom Christ came to establish for us. What was His expectation as He preached to them? That they should give Him audience, of course! And implying further that they should leave their businesses to learn about the ways of the Lord first - a new kingdom was about to be unveiled, and with this comes new sets rules of engagement:

- Serving God in truth and in Spirit.
- Doing business, without cheating one another, and holding God in high esteem.
- Marriage, as there are stricter rules that prevent divorce, and the need for men to take care of their family, unlike waiting for their wives to become virtuous women, who would meet all their needs, while they boast outside, as if trying to set the women into competition by their polygamous practices, etc.
- Sanctifying of the hearts - 1 Peter 3:15: *But sanctify the Lord God in your hearts: and be ready always to give an answer to every man that asketh you a reason of the hope that is in you with meekness and fear.*

CHAPTER ONE

This is the beauty of the Kingdom of God where God is fully in charge of all we would do as it was in the Garden of Eden, where God provided all that Adam ever needed, just as He is providing for the Angels in heaven. The Book of Lamentations in the Bible explains the adversity that comes upon humans once we are out of tune with the Kingdom values of heaven.

The Lord spoke in Zechariah 11:7: *And I took unto me two staves; the one I called Beauty, and the other I called Bands; and I fed the flock.* He took two rods – **Beauty** and **Bands**. What do these represent, and what is God trying to do with them? The answer to what He would do with them is just there – *and I fed the flock,* with the two staves (rods) – the one called **Beauty** and the other called **Bands.** The one called 'Beauty' represents 'Favour' and this would mean the presence of the knowledge of God in our midst, and the other, called 'Bands', represent 'oneness, or union' perfecting our understanding of God's precepts, which brings unity amongst His children**.** The Lord says in Jeremiah 3:15: *And I will give you pastors according to mine heart, which shall feed you with knowledge and understanding.* And the flock would be fed with these two rods so that the wisdom of the

Lord will be established in the hearts of His children. This would make them worship Him in truth and in Spirit, thus propagating His Kingdom here on earth. God is looking for someone who can do this job in His name.

God found Abram after when evil had increased, even after the flood, which would have rendered the Earth free from evil. The appearance of evil after the flood, points to the fact that the evil was not in the society per se, but in the values of lives people live, for the children of Noah had lived a life in the world God ruined with water, and as such, the thought of evil lives in them, manifesting in the lives of every child they would born, even after they harkened to the voice of God and were saved from the flood. We still do same today, repented yet still repenting. And the Bible concludes thus – *All have sinned and come short of the glory of God*– Romans 3:23. This simply implies that sin and evil defaces us to the extent that the glory of God that makes us His image, diminishes by the day as we heap up scores of sins into our hearts. When God found Abram, His main apprehension was how he would take over authority from the heathen. And to establish this fact, his name would have to be changed from Abram to Abraham.

CHAPTER ONE

It was my knowledge of the ant kingdom that first made me understand what it takes to live in a kingdom. Every one of those ants is busy in that colony to ensure they maintain and live daily, by the culture that makes them ants. As I write these lines, on the 20th of March 2013, my 41st birthday, at about 8:05 pm Nigeria time, I can see in my inner mind ant hills scattered all around a field with each of these hills managed by similar sets of ants' colonial rules and regulations, though distinctly located with territorial boundaries of influence. These ants would eventually return to their colony at the end of the day in organised lines, which beats human imagination. No matter what may get them in the way as they return back to their anthill, they will strive to make it. In the same way, we often undergo trials, but they are there for us to become stronger and pure as gold (Job 23:10).

CHAPTER TWO

THE PROMISE OF A KINGDOM

Nothing is possible unless the Lord decrees it to be, and this is what anyone would learn from the story in Daniel 5:21: *...till he knew that the most high God ruled in the Kingdom of men, and that he appointeth over it whomsoever he will.* The last statement there says that God appoints whomsoever He will, to rule over His kingdoms on earth. Even today, as God raises servants, these servants acts as kings, overseeing the Kingdom of God here on earth.

A kingdom in simple terms can be seen as the **King's Domain** of influence. In Genesis 17:6, God made a promise to Abraham and in that promise God said He would raise kings through him: *And I will make thee exceeding fruitful, and I will make nations of thee, and* **kings shall come out of thee**.

Though Isaac and even Jacob did not wear a physical crown of kingship, that didn't mean that they were not indeed kings of a heavenly order. Today God is raising disciples, the angels of His churches worldwide (see Revelation 2 and 3), unto Jesus, who are now the kings that would rule each of the Kingdoms that belongs to Christ - the King of kings, as detailed in the gospel of Luke 22:29-30: **And I appoint unto you a kingdom**, *as my Father hath appointed unto me; That ye may eat and drink at my table in my kingdom.*

Let's take good note of the first statement in verse 29 and the first statement in verse 30. Jesus first handed over a **kingdom** to them to manage and that would qualify them to dine with Him in His own kingdom as further explained in, Luke 13:29: *And they shall come from the east, and from the west, and from the north, and from the south, and shall sit down in the* **Kingdom of God**.

I had a dream sometime in 2012, which when interpreted, would mean that I had not been able to raise anyone who would make it to the dinner of the Lord. In the dream, when I got to the banquet, Jesus was seated at dinner with candles on the table, but no one sat on the chairs. I went in happy, but when I saw His countenance, I felt guilty that I hadn't come with anybody. What actually happened in that dream was that while I was preaching, many did not listen to me. However there were some that listened and were ready to repent and make heaven. I however left them while I was going to the dinner with the Lord and they eventually drowned in a river, which I had crossed because they didn't know I had walked through after the water had parted. They went into the river trying to catch up with me without knowing it was parted for me to cross. This meant I had not managed the Kingdom he appointed to me in such a way that kingdom values would rule the hearts of those He kept under my care. And He keep on telling me, they are there for you, if you would not teach them to obey me, you will have yourself to blame on the day of judgement. For every soul He attracts into His Kingdom on Earth, He expects that His servants should give account of them.

This further buttresses the fact that not until the church begins to live God's kingdom rules and principles may we really please God and do His will on earth. This is what the sovereign Lord says in Exodus 19:6: *And ye shall be unto me a **kingdom of priests**, and an holy nation.* A priest is a servant of God, who officiates in His tabernacle, teaching the children of God the ways of the Kingdom of God, with the authority to forgive sins on behalf of God who call him to serve. The book of Revelation 1:6 says: *And hath made us kings and priests unto God and his Father; to him be glory and dominion for ever and ever.* Priests support the king. This is why the Bible would say that God wants to see royal priests, a peculiar people, and holy unto the service of God (1 Peter 2:9). Melchizedek was referred to as the priest of the most high God and He was the king of Salem, meaning that God was actually referring to a kingdom ruled by kings who would surrender to the King of kings. The King of kings rules all over the earth, given instructions through His anointed, yet everyone feels His presence. This is well captured in Luke 17:24: *For as the lightning, that lighteneth out of the one part under heaven, shineth unto the other part under heaven; so shall also the Son of man be in his day.* This refers to information. This is one way to test if your pastor is really genuine. In certain seasons, when the Lord releases information, you would hear the servants of God preaching or teaching the same sermons with similar Bible quotations, and giving out the same revelations of events about to happen in the world.

I am not writing this book to teach us how to feel the presence of God and have the consciousness of Him, but to teach us how we can become the consciousness of God in whatever we do – John 10:34-35.

Spiritual Illumination

From the passage in Luke 17:24 we just read, we see that the wisdom and consciousness of Jesus is in the world as streaks of lightning subduing the world. Everyone created by God has an element of light in him or her. This light has what I would refer to as 'Spiritual Lumina' characterised by its luminous intensity. This is why the Kingdom of God is also call the Kingdom of Light. And Jesus says that anyone who is begotten of God is a light to the world - Matthew 5:14. Spiritual illumination is what characterises every citizen in the Kingdom of God. The aim, therefore, of the Kingdom is to emit lights of love, togetherness and dedication to the purpose of Heaven, which is the will of God, ensuring that all humans are caught up in their thoughts into the thoughts of God in heaven, creating a kingdom of sonorous uniformity of 'sounds of unspeakable joy' in the hearts of all and sundry.

The life we live in Christ is a life of glory, the same glory Christ had while on earth. So we are the same as the Christ that lived on earth in authority and glory – with the same power and wisdom. This we can affirm from John 17:22 - *And the glory which thou gavest me I have given them; that they may be one, even as we are one.* It is this glory that links us to the plan and purpose of God so that we would not walk through darkness and groping (Isaiah 42:16). It is the perfect will of God, that we all would become His consciousness and live to appreciate His being nature in us.

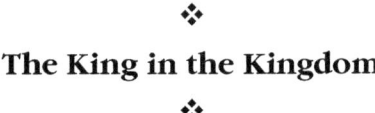

The King in the Kingdom

The king in the Kingdom of God here on earth is the servant God and God expects even the nations to submit under his authority as given to him by God, so that they can be blessed. We have seen all over the world how presidents and world leaders submit to the authority of God through His servants. This was the promise upon Abraham (Genesis 12:3), and God is still raising kings after Abraham and filling them with the spirit of Christ, so that they would operate with the purpose of God here on earth.

We would see an instance where we would have a clue of what God expects once He call His servant, institute his authority and establish his kingdom, in the book of Jeremiah 27:6-8: *And now have I given all these lands into the hand of Nebuchadnezzar the king of Babylon, my servant; and the beasts of the field have I given him also to serve him. And all nations shall serve him, and his son, and his son's son, until the very time of his land come: and then many nations and great kings shall serve themselves of him. And it shall come to pass, that the nation and kingdom which will not serve the same Nebuchadnezzar the king of Babylon, and that will not put their neck under the yoke of the king of Babylon, that nation will I punish, saith the Lord, with the sword, and with the famine, and with the pestilence, until I have consumed them by his hand.* God says that

Nebuchadnezzar was His servant, and that He expects all nations to submit under Him. When Christ was about to leave earth, knowledgeable as the disciples were, Christ handed them over, under the care of Peter, a fellow disciple like them. Because of the authority Elijah commanded, when Jesus called out to God in Mark 15:34, the soldiers thought He was calling on Elijah to rescue Him and because they feared that the presence of the spirit of Elijah could liberate Him, they decided to give Him acid (vinegar), so that He would die before the rescue – Mark 15:36: *And one ran and filled a sponge full of vinegar, and put it on a reed, and gave him to drink, saying, Let alone; let us see whether Elias will come to take him down.* Throughout this book, we will understand what God is expecting in this era where the Kingdom of God is now in and with us through the presence of the Holy Spirit. Those who understand the working of the Kingdom of God here on earth are closer to the servants of God, for the Arm of the Lord to be stretched towards them, and they have for years, all through their generations, experienced the increase of the Lord. Societies that disregard these spiritual authorities have also had to struggle to survive, while they also lose their lands to the control of those who are submissive to God's servant – commerce and entrepreneurial power. The reason is that God sees the acts of not submitting under authorities as rebellious, and He hates it (Numbers 14).

The Lord want to dwell among us, and that is the everlasting wish of heaven – Revelation 21:3: *And I heard a great voice out of heaven saying, Behold, the tabernacle of God is with men, and he will dwell with them, and they shall be his people, and God himself shall be with them, and be their God.* The Lord wouldn't release His tabernacle to us when He is not interested in us.

With the coming of Jesus, the church became the Kingdom of God, and the old form of kingdom was discontinued. God gives kingdoms to whomever He wishes: … *till he knew that the most high God ruled in the Kingdom of men, and that he appointeth over it whomsoever he will* – Daniel 5:21. When God raises a servant, He uses him to set up a spiritual cloud and fire – usually referred to as a pillar of fire and of cloud. These are a spiritual presence that creates the immortal realm within the mortal. What people should do is to cluster around to hear what the Lord has to say through him.

Imagine what would have happened if all the children of Israel were to stretch forth their rods towards the sea. Or imagine if everybody was to carry the ark across the river Jordan. When an individual sets up fire in a desert alone, it would be blown away by wind. If we gather more wood into an already burning fire, the flame will be much to give more people warmth. This is the purpose of a Kingdom.

Within the large church worldwide we have specific callings which are represented by the anointing duty-call upon the servant of God who institutes the church in place, which would now become his kingdom or domain of influence. The moment the faithfulness and wisdom of Joseph was discovered, though he was bought as a slave, Potiphar made him ruler over his household – Genesis 39:3. Even in the prison he was made more of a supervisor – Genesis 39:22. Daniel was a captive, one who was to be in a refugee camp, but his faithfulness to God and the display of supernatural wisdom announced him before King Nebuchadnezzar, and he was made a ruler over the wise men, who held the destiny of Babylon in their hands and tongues – Daniel 2:48. Referring to this phenomena, Jesus says in Matthew 24:45 - *Who then is a faithful and wise servant, whom his Lord hath made ruler over his household, to give them meat in due season.* Every faithful and wise servant of the Lord acts in the Kingdom of God on earth, to feed the congregation with meat, as a king who reports to the King of kings and the Lord of Lords. This is why Saint Paul was angry with those amongst the congregation who love to drink spiritual milk only - Hebrews 5:12-14. What is this meat that they cannot receive and who are those who cannot receive it? They are those running from one prayer house to the other. We eat spiritual meat when we have the anointing. 1 Corinthians 3:2-3 says: *I have fed you with milk, and not with meat: for hitherto ye were not able to bear it, neither yet now are ye able. For ye are yet carnal: for whereas there is among you envying, and strife, and divisions, are ye not carnal, and walk as men.* In my book *Gifted and Anointed*, I explained the anointing, what it represents and its administration.

As I recounted in the introduction to this book earlier, I saw myself wearing a crown in a dream sometime in 2008 and I was wondering what it was. The Lord made me to know that the crown I saw was my current status and position in His kingdom, but the more I would do the work He has assigned to me, the more I will grow and get a better crown, then live in a mansion here on earth and later in heaven, at the gathering and sealing of the foreheads of the saints and servants of God. It was at 5.30 am on the 14th of December 2008 when I saw myself in the learning environment, more like in the wilderness, with many tents. Each of these tents had a teacher disseminating the heart of God to his students. I came into the tent that was close to the entrance of the camp, and my teacher instructed me to get a notebook to write down whatever he said. This was when I got admitted to learn the secrets that establish the Kingdom of God here on Earth. On the 20th day of October 2013, at around 4 am, I saw myself in another learning environment with other people, some I recognised to be those who preached to me while I was not yet in the Faith, and other pastors. I came into the class late but completed all my studies and exams in about 5 days, and was issued a certificate. It was surprising to many and even to me, because it was so quick and fast. When I woke up from the dream, I heard a voice saying that I have learnt so fast that I should go and invest what I have learnt – that was my graduation from the spiritual training school, in

CHAPTER TWO

the 5th year of my calling. On the 21st night, a day after the certificate was given, I saw myself in a beautiful apartment, in a beautiful story building. It was so lovely, representing the new life in ministry that I would experience. Then as I woke up on this day, I heard a voice – as from today, you must become calm always, dressing with honour and respect – 'you cannot wear anything filthy again – you must limit your discussion with people. It is time to be quiet and act maturely. Don't be too fast to give answers to questions pushed at you – never again.'

God is sealing those that would eventually merit His reward due to their service in His vineyard: *Saying, Hurt not the earth, neither the sea, nor the trees, till we have sealed the servants of our God in their foreheads* – Revelation 7:3. These are the servants who have been kings and priests of salvation on earth. The servant of God runs the Kingdom with the authority in the anointing he bears. We would want to have a better understanding of this fact in Revelation 2:17:*He that hath an ear, let him hear what the Spirit saith unto the churches; To him that overcometh will I give to eat of the hidden manna, and will give him a white stone, and in the stone a new name written, which no man knoweth saving he that receiveth it.*

This is where my authority comes from, for instance. God empowers us with secrets of life so that we can shine for Him. The hidden manna, also known as the 'hidden wisdom (1 Corinthians 2:7),' is spiritual food to strengthen us for the works of truth. The white stone is diamond – pure, resolute, determined, and beautiful- a shining white stone of authority. This is the mantle of the authority of the Power and Wisdom of God that lives and works in me as one who is filled with the hidden manna.

In the book of Job 1:20, and Job 2:12, we are told how it was the practice in those days of men carrying their mantles about. From both verses, Job and his friends rent their mantle, as if saying – 'why didn't this mantle save Job?' which means the devil wouldn't have had power over Job if God hadn't taken away His arm from his mantle. Prior to Job's predicament, we are made to know what the mantle did for him in Job 29 – he had the power to rule, acquire wealth and command respect from everybody. One special thing about mantles is that their effectiveness lies in the presence of the Lord. Through the Bible, mantles were rent when it was obvious their presence didn't save a situation (also see Ezra 9:3). I will want to talk about the mantle a little, and how it explains the Kingdom identity. Whatsoever a mantle touches is possessed by it, and used for the work of God – 1Kings 19:19. A mantle paves way for you when you encounter an obstacle -2 Kings 2:8. It is a symbol of authority, and when it works for you, shows that the spirit of God, who is the bearer of the anointing, is already working for you – 2 Kings 2:13 - 14.

Mantles were worn by priests (Ephod), kings (Saul), the rich (Job and his friends), and prophets (Elijah). The robe Jesus wears to the cross qualifies as a royal mantle, hence the shroud of Turin, being preserved as a sacred relic, because it is believed to be the covering used when Jesus was buried. It was also called a cloak. The benefits of mantles can also be seen from verse 3 of the hymn *O Worship the King*:

The earth with its store of wonders untold,
Almighty, thy power hath founded of old;
Hath established it fast by a changeless decree,
And round it hath cast, like a mantle, the sea.

The sea existed before God started creation upon the surface of the earth. The dry land came out of the sea. The sea brought forth and multiplied every living creature in it. If the mantle is likened to the working power of the sea, and believing that the writer was deeply inspired by the Lord's spirit, it also buttresses the fact aforementioned, that mantles command spiritual authority and power. The sea connects us to new opportunities as we meet people from other nations, as also does the mantle – we would see Elisha following Elijah after the latter threw his mantle on Elisha. The sea beautifies the landscape with its waves and cool breeze, so also the mantle.

Now let us read further through the book of Revelation 2:26-28:*And he that overcometh, and keepeth my works unto the end, to him will I give power over the nations: And he shall rule them with a rod of iron; as the vessels of a potter shall they be broken to shivers: even as I received of my Father. And I will give him the morning star.*

We would notice that God gives power to those who overcome the devil's temptation and have also worked the work of salvation to the end, without deviating. What is the power meant for? We are told that a rod shall rest upon our hands, as it was with Moses, and with this rod we shall rule the Nations of the Earth; we know that only kings have powers over nations or kingdoms. This proves that in God's Kingdom on earth, we shall have servants of God, who are angels of the church, as kings with a rod, or more adequately called 'a staff of office,' to ensure that they subdue the world under the works of God forever. And further, these faithful witnesses of Christ would receive a 'Morning Star.' What is this Morning Star? It represents light bearing and life. In Revelation 22:16, Jesus calls Himself the Bright and Morning Star. The only difference is that while the servants of the Lord become morning stars (kings), He reigns over them as the 'bright and morning star (King of kings).' The bright and morning star in heaven feeds the morning star here on earth with power and wisdom. 'Bright' represent authority and the 'morning star' represents power. This is why Satan also disguises himself as this light, so that the very elect may be deceived, because without the light of righteousness, man have no future.

As John would say in 1 John 2:27: *But the anointing which ye have received of him abideth in you, and ye need not that any man teach you: but as the same anointing teacheth you of all things, and is truth, and is no lie, and even as it hath taught you, ye shall abide in him.*

The servants of God are to display the character of nobility, which they receive from the Almighty God, whom they represent. And their duties would be seen as that which has to do with enlarging the Kingdom of God on Earth. This is well captured with the parable of Jesus in Luke 19:12-13: *He said therefore,* ***A certain nobleman went into a far country to receive for himself a kingdom****, and to return. And he called his ten servants, and delivered them ten pounds, and said unto them, Occupy till I come.* Jesus establishes kingdoms and appoints kings to oversee them – the angels of the church (Revelation 2, 22:16). And as such He also expects us to do what the noble man did above, which is why He says in Luke 18:29-30: *And he said unto them, Verily I say unto you, There is no man that* ***hath left house, or parents, or brethren, or wife, or children, for the Kingdom of God's sake****, Who shall not receive manifold more in this present time, and in the world to come life everlasting.* Nobility is the character of discipleship. It is the beauty of the throne of God. Every servant of God acts as a king who conquers kingdoms for Christ, the King of kings. These kingdoms are both physical and spiritual.

CHAPTER TWO

Worldly kingdoms' values are seen in the character and life of the people such as lying, stealing, gossip, murmuring, etc, which are the characteristics of disunity with God, resulting in a popular phenomenon often used to deceive many that they are into a competition - survival *of the fittest*. Spiritual kingdoms are all over the place and some have been established by the devil where he rules through his agents who are also kings, in charge of the world. But Jesus has overcome the world when He saw Satan fall - Luke 10:18, and He is receiving back His lost kingdoms - Luke 19:12, and handing them over to His servants who must exercise the Kingdom of God's authority in order to enlarge their respective kingdoms through the teaching of God's oracle as contained in the anointing that is in them. Christ reviews their progress periodically. The Lord reviews my performance in the month of March in every year, which is the season my star appeared in heaven, when I was born, and after this review, He would give me more secrets and mysteries of the Kingdom. He also visits our kingdom in the month of October, the month that is officially recognised as the starting month of our kingdom. A church anniversary is a period of celebrating the strength of the Kingdom God has handed over to His servants to oversee. This is why in some churches the servant of God is called General Oversee. This title is true and real as Paul will recount in 1 Corinthians 3:10: *According to the grace of God which is given unto me, as a wise masterbuilder, I have laid the foundation, and another buildeth thereon.* And Jesus would be the Grand Commanding General Oversee (GCGO), because He is the King of kings and the Lord of Lords. Many people frowned at recognising the servant of God, but we would borrow a leaf from 2 Kings 1, the third captain of fifty came kneeling before the servant of God, and his life was preserved, unlike the first and second captain, who treated the Servant of God without respect. Elijah was honoured with a whirlwind into heaven - he never tasted death. Jesus was honoured – John 12:3: *Then took Mary a pound of ointment of spikenard, very costly, and anointed the feet of Jesus, and wiped his feet with her hair: and the house was filled with the odour of the ointment.* Jesus admonish us to bless whoever come in the name of the Lord – Luke 13:35: *Behold, your house is left unto you desolate: and verily I say unto you, Ye shall not see me, until the time come when ye shall say, Blessed is he that cometh in the name of the Lord.* Jesus is the Lord; those coming in His name are His servants, whom He is raising among you to lead you to Him. This implies that if we don't recognise those the Lord is using to do His work, we would experience desolation. If showing respect to a servant of God is wrong, Jesus wouldn't instruct His disciples not to enter into unworthy homes – but He told them to only abide in worthy homes – people with respect and honour – Matthew 10:11: *And into whatsoever city or town ye shall enter, enquire who in it is worthy; and there abide till ye go thence.* Severally, St. Paul talk of those who took care of the material needs of the apostles – Romans 16:1-2: *I commend unto you Phoebe our sister… for she herself also hath been a helper of many, and of mine own self.* The midwives in Egypt preserved the lives of the Hebrew children and that earned them the provision of God – Exodus 1:21: *And it came to pass, because the midwives feared God, that he made them houses.* Which life did they actually preserve? It was the life of Moses, the messenger of deliverance. And as funny and tactful as it could be, the deliverer was in Pharaoh's house, learning about the secret of his kingdom as a prince. So Moses was a king, who has to lead the Israelites to God. And that wasn't all, God made Moses a God to Pharaoh – Exodus 7:1: *And the Lord said unto Moses, See, I have made thee a god to Pharaoh: and Aaron thy brother shall be thy prophet.* So, who is your servant of God? He represents God and when you see him, expect a word from God. In fact, Jesus says those who neglected His disciples have neglected Him.

Sometime in the month of April 2014, the Lord spoke to me, demanding that I should raise fifty saints for Him, and that suffices. And since that day, I have being wondering how these fifty saints would be raised when many are not ready to hear the gospel of truth – a confirmation from John 3:19 says; *And this is the condemnation, that light is come into the world, and men loved darkness rather than light, because their deeds were evil.* All the while, spanning six years now, that the word of the Lord came to me, doing this work of restoration, hardly have I found anyone ready to listen and to hear what the Lord says, and yet, as many would claim, they are indeed Christians, but a little check in their lifestyles would prove otherwise - they hadn't known Christ.

CHAPTER TWO

Anyone who is not in a Kingdom would usually find it hard to serve God because he/she would be hunted by the devil day and night. This is the reason why many of us still cry and pray without answers. When people are in need, what God does is to lead them to one of His Kingdoms and ensure that the king there has what it takes, which is the anointing, to make them have peace. The anointing increases with the demand in place – Luke 5:17: *… and the power of the Lord was present to heal them.* That would make the servant of God a father unto them because he begat them through Christ, as Paul would say in, 1 Corinthians 4:15-16: *…yet have ye not many fathers: for in Christ Jesus I have begotten you through the gospel. Wherefore I beseech you, be ye followers of me.*

This anointing upon the servant of God bears the peace in Christ and it can be released upon people for them to experience peace when they follow through as Elisha followed Elijah, and when the spirit realm confirms that they already have the foundation to receive it –Luke 10:6: *And if the son of peace be there, your peace shall rest upon it: if not, it shall turn to you again.* On the 31st of March 2013, the Lord led me to conduct an anointing service

CHAPTER TWO

and after this event, on the morning of the 5th of April 2013, He instructed me to start teaching the congregation how to invest, act and to live the anointing, to positively affect lives and become a blessing to many as they teach more people His kingdom principles and values. On the 26th of September 2014 at about 5am, He further instructed me to tell the congregation to follow Him so that He can change their lives, and give them a better and promising future.

The whole essence of teaching Kingdom values is to ensure the foundation is repaired so that our thoughts and doings will reflect the fact that we harbour Christ in our hearts, as the righteous can do nothing except the foundation is set aright - Psalm 11:3. The king in the Kingdom must point everyone to the Lord, no matter his achievements, and we would borrow a learning from Gideon – Judges 8:22-23: *Then the men of Israel said unto Gideon, Rule thou over us, both thou, and thy son, and thy son's son also: for thou hast delivered us from the hand of Midian. And Gideon said unto them, I will not rule over you, neither shall my son rule over you: the Lord shall rule over you.* No servant of God has the power to rule except that the Lord permits Him. Even as the Holy Spirit glorifies Jesus, so also every action of a king must glorify the King of kings.

The place of the Queen

In every kingdom, there is a queen. The Bible recorded that the children of Israel did worship the queen of heaven. The Lord didn't say the queen does not exist, His anger was that the children of Israel had decided to give His glory and honour to the queen, hence they had committed treason, and should be punished for that – Jeremiah 7:17-18: *Seest thou not what they do in the cities of Judah and in the streets of Jerusalem? The children gather wood, and the fathers kindle the fire, and the women knead their dough, to make cakes to the queen of heaven, and to pour out drink offerings unto other gods, that they may provoke me to anger.* If the queen never existed, there wouldn't be any need for God to be angry, but the fact that He kicked against it showed that there is indeed a queen somewhere in heaven. This is idolatry and it must be discouraged. The reason why I brought this up is that while we talk about the queen in the

Kingdom as a representation of the wife of the servant of God, who should follow him wherever he goes to do the work of God – 1 Corinthians 9:5, she shouldn't be worshipped. The Eden kingdom was started with Adam and Eve. We are getting to the point where we would really begin to appreciate the role of mothers in the building of a virile kingdom unto God, here on earth. Eve was created after a form and likeness – her bones and flesh were of Adam, though it was only the rib (bone) God took, but we see Adam referring to 'his flesh' as a metaphor for human. The form and likeness should be after the queen in heaven, I suppose. Eve was made to help Adam, meaning the form she was made after was also offering help in heaven – these are my thoughts though. The woman wasn't created less than man except after the sin – Genesis 3:16: *... and thy desire shall be to thy husband, and he shall rule over thee.* And if we believe that once we receive Christ, the curse in Eden is lifted, then the woman too has received her original rights back, and would really become that perfect help in the Kingdom of God – 2 Timothy 2:15: *Notwithstanding she shall be saved in childbearing, if they continue in faith and charity and holiness with sobriety.* A woman is saved continually provided she continue in:

1. Faith: which is putting trust in the helping arm of the Lord

2. Charity: care and love to the work of God

3. Holiness: being sanctified for the service of the Lord, and dressing with moderation, not to entice and seduce men, but to always seek ways to uphold the fruit of the Lord in her life.

Though many women are yet to understand this as they yield their hearts to material needs. The fact above would mean that the cultures that treats women as less important than men must have been ruled by the devil, who want the woman to be subjected to the curse, which Christ has taken away, therefore making her salvation inferior to that of the man. And in such cultures, it is not really hard to discover that the men don't really mean well. Jesus once frowned at the wanton deprivation inflicted on widows – Matthew 23:14. If we look closely again at what God told the Serpent, we would see a clue to the origin of Eve – Genesis 3:15: *And I will **put enmity between thee and the woman,** and between thy seed and her seed; it shall bruise thy head, and thou shalt bruise his heel.* The highlighted text says - **put enmity between thee and**

the woman, showing that, *ab initio,* the Serpent and Eve were friends, or knew each other so well, or Eve was created after a kind that lives where the Serpent had existed. And if we see, as we have always believed, that the Serpent is the anointed Cherub – Lucifer - we would say that Eve, or her form, existed in heaven where Lucifer knew her. And again, if we see Genesis 6:2, as angels came to take wives, we may say that indeed there are damsels in heaven, and that because no one is permitted to marry in heaven – Matthew 22:30: *For in the resurrection they neither marry, nor are given in marriage, but are as the angels of God in heaven,* we would say that the angels only decided to have the taste of what humans were doing – and the result was the birth of a superhuman, which was against the will of God. Jesus also in His teachings gave us a spiritual clue to what happens in heaven – Matthew 19:12: … *and there be eunuchs, which have made themselves eunuchs for the Kingdom of heaven's sake. He that is able to receive it, let him receive it.* Which shows that for the sake of the will of God that must be done in heaven, marriage is thus prohibited. Hence we would say that all who dwell in heaven are made eunuchs for the sake of the gospel – Revelation 14:6.

CHAPTER TWO

While God was initiating the new Kingdom through Abraham, He recognised the importance of the queen and king mother, Sarah: *And God said unto Abraham, As for Sarai thy wife, thou shalt not call her name Sarai, but Sarah shall her name be. And I will bless her, and give thee a son also of her: yea, I will bless her, and she shall be a mother of nations;* **kings of people shall be of her** — Genesis 17:15-16. Abraham have a duty to effect God's promise of establishing Sarah as the Queen, and that would be changing her name from Sarai to Sarah.

We would see that Isaac never wore a physical crown, but that didn't stop him from being a king as recorded in the above Bible extract. This explains that the kingship is more of a spiritual administrative authority, over the manipulations of darkness. Between Esau and Jacob, neither of them wore a physical crown, but that didn't take away the fact that they are kings, and they indeed had their own domain of authority and influence, hereby known as the Kingdom. Let's take a look at the plural, 'kings,' in the last verse we just read, and what will come into our minds is, 'who makes kings?' God does, and brings them forth to life through the woman, who takes the responsibility of weaning the baby king until he grows. A look at Proverbs 31:1-9, we would see an instance of the king's mother giving a prophetic revelation on what is required of a king to her dear son, the king Lemuel. The advice started thus - *The words of king Lemuel, the prophecy that his mother taught him.* I argue this often in my books, because I strongly feel that our mothers, the king bearers, have neglected their duties in a child's upbringing. They have seen kingship as more of a physical affair, that the children are also thought to fight for recognition and obtain power by force – this has led to the high level of crime and atrocities in society today. The woman is to the man what the ribcage is to the heart. The fame of a man is often known through the brilliance of his wife - Proverbs 31:23. Before the call of Abraham, as the Kingdoms grew, the capacity and strength of the women who survived the harsh lives they lived were being forgotten. Yes! It wasn't mentioned, not even once. In one of my widest meditations, I had looked at the ant colony again, and could see the queen, and how she was revered, leading to the colony being united and strong, dedicated towards the actualisation of the vision they drive to finish. Nimrod was strong, and a mighty hunter. The question is, who was the woman behind him, and one that bore him in her womb and also gave him the early education about survival that he grew with? Who was he trying to please in all the wild strength that made him? Who was the woman sending him out to hunt down animals? She was strong and powerful, I suppose. The power of the queen could be estimated from the power of Esther in the book of Esther. Yes! Esther took hold of the Kingdom. We would see how even Jezebel was in charge and Elijah had run for his life at her threat. There is always a woman in charge in every kingdom, because she bears the children that become kings and queens. She gave them milk while they were young, and often the children try to please her. She has strong control in the day-to-day culture that exists in a kingdom. How did she invent the foods she cooks? She may have had an angel teaching her (we are told an angel gave food to Elijah in 1 Kings 19). She is powerful, with enormous strength, and she gave birth to the Kingdoms we see all over the world today. The Governors, Presidents, Managing Directors, CEOs, etc, all exhibit the character their mother may have sown in them. This is why cultures that neglect the roles of mothers would hardly see increase and peace, as they are submerged in

CHAPTER TWO

wanton wars. Increase and peace have always been, and will always be, the bearers of societal stability.

Jesus said that His time was not due, but she turned water to wine at the request of her mother. There is no kingdom without a queen - from the home, society and church, even in our industries, the CEOs and MDs have a queen behind every decision that is made – *the woman behind the successful man*. Through the queen mother, the daughters and women in the Kingdom learn kingdom values, and that enables them to give birth to princes, princesses, priests and kings. Naturally, the first disciple of every pastor, for instance, is usually his wife. We would also see that the mother of the pastor has much to do in the success of the calling of God upon the servant of God as seen through the Bible. Jesus handing over His mother to John is a clear demonstration of such regard to the queen mother – John 19:26,25. If we look at verse 26 carefully, you will agree that Jesus actually handed the disciples in the care of Mary, His mother, when He said – *Woman behold thy son*.

When the queen mother in a kingdom does her job, the righteous will fill the face of the earth, and once again we see that everyone is then begotten of the father - 1 John 2 23-24, 29 says: *Who is a liar but he that denieth that Jesus is the Christ? He is antichrist, that denieth the Father and the Son. Whosoever denieth the Son, the same hath not the Father: he that acknowledgeth the Son hath the Father also. If ye know that he is righteous, ye know that every one that doeth righteousness is **born of him**.* This is what the term 'born again' implies, which is having the mind of Christ– the heavenly kingdom values. Like Lemuel's mother, the queen must inculcate this value in the children early enough, and when they grow they will not depart from it.

Who tells the histories and stories that establish a kingdom under the full moon? The queen mother does! The church will reap a greater harvest of souls when the mothers are trained and equipped in such a way that they can teach the children about the values of the Kingdom of God early enough.

Often we see that the wives of most servants of God have not seen themselves as building a kingdom for God and they would use their worldly unrepentant character to run down the Kingdom. Many of them, who are under the influence of the seed of the devil in them, because of the lives they had lived earlier, really do not know the value they must bring to bear, as they administer Kingdom values in the Kingdom. We have had cases of many queen mothers who lure young women into lesbianism. The Lord spoke to me that the wife of His servant is a queen and that is why He defends them – from Abraham to Isaac, when these duos lied to save themselves by trading off their wives.

Why we ought to recognise the wife of the servant of God

Since the Bible made reference to a wise woman being the brain behind every successful home, and a foolish woman being the reason behind homes being reduced to ashes, we would take this by inference, to imply that even in society and the church, there would be a woman, the king mother, sowing seeds of cultures that would eventually mature into what we see being exhibited in society and church – if they be good or bad seeds, the evidence is all over the place for us to see – Proverbs 14:1: *Every wise woman buildeth her house: but the foolish plucketh it down with her hands.* In Africa, because of polygamy, many a mother tries to defend their sons and daughters so that their father and society would see them as good children, even when it is a clear fact that these children have unhealthy traits and habits. This has continued even in the era of monogamy, so that many Christian mothers even connive with teachers and lecturers to buy marks for their children. The mothers have often been the ones changing schools for their children, just to hide the children's poor academic performances in some cases. Sooner they would also teach their daughters these ill traits, and then the cycle of falsity will continue unabated.

My wife used to sit with the congregation, until one day I heard in my heart that I should anoint her to sit by my side. I hesitated but soon, the voice enveloped me for days and I had to anoint her – and I have not regretted that action, since she has always been the one to know early when people who don't mean well, who are actually devourers, are in my circle of decision making to pull down the Kingdom. The Lord spoke to me some time ago, saying that He made me anoint my wife so that she is separated from the congregation because of the value He places on the wife of His servants. She would have had quarrels and fight with the women who would have disregarded her because every woman wants access to the servant of God, and they often see the wife as an obstacle and as such they would hate her out of jealousy. And He said – 'stand to defend her always. She is always right. I have given her to you to watch your back else this ministry would fail.' So the Lord values the wife of His servants and will not forgive any church that treats her less than the husband.

The woman is the first disciple of the servant of God, as he receives instructions from God. Neglecting her role could lead to God even refusing to answer the prayers of His servant – Malachi 2:13-16. She knows so much about this calling and how it all started. If a journalist wants to know about me, or a historian, the first source of information would be my wife, before any other person at all, so she deserves respect too.

The women ministry in many churches is failing in its duty as the mothers of the princes, princesses, kings and priests, and we are not seeing the kind of increase we need because there is a gap between them as they disregard pastors' wives and kingdom revelations, which unless taught by the servant of God himself, remain unlearned. We would also see that the children of many servants of God do not even show the character of those with the fear of God. We are informed how the mother of King Lemuel instructed him in Proverbs 31:1-3. So the role of the queen mother or the pastor's wife in ensuring that heavenly values are transferred to the younger generations cannot be overemphasised.

A case in our church some time ago showed that things weren't going well as I have asked my wife time without number of the outcome of the women's meetings and she would say the women leadership don't tell her anything or even come to her office to discuss it with her –I saw that as pride. As long as this went on, the women in the church were disconnected from the vision I was bearing. What I did was to stop every gathering in the church until the Kingdom values were taught and understood. The women meeting are to help her to achieve, as a *'mother in Israel'* – Judges 5:7. They are to support her as a mother whom God has chosen as a result of the anointing upon the husband. She is in the heart of her husband because both of them are one and the same, and therefore, she knows my heart because I often complain before her.

A church that does not regard its Pastor's wife should repent. God cannot increase such a church. If we disrespect pastors' wives, we disrespect the pastors also, and the anointing upon them, and the God who anointed them.

❖

The Manner of the Kingdom

❖

Before the first coming of Christ, it was difficult for the world to understand what the Kingdom of God was all about. Many felt they had to die before they could experience the beauty and luminance that the Kingdom of God reflects on those who have entered into the presence of God's glory. But Jesus explains what it is all about in the Lord's Prayer and His reply to the Pharisees –

- Matthew 6:10: *Thy kingdom come, Thy will be done in earth, as it is in heaven.*

CHAPTER TWO

- John 10:9: *I am the door: by me if any man enter in, he shall be saved, and shall go in and out, and find pasture.*

See these two verses of the Bible – The Kingdom of God is here on earth already since Christ instituted it - *the Kingdom of heaven is at hand* – Matthew 4:17. This was a task that was difficult for all the prophets of old to carry out. We could see what Jesus says: *All that ever came before me are thieves and robbers: but the sheep did not hear them – John 10:8.* So, since we have become the consciousness of Christ (Galatians 4:6), through receiving Him into our lives, we are therefore citizens of God's Kingdom, where we carry out our activities freely, relating to the will of God, as represented in John 10:9: *... and shall go in and out, and find pasture,* in such a way that we would oversee the Lord's estates united as one entity all over the world, which Satan came to put in ruin (Revelation 12:12). This we must carry out with the authorities of kings and priests unto God, the father of our Lord, Jesus Christ, and to reign on earth so that our lights would shine forth before men, and through our earthly exploits of making the society a peaceful habitation for God's children - through the preaching of the message of salvation to the disoriented in society, God would eventually receive Glory and Dominion forever and ever in our hearts (Isaiah 61:6, Matthew 5:9, Matthew 5:16, Revelation 1:6, Revelation 5:10). He vowed sometime that one greater than the temple was in their midst, which implies that if people were bowing down in the temple, then they should worship the one greater than the temple – the fullness of the consciousness of God; Matthew 12:6 - *But I say unto you, That in this place is one greater than the temple.*

Rehearsing the word of the Lord in John 10:9 again: *... and shall go in and out, and find pasture,* also reminds me of the promise of God to all those who will desire to live in His Kingdom, and this can be affirmed severally in verses all over the Bible – the authority of the Faith we profess as children of God.

Let's see such proclamation of what God is expecting to see in our lives as we live and imbibe the characters and expectations of the culture of His Kingdom - Deuteronomy 28:6:*Blessed shalt thou be when thou comest in, and blessed shalt thou be when thou goest out.* This expectation of God concerning us – the thoughts of good and not of evil (Jeremiah 29:11) - is supposed to manifest all around us, all year round - *And all these blessings shall come on thee, and overtake thee, if thou shalt hearken unto the voice of the Lord thy God* (Deuteronomy 28:2). But we need to understand what God is expecting from us to enjoy this lasting peace and joy from His throne.

We can make choices here on earth, but this is not possible in heaven. The life we would live in heaven is determined by the life we lived here on earth. Anyone is free to live a life that he/she desires and also to worship God the way he/she deems fit, but the truth remains that we would all have to account for the life we lived on earth. It is expected that a first-time visitor to my house must seek to know the direction to my house, and usually the direction(s) would be described by me or some other persons who have been to my house before. This is what Christ did by teaching us what we should have done or should do to please God. Christ lived with God from the foundation of the earth and knows exactly what God expects from us; hence He said that He is the good shepherd - John 10:11. He still raises people who He teaches these secrets and they would become the Servants of God in His churches. When Christ lives in us

CHAPTER TWO

and we become the consciousness of God, we live our lives daily to please God and also fulfil our tasks here on earth. We can make all the effort to labour on earth to enjoy a certain standard of life that we desire. This is not so in heaven. Our standard of living in heaven is determined by how far we fulfilled our destiny here on earth. If we merit one room in heaven for instance, as a reward for our earthly life, so it would be from eternity to eternity. There are people who will perambulate in heaven, as we see also on earth. Here on earth, we may decide to attend college to be trained in a specific profession in an attempt to live a more prosperous life. In Heaven there is no such opportunity to change our status. What we earn is what we would live with - the Lord is a righteous judge. This is why anyone who is responsible for us not to have had a destiny fulfilling life on earth would receive punishment - the more reason why we seek for forgiveness from those we hurt daily.

Most people find it hard to receive these codes and the conduct that is expected of those who would enjoy the good life the Kingdom of God has to offer, because they must be discerned spiritually (1 Corinthians 2:14). I have also seen people who would come to the house of God to meet a servant of God to help them with money and other welfare needs, for instance. What they really need is the secrets – the hidden wisdom - to make life more liveable. It is common to have churches without these hidden life secrets and wisdom getting filled to the brim with multitudes expecting miracles on Sundays which they hardly get, but to rest their hopes on the testimony of a Christian brother or sister which was announced, with all joy by the pastor, as a show of his power to work miracles. What a decimation of the glory of the Kingdom of God, which bears the truth and answer to life's unending sorrows. While miracles are necessary, they are signs meant to convince those who are hard-hearted towards God, who are still outside the Kingdom, so that they would yield their hearts to God. Once we are in the Kingdom, we don't look for signs and miracles anymore because we are bearers of signs and wonders. Everything about us is a manifestation of the works of God that live in us once we are saved by the blood of Christ. We would see that the reason a sign for a miracle was given to Moses was to convince the children of Israel that God sent him to deliver them (Exodus 4:1-9), and to persuade Pharaoh to let the Israelites go (Exodus 3:19). After the miracle, we are supposed to begin a three-day journey into the wilderness to serve the Lord with wholehearted sacrifice (Exodus 3:18) – which means, you are to start having a relationship with God. This is the whole essence of the reason why God is interested in delivering us; to serve Him. When Jesus was about to raise Lazarus from the dead He opened up the fact that miracles are only a means through which God convinces unbelievers about His power, so that they can believe and turn away from their evil ways: *And I knew that thou hearest me always: but because of the people which stand by I said it, that they may believe that thou hast sent* me - John 11:42. In another place in the Bible, He clearly said that signs are demanded by a perverse generation – Matthew 16:4:*A wicked and adulterous generation seeketh after a sign…*

The poor should know that they are not permitted to remain poor the moment they have given their lives to Christ and have also made up their minds to live according to the dictates of the Kingdom of God. So it is not about accepting Christ, but also living by Christ – we all should abide in Him. The solution to coming out of poverty is to accept the good news of restoration and freedom – Luke 4:18: *The Spirit of the Lord is upon me, because he hath anointed me to* **preach the gospel to the poor**. This implies that the poor have to be ready to hear in the house of God (Ecclesiastes 5:1). People can be poor mentally, which implies they have a low reasoning faculty. Poverty brings humility, sometimes, and making oneself willing to serve as long as bread will come from the table. But in all, poverty is a sense-dulling factor, and often leads people into taking foolish decisions. The act of preaching is the act of communication, and communication involves encoding, decoding and feedback. Christ's expectation of them is also captured in John 6:26-27:

*Jesus answered them and said, Verily, verily, I say unto you, Ye seek me, not because ye saw the miracles, but because ye did eat of the loaves, and were filled. Labour not **for the meat which perisheth**, but **for that meat which endureth unto everlasting life, which the Son of man shall give unto you**: for him hath God the Father sealed.*

The purpose of what Christ said was to enable them to desist from seeking after what is not important to living a life that would please God. What are miracles? This should be the first question anyone desiring to live in the Kingdom of God should try to answer correctly. In John 6:26 Jesus says *Ye seek me, not because ye saw the miracles...* If they had seen the miracles with the heart of meeting God to helping them live a life of fruitfulness, they would have seen the power behind the miracles and then yield their lives to the Power of God, to be controlled and directed by God to fulfil His desire to direct their lives as captured in Isaiah 42:16:*And I will bring the blind by a way that they knew not; I will lead them in paths that they have not known: I will make darkness light before them, and crooked things straight.*

We would discover that while Adam was in that Garden, God presented him with a help to support him and to make him fulfil his task to tender the garden. In the same way, we all have one garden or the other to tender for God, and if we fail in our responsibility to do this, we will not be qualified for His glorious reward set for the righteous. The poor should be made to know that there is a value of living called 'righteousness,' and that they must seek to live it, whether they like it or not. It is God's standard for all mankind.

Every kingdom has a set of rules, regulations and way of life and culture, which spells their uniqueness. This is spelt out in the book of 1 Samuel 10:25:*Then Samuel told the people the **manner of the Kingdom**, and wrote it in a book, and laid it up before the LORD.*

Earlier in 1 Samuel 7, we were informed how Samuel visits all the clans that makes up the Kingdom, which is similar to what a General Overseer does, ensuring that the Kingdom is healthy. In this sub-section we will explain the manner of some kingdoms of God, which were administered by God's Servants in the book of Revelation 2 and 3, so that we can have a clear picture of what the Kingdom of God on Earth represents and stands for. Every Kingdom of God on Earth is represented by a candle light before Jesus and this we can get from Revelation 2:5: *...else I will come unto thee quickly, and will **remove thy candlestick out of his place,** except thou repent.*

Kingdom of God at Ephesus

This church had some peculiar character that made God choose them as heirs of His kingdom, though they had some short comings later on, but our concern is seen in the qualities and the culture of the Kingdom as seen in Revelation 2:1-3, 6: *Unto the angel of the church of Ephesus write; These things saith he that holdeth the seven stars in his right hand, who walketh in the midst of the seven golden candlesticks; I know thy works, and thy labour, and thy patience, and how thou canst not bear them which are evil: and thou hast tried them which say they are apostles, and are not, and hast found them liars: And hast borne, and hast patience, and for my name's sake hast laboured, and hast not fainted. But this thou hast, that thou hatest the deeds of the Nicolaitanes, which I also hate.*

From this portion of the Revelation we would be seeing the emblem and culture of this Kingdom of God on Earth:

The **'Identity'** of this kingdom is Jesus, as one holding seven stars in His right hand and walking in the midst of seven golden candlesticks, so we would expect to see this reflected in their flag, anthem and their kingdom pledge if they have one.

This kingdom showcases a **'Culture'** of hard work for the sake of the gospel, patient in waiting for the day of the Lord, hates evil, reject false apostles and continuously defends the name of the Lord.

This kingdom exists to showcase the beauty of the Lord as their only source of hope. So the angel of the church, who is also the king of the Kingdom or the pastor of the church, is one who encourages steadfastness in the Lord, no matter the circumstances. He defends his kingdom from heresies. He does not invite anybody in the name of servant of God to minister in his altar before the Kingdom citizens, the congregation. As seen in the verses we just read, the angel, the king of this kingdom, may have been engrossed with chasing after fake apostles and comparing doctrines that the Kingdom is gradually losing its value as seen in Revelation 2:5. This king or angel as he was referred to here would have done well by training his kingdom adherents the true way of the Lord in line with the values explained earlier until it becomes a song in their lips rather than allowing other apostles to counterfeit what they had heard.

❖

The Kingdom of God at Smyrna

❖

This is another kingdom that has a manner of life that pleased the Lord. We can see this captured in Revelation 2:8-10: *And unto the angel of the church in Smyrna write; These things saith the first and the last, which was dead, and is alive; I know thy works, and tribulation, and poverty, (but thou art rich) and I know the blasphemy of them which say they are Jews, and are not, but are the synagogue of Satan. Fear none of those things which thou shalt suffer: behold, the devil shall cast some of you into prison, that ye may be tried; and ye shall have tribulation ten days: be thou faithful unto death, and I will give thee a crown of life.*

In this kingdom, their **'Identity'** is Jesus, seen as the first and the last, which was dead, and is alive. This implies that the message the citizens will understand is that of resurrection of the dead.

The **'Culture'** inherent in this kingdom is also seen as the defence of the faith they professed in Christ even when some Jews attacked their doctrine. They were comforted by Christ not to bother but to continue in the revelation that set their kingdom in place.

❖

The Kingdom of God in Pergamos

❖

This kingdom is also unique as one standing for the truth as seen in their emblem – Revelation 2: 12-13: *And to the angel of the church in Pergamos write; These things saith he which hath the sharp sword with two edges; I know thy works, and where thou dwellest, even where Satan's seat is: and thou holdest fast my name, and hast not denied my faith, even in those days wherein Antipas was my faithful martyr, who was slain among you, where Satan dwelleth.*

Their **'Identity'** would be a man holding a sharp sword with two edges, representing judgment. This may also feature in their flag, anthem and kingdom pledge. They also have a **'Culture'** of standing by their faith even when they dwell where Satan had authority to silence their voice.

We can also see other kingdoms recorded in Revelation 2 and 3 as we read further.

❖

The Royal Diamonds International Church

❖

Our church, the Royal Diamonds International Church, stands to raise God-loving leaders while building a kingdom of saints, who will do the will of God on Earth. Our **'Identity'** is the Diamond and Royal robe of purple, where the name Royal Diamonds comes from. Our desire is to live the values of the Kingdom of God on Earth so that we would merit the new Heaven and Earth that the Lord would fashion after His heart at the end of the day. Our **'Culture'** is royal culture where the pastor and his wife act as king and queen respectively, and this is replicated in the lives of the members of this royal kingdom,to show forth the grace of the Lord Jesus, who has called us unto himself. Who are the Saints? Ezekiel 44:7-9 explains whom God is interested in. They are those who are no longer strangers to the oracles of God. They are circumcised in both heart and flesh, and are willing to carry the message of Christ in their lips wherever they go, while caring less about their physical needs.

Kingdom Truths

On no account should we compare kingdoms because they have different callings, though with one purpose - Heaven seek. Saint Paul was sent to the Gentile nations - Acts 22:21: *And he said unto me, Depart: for I will send thee far hence unto the Gentiles,* while the twelve disciples were sent to the Jews - Matthew 10:5-6: *These twelve Jesus sent forth, and commanded them, saying, Go not into the way of the Gentiles, and into any city of the Samaritans enter ye not: But go rather to the lost sheep of the house of Israel.* God raises His servants after His heart to meet the needs of specific sets of people, which we refer to as nations or kingdoms. In our universities, people study different courses to meet the requirements of the profession they want to practise and through which they would earn a living. In the same way, God's children have various, onerous tasks to fulfil on earth and they are adequately mapped to God's kingdoms on earth that have the capacity to oversee them and provide spiritual training and consultancy support from the throne of God.

In the Book of Lamentation one would see the prophet recounting the culture of the Kingdom of Judah before its fall. We would at this juncture see this book and list out some of the expected lives of those in God's kingdom on Earth. We shall be taken the ideal case as shown in the book of Lamentations.

CHAPTER TWO

- **The Kingdom must be full of people, with the evidence of the presence of Christ, the Groom, and must be great among nations – as a fruitful princess in the midst of other Kingdoms of Christ:** It is the desire of God that we increase in number and strength, and that He should be present with us (John 14:18). We must occupy till He comes, winning every soul to Him. In reference to the absence of this, the Prophet said: *How doth the city sit solitary, that was full of people! how is she become as a widow! she that was great among the nations, and princess among the provinces, how is she become tributary!* – Lamentations 1:1.

- **The enemies of the Kingdom do not prosper as long as the Kingdom is in good relationship with God:** As long as we live by the standard of God, we would have no need to be afraid of the enemy. I find it difficult to comprehend why many churches spend so much time fighting the enemy in their prayers. I hear warfare prayers in every nook and cranny, as if this is the essence of Christianity. And this is as a result of these believers not having the authority of Christ in them, which comes with the continual hearing of sound doctrine of Faith. The Prophet also lamented this derogatory state in Lamentation 1:5: *Her adversaries are the chief, her enemies prosper; for the Lord hath afflicted her for the multitude of her transgressions: her children are gone into captivity before the enemy.* I prefer to do the will of God and allow God to fight His battle ahead of us, rather than waste my energy in entering into a context with a looser – the devil.

- **Citizens of the Kingdom are supposed to live a life of abundance**: We can also affirm this in John10:10 – *Have life... have it more abundantly.* We cannot be hungry. We cannot live a life of 'Want' as long as the Kingdom pleases God in context and their everyday living (Psalm 23:1). The Prophet knew that those who live in God enjoy His abundance, hence he cried for help from God: *All her people sigh, they seek bread; they have given their pleasant things for meat to relieve the soul: see, O Lord, and consider; for I am become vile – Lamentation 1:11.*

- **The Kingdom experiences the availability of mighty men who make things happen in the world**: These mighty men are the movers and shakers of society, presidents, governors, MDs, CEOs etc. They make the rules that set everything rolling wherever they are. Job confirmed this in the book of Job 29:21-22; - *Unto me men gave ear, and waited, and kept silence at my counsel. After my words they spake not again; and my speech dropped upon them.*

They are the righteous in power who must rule with the purpose and plan of God to bring succour to society. When the Kingdom pleases God, He in turn gives such a kingdom mighty men. This implies that when a servant of God leads his congregation into greener pasture of good and sound doctrine of God in knowledge, and understanding, and they apply this knowledge as the wisdom that guides their living, then such a servant of God would boast of having mighty men in government and private sectors, changing society to what God expects. The Royal Diamonds International Church is committed to preaching and teaching the word, raising God-loving leaders and building a Kingdom of Saints unto God. Every servant of God who has no God-fearing presence in the affairs of the government and private sectors should plead for the Lord's intervention as the Prophet did in Lamentations 1:15-20: *The Lord hath trodden under foot all my mighty men in the midst of me: he hath called an assembly against me to crush my young men: the Lord hath trodden the virgin, the daughter of Judah, as in a winepress....Behold, O Lord; for I am in distress: my bowels are troubled; mine heart is turned within me; for I have grievously rebelled: abroad the sword bereaveth, at home there is as death.*

Anyone who gathers with Christ – Matthew 12:30, and save humans from the eternal destruction of their souls is one who would be rewarded in heaven with a heavenly banquet - Luke 22:29-30 – *And I appoint unto you a kingdom, as my Father hath appointed unto me; That ye may eat and drink at my table in my kingdom.* It is my responsibility as a servant of God to look after His Kingdom here on earth as a requirement for me dining with Christ in heaven. This was the very meaning of the last words before His arrest. This is very key to our responsibility, as we know that the last words from someone dying are to be taken very seriously as commandments that must be done in honour of him/her.

These verses also show that what God is interested in is how we can live in royal patterned kingdoms here on earth.

CHAPTER TWO

The question is, why has it been difficult for us to live these heavenly values here on earth? If we came from heaven, how come we couldn't remember any of the values of heaven and live them here on earth? The answer is found in Romans 3:23: *For all have sinned, and come short of the glory of God;*

We have come short of that illuminative glory of God which should have enabled us to walk through this world (darkness) without hindrance and the groping characteristics of walking in the dark – the mistakes we make daily. Without the help of God through Christ, who is the only authorised way to salvation, we would live to please Satan all the days of our lives. Satan stains our glory when we obey his voice by sifting us as wheat – a characteristics of murmuring against God, doubting God, and quenching our thirst for the things of God. Let us take a look at what Satan does with anyone he uses in, Luke 22:31: *And the Lord said, Simon, Simon, behold, Satan hath desired to have you,* **that he may sift you as wheat:** To sift, is to sieve, filter, separate, strain, etc. Peter would be used to cause division among the brethren by Satan because Satan seeks pleasure in the things of men as confirmed in Jesus' statement in Matthew 16:23 - *Get*

CHAPTER TWO

thee behind me, Satan: thou art an offence unto me: for thou savourest not the things that be of God, but those that be of men. But Christ helped him succeed by praying to God to strengthen him so that his faith will not fail (Luke 22:32) - *But I have prayed for thee, that thy faith fail not: and when thou art converted, strengthen thy brethren.* So the whole essence of being in the Kingdom of God is to reach out to others and bring them into the fold.

So far, we have seen that:

- A kingdom is the domain of a king where he exercises dominion and control.

- The Lord wants us to learn kingdom values in His church and extend it to our homes where the husband becomes the king and the wife a queen. And the children would learn about kingdom ways of greeting, manner of eating, royal dressing, etc, in order to please God. So that every man would indeed be a ruler in his domain of authority, to the glory of God. The name, husband, has nothing to do with the bride price men give or the dowry when they marry, it is more of bearing a responsibility and being committed to that responsibility as the head, who must protect, provide, and be present when called upon to act in like manner. An earthly king once instructed thus: *For he sent letters into all the king's provinces, into every province according to the writing thereof, and to every people after their language, that every man should bear rule in his own house, and that it should be published according to the language of every people.*

- So, here, the church is a 'training and culturing' ground. Our heavenly task is to say and do what God wants as it is done in heaven. We practise it in the church first. And we take it home to practise. So every time, this is what we should be expecting; building 'according to pattern,' the church of Christ; the Kingdom of God on Earth.

- Our God is a great King. He is the Lord of hosts –a mighty heavenly army. He is dreaded among the heathen – unbelievers (Malachi 1:14b). He is the King of kings and Lord of Lords. We can see the fulfilment of Daniel 2:44, that God has raised His kingdom when Christ died. This kingdom extends from heaven to earth. So we have the Heavenly Melchizedek Order and the Earthly Melchizedek Order.

CHAPTER TWO

- We have to conquer more lands for Christ and crusades are avenues for conquering new kingdoms and enlargement of the domain of influence, to increase love and opportunities for everyone. We should be able to have our own hospital, school, swimming pool, camping ground, hotel, etc. We dress in a pattern and talk in a manner identical with heaven - Titus 2:1-10.

- Everything is according to the laid-down pattern shown to His servant, the king, serving under Him. We see the Kingdom when we are born again – meaning that one is yet to belong to any Church. We are not members yet, we have accepted the doctrine of Jesus but yet to be located in any of His earthly kingdom to be taught Kingdom values, so that we can reign here on earth to His glory - Revelation 5:10. This is why we groan and pray so hard to be led to the Kingdom that would provide the healing we require for our weak soul to be strengthened. The moment He leads us to any of His servant according to His heart, all He wants from us is our obedience to His instructions through His servant.

And we conclude that the church of Christ represents the Kingdom of God here on earth. And for every church gathering, there must be an institution of service. In the book of 1 Chronicles 28:19-21, we would see an order of the kind of service the Lord expects from David, and being the king of Israel, such service is what God is expecting from His people:

All this, said David, the Lord made me understand in writing by his hand upon me, even all the works of this pattern. And David said to Solomon his son, Be strong and of good courage, and do it: fear not, nor be dismayed: for the Lord God, even my God, will be with thee; he will not fail thee, nor forsake thee, until thou hast finished all the work for the service of the house of the Lord. And, behold, the courses of the priests and the Levites, even they shall be with thee for all the service of the house of God: and there shall be with thee for all manner of workmanship every willing skillful man, for any manner of service: also the princes and all the people will be wholly at thy commandment.

At the end, we are told how King Solomon brought down the presence of God with the temple he built and the sacrifice he performed in the presence of God's children. So also, every servant of God is giving an order of service to enable him to lead the children of God. In most cases the order of service as instituted by the servant of God is a reflection of the covenant he has entered with God, so he acts as instructed. Any breach of this order would mean disobedience and would render the covenant null and void.

Every Kingdom also bears a message, and this message is also a reflection of the covenant between God and the servant of God who oversees the Kingdom in his care. In the book of Matthew, from chapters 5 to 7, Jesus taught about the message of the Kingdom. The whole essence of the message is also explained in John 4:23-24:

But the hour cometh, and now is, when the true worshippers shall worship the Father in spirit and in truth: for the Father seeketh such to worship him. God is a Spirit: and they that worship him must worship him in spirit and in truth.

We are admonished to be quiet in the presence of God - Ecclesiastes 5:2. The more we allow God to talk, the more we become quiet. He has called for a meeting by sending us salvation in Christ, to reason with Him, let's give Him the opportunity to talk. Many people are used to complaining before God. This is not a good character for anyone in the Kingdom.

It is easy to know a servant of God by what He writes. As Jesus said - *For had ye believed Moses, ye would have believed me: for he wrote of me. But if ye believe not his writings, how shall ye believe my words - John 5:46.* And since he does not exist on his own, passing the words he teaches through fire will tell of what sort it is made of. To do the will of God requires strength and good courage, and these have been the characteristics of all successful servants of God who oversee His kingdom here on earth. If they look at all the discouragements from those they lead and the outside, they would faint. But with God strengthening them, they are able to succeed beyond human understanding, to the amazement of their enemies.

Visiting the Home Kingdom

Every kingdom extension must deem it necessary to point her citizens to the home kingdom. It is the responsibility of the king of the Kingdom extension to visit the home kingdom, at least once in his lifetime. In John 14:4, we saw a reference to Jesus informing his disciples that they knew where He was going, because they knew the way, meaning they had visited or had perfect knowledge of where the Kingdom of God is: *And whither I go ye know, and the way ye know.* And indeed, Stephen saw heaven before he died. The devil did visit God on a meeting with Him - Job 1:6. Apostle Paul talked of being caught up to the third heaven - 2 Corinthians 12:2. Jesus was always seeing what the father was doing, meaning He was in contact with the home kingdom. Moses left to the home kingdom where he saw the pattern of the tabernacle. If God was with him on that mountain top, the Israelites would have know because they indeed saw His presence often as a cloud, and then when He came, the thunderous sounds made them to know that God was in their midst, but the quietness that existed at the foot of the mountain, which made them beg Aaron to make a God for them, tells of the fact that Moses was indeed far away from the mountain top - Exodus 25:9. If the devil can ascend to talk with God, it is a requirement that we should desire this daily.

CHAPTER THREE

THE KINGDOM WARS

If the scripture had not been fulfilled, Jesus would have engaged the services of angels the night he was being arrested – Matthew 26:53:*Thinkest thou that I cannot now pray to my Father, and he shall presently give me more than twelve legions of angels.* Again, looking at this verse of the Bible tells us what it seems like to engage the Kingdom of darkness in a war. Jesus gives us the number of angels God would dispatch to push the devil away and make him flee – more than twelve legions of battle-ready angels. Is the devil easy to deal with using human wisdom? No! If we read the book of Matthew chapter 4, carefully, during the temptation of Jesus – the wilderness is far from the pinnacle of the temple, how did the devil get Jesus into there? It was a spiritual battle. If it had been a physical fight, at least people would have witnessed the argument between both of them right at the pinnacle of the temple. As we read, the devil came when Jesus was worn out after the forty days fasting, and He was hungry. Many of us would expect that after forty days fasting, peace would automatically come – but that was when Jesus' temptation started.

Why did Jesus refer to the Jews as the generation of vipers – Matthew 12:34? And why would Babylon become the habitation of devils – Revelation 18:2? This is as a result of the multiplication of evil. We would discuss this within the context of kingdom wars, and to know why the human race is gradually facing extinction.

Within the invisible cosmic abode lie the realms of spiritual authorities. Layer upon layer of spiritual consciousness exist beyond our atmosphere, and even beneath the earth we tread on daily. These spiritual authorities want to interfere with humans when invited to do so. In most cases, they just live their lives in the order in which they have been constituted. But the knowledge of good and evil which now lives in the heart of humans has also made those spirits within the evil realm of disloyalty attack the purpose of God, rendering spiritual assistance to wicked humans on earth to undo others. This is where the cry for righteous judgement emanates from, and the hosts of the righteous abode are hence invited to free humans from the attack of the wicked world. The devil is fighting tooth and nail these last days. The world over, there is increasing moral decadence. It seems as if God has covered himself with a blanket of cloud that He no longer answers prayers - Lamentations 3:44. As I mentioned in the introduction to this book, the voice of the Lord echoed in my night vision on the 26th of May 2012: *Who will go before me like Moses and Elijah did, to tell this generation their sins so that they would repent?* World economies are crashing down. Nothing short of what the Bible reveals in Revelation 12:12: *Woe to the inhabitants of the earth and of the sea! for the devil has come down unto you, having great wrath, because he knows that he has but a short time.* The devil knows he has but a short time and he wants to drag as many people he can with him to eternal destruction where he belongs. It is his expectation that if the entire world is in sin, then God may want to have mercy and have a second thought not to end this evil world with the calamities predicted in the Book of Revelation – Smart thinking, I guess. But the devil is wrong always, about everything. His modus operandi was revealed by Jesus when He spoke of how the devil would try to tempt Peter as earlier discussed – Luke 22:31: *Satan hath desired to have you, that he may sift you as wheat.* To sift as wheat is to examine critically. And again, it implies that the devil works with our minds – trying to convince us not to accept the gospel, or to make us feel that our salvation is not real, or to try to prove to us that Jesus wasn't divine, and therefore not God. The devil works with arguments, just as the serpent did to Eve in the garden.

But before the devil left heaven, there were evil forces already inhabiting the earth as would be seen in Genesis 1:2: *The earth was without form and void, and darkness was over the face of the deep. And the Spirit of God was hovering over the face of the waters.* Formlessness, void and darkness are only but the description of oppression and evil that existed in the primitive earth kingdom. It was so disgusting that all the Spirit of God could do was hover without a resting place. Many people have had dreams of images appearing with disgusting faces to them and often these were the images of the idols that placated the earth and were served as idols that protected the heathen kings of old. These images are those of the spiritual authorities that existed *ab initio* on earth that caused the earth to experience such formlessness, void and darkness. Though when the devil rebelled and left heaven, these authorities submitted to his control as a means to end the creation of God on earth, it should be understood that the devil is not the same in image and likeness as these idolatry images. The devil only uses them as agents to administer woe upon the inhabitants of the earth - Revelation 12:12. We should also know that because the Lord claimed this earth from the forces that existed prior to God pronouncing light upon the earth, these forces, as they have claimed to be the original owners of earth, have always wanted to extinct the existence of the creation of God on earth. This could be understood from the way God took the land of Canaan from her original dwellers and gave it to Abraham's descendants. So God only took a part of the deformed world, made it beautiful and kept Adam to oversee it. Adam by this became the first king on earth, to report to the King of kings. When Abraham also had the opportunity of working with the Lord, he rejoiced as

CHAPTER THREE

Jesus confirmed in John 8:56 - *Your father Abraham rejoiced to see my day: and he saw it, and was glad.*

I propose that the so-called dinosaurs were the ancestors of the serpent we see today, which the evil forces used to deceive Eve. Dinosaurs are depicted like dragons, from fossil evidence seen so far. The Bible refers to the devil as a dragon – Revelation 12:13: *And when the dragon saw that he was cast unto the earth, he persecuted the woman which brought forth the man child.* The dragon is a reptile, and reptiles are cold-blooded animals – humans are warm blooded, so if the devil is depicted with cold-blooded animals, it shows that the devil cannot give life to humans. I also propose that it was after its fall and losing its limbs and through years of mutation, it became the present day form of serpent we call a snake, and that to adapt to its new state of crawling, its body had to become the size we see today. We have had snakes growing up 50 feet long and weighing up to 600 pounds.

I also propose, from evidence in the Bible, that after God created the Heavens and the Earth, He resided in Heaven as it has always been, being His throne, and created the angels to live in heaven. During these periods, the earth with its forces trying to disintegrate the earth to its original separate elemental form, prior to God creating it into a uniform shape, which He moulded into a sphere in His potter's wheel, multiplied as a result of electromagnetic forces created within the elements within. The result of this was fusion, fission and the dissolution of substances in the waters that were formed from the reaction between oxygen and hydrogen on the surface of the earth, and this later filled the earth surface. The solid part of the earth sank to the bottom, retaining water within, and then also dissolving every element, as water dissolves solid elements. We still have water gushing from rocks all over the world. Yet there was heat in the middle of the earth caused by the fusion and fission of the elements that God had forcefully brought together into one spherical form. These forces causes all the spiritual currents that exist on earth, as the elements on earth have potential to maintain territorial control. Metals and non-metals alike have spiritual relevance as they do physically – Daniel 2:31-45. These elements have formed human's weaponry of destruction for years now. They have also become the structures upon which every world civilization has evolved.

CHAPTER THREE

Continuing with my allegorical treatise, when God brought them together as one entity to make a spherical earth, the war that emanates from them turned the earth into a deformed, void and dark entity – which means they had stopped reacting with one another, because they had formed compounds with one another. When God spoke light into the earth, He increased the temperature of the earth and set every element into a reactive mode so that further new substances could be created. The earth, through a volcanic eruption, pushed rocks forth from beneath the waters and it was time to make the earth habitable. It is true that humans have made idols of iron, bronze, etc. And these have also become intermediaries between the spirit world and man; this is as a result of the inherent forces that exists in the elements that makes up the earth. These elements are also in the body of man – iron in the blood. We have the element zinc also living in the human body. Science shows that iron has magnetic properties, and because this element is present in our bodies, we are also manipulated by magnetic fields. All these resist God, hence the body is weak – Matthew 26:41: *...the spirit indeed is willing, but the flesh is weak.* And every food we eat on earth is to replenish these elements in the body. The presence of these elements in our body makes us mortal. What make the flesh weak are the elemental substances in the body, which try to return the body to an unreactive mode. And I propose further that the knowledge that these elements have spiritual manipulative forces only came from the fact that since God formed the earth from them, He must have breathed His spirit upon every element on earth, to be able to listen to Him and act in accordance. Today, we would see all over the world how these earth substances have changed lives around. No wonder the early scientists were alchemists who tried to use their knowledge to explain God's creation. It is the wrong use of the forces residing in these substances that we now call evil.

Now, going further into knowing what the devil came to represent in the life of humans, and their relationship with their creator, we would suppose that the devil being an enemy of God fits into one who would become the evil warlord who would eventually help them to take over the earth after putting out life, and once again return the earth to the original state of formlessness, void and darkness. This is the battle for control upon the earth,

CHAPTER THREE

and every Christian should be grateful to God who has given us the power of His spirit to take possession of the earth. Evil will stop influencing us only when we stop interacting exploitatively with the substances that make the earth. This is why, during fasting and praying periods, humans usually want to have rest. Our homes are made of silicon, iron, etc., and these elements create forces that affect our living and reasoning, hence Jesus says – Matthew 8:20: *And Jesus saith unto him, The foxes have holes, and the birds of the air have nests; but the Son of man hath not where to lay his head.* This is why He also says we should store our treasures in heaven. Interacting with the elements that make the earth will always make us experience evil spiritual currents, affecting our godly reasoning. Caution is the right word! If our desires rests in the substances that exist on earth, we will be interacting with forces of darkness on earth – the forces that existed on the face of the earth before God took over, and took man into a special environment where these forces wouldn't have control on him, until he was deceived by the enemy of God and then thrown out into the forces from which he had hitherto been protected.

In heaven, until the devil challenged God and wanted to

build a throne above that of God, there was only one kingdom. When the earth came to be, the Kingdom of God was extended to the Garden of Eden, which would eventually serve as the colony of God, because He actually sent His Holy spirit to envelop the earth before He acquired the lighted part and then invested His anointing and later made the Garden of Eden His administrative unit on Earth. The immortal was then fully present in the affairs of man. The absence of this made man become subjected to the devil, until the appearance of Jesus returned these anomalies to status quo, as it was in the beginning – 2 Timothy 1:10: *But is now made manifest by the appearing of our Saviour Jesus Christ, who hath abolished death, and hath brought life and immortality to light through the gospel.* When the devil challenged the authority of God in heaven, because of the anointing the devil possesses (Isaiah 14:12-14) and when he was chased out of heaven, his anointing gave him the upper hand over man, and he took over the Kingdom of earth, teaching men his character of disloyalty. He ensured he mutilated the image of man so that God would eventually hate His creation. Though the devil couldn't receive a kingdom above the throne of

God, which he desired, he indeed had the throne beneath God's kingdom. Even as Jesus walked in the midst of seven candlesticks in heaven (Revelation 2) so also the devil did walk through the stones of fire. He was well respected above all the creations of God until he fell from grace (Ezekiel 28:14). Why was he cast out? Jesus gave us a clue in Matthew 5:13: *Ye are the salt of the earth: but if the salt have lost his savour, wherewith shall it be salted? it is thenceforth good for nothing, but to be cast out, and to be trodden under foot of men.* The devil lost his saltiness, which is the sanctified life that would make him stand before the face of God, and since the cord of relationship between him and God was broken, he was no longer useful in God's Kingdom; hence he was cast down to earth - brought under the feet of the Lord. So it is with anyone who feasts with the devil - they are not regarded as God's Kingdom adherents.

Contending with the devil without the anointing of the Lord (Psalm 89:20), is a suicide mission because he is anointed already, though now in mutilated form devoid of the light - wisdom - of God, and he has replicated this kind of anointing in the hearts of those under his control. Every child that is born into this world inherits the

CHAPTER THREE

anointing upon the devil through his/her parents – Romans 3:23.

This implies further that everything we need on earth has to be begged for, including our daily bread, because the devil has set himself in high places, in government, to ensure God's blessings don't come to us (Daniel 10). We now wrestle with him and his angels (Ephesians 6:12), in order to live on earth, even for a bite of food – hence many people lie daily for their stomachs' sake. The only way to ensure we don't struggle is moving into the Kingdom of God here on earth, where His angels would come providing for our needs.

As a matter of emphasis, we must know that the moment the devil left heaven, he came down to earth to establish his own kingdom where men would eventually live his character of disobedience, rebellion and self-praise. In the Kingdom of God there is no lack, but because the devil is a thief, everyone ruled by the devil experiences a sense of lack and dissatisfaction.

We would now have a good understanding of the devil, and his kingdom character and values. In order to understand what the Kingdom of God is all about, we need to first talk about the Kingdom of darkness, and to do that we must talk about the devil.

What the Devil is

Who is the devil? For the purpose of gaining preliminary knowledge, you would have to read the books of Isaiah 14:12-15, Ezekiel 28 and Revelation 12 on your own before continuing. These three chapters of the Bible give us a clue who the devil is. The devil is known as the adversary, opposer, slanderer, or false accuser. This means the character of someone who stands against your success, to oppose you; someone who challenges you for no just cause, and who does not give you an opportunity to defend yourself. The devil is a spirit, hence unseen, so he possesses people to carry out all these. When you see people who slander, oppose the good things you are about to do and your dedication to the work of God, people who are just there to condemn you, in the workplace, for instance, the devil is in action. The devil does not believe in 'us,' it is always, 'I' he knows.

CHAPTER THREE

❖

How the Kingdom of the Devil came to be

❖

The devil was known as the anointed cherub, meaning he was greater than the angels. He was very close to God, until he challenged God over His authority, in Isaiah 14:12-15.

In heaven there was order, but the devil does not like order, so he challenged the authority of God that he wants to be above God, and then he was thrown out by the other loyal angels to God. The powerful angel that brought him down was Archangel Michael. The devil was higher than them in rank, as the anointed Cherub, but when he disobeyed God, they grew angry and threw him down. As he was going, one third of the angels in heaven who were also loyal to him left with him. For the purpose of illustration, if we have ninety angels, for instance, thirty left with him. The attitude of the devil is also seen in many churches today. An assistant pastor breaks out and all of a sudden he builds his own church, leaving with one-third of the church members, so to speak.

CHAPTER THREE

The attitude of the devil is stealing (John 10:10), as we can see from the angels that he seduced to follow him down to earth. Now, when he left heaven, he went straight to the Garden of Eden.

Adam and Eve didn't know who the devil was. When God was creating the Garden of Eden, he used the angels to plant it. And the devil went there to plant the seed of good and evil I suppose, and he planted the seed in the middle of the garden, and the tree started blossoming. So when it was time to bring the downfall of man, the devil went straight to possess the serpent that was on the tree of good and evil, and after he deceived the woman therewith. The Bible says in Ezekiel 28:13: 'every precious stone was thy covering.' So he was shining. We have heard of diamond pythons with body markings as shiny as a diamond, which are often seen around coastal areas, living close to human residences. The diamond python is a popular non-venomous snake which often takes up residence in the roof spaces. The woman saw the shining beauty, I suppose, and wondered what it was, but when she got there it was the serpent. The devil went to Eve because he knew she didn't have the original information from God; the devil didn't disturb Adam, because he knew he was filled with the original information. Satan knew that the moment the information is not from the original source, there is bound to be inconsistency with what God said, and that would mean lying, which would be a sin against God. The moment Eve said in Genesis 3:3: *God hath said, Ye shall not eat of it, neither shall ye touch it, lest ye die,'* she lied and because she lied, she was now under the control of the devil. Compare her statement with the original voice of God to Adam in Genesis 2:17: *But of the tree of the knowledge of good and evil, thou shalt not eat of it: for in the day that thou eatest thereof thou shalt surely die.'* Eve, added, *'neither shall ye touch it'* to God's command. Despite her remark being of a more stringent condition, she had sinned. Many times we try to make God's ways too stringent and difficult to follow, as is seen in most of our over-popularised spiritual warfare prayers, when we shout as if God is deaf. The moment Adam and Eve yielded to the devil's deceit, they fell from God's grace, and they couldn't cling to the vine of life. The moment they fell like a falling star, Adam and Eve couldn't face the presence of God any more. They started thinking about themselves, and the first thing they did was to provide clothing made out of fig leaves to

CHAPTER THREE

cover their nakedness. So they were no longer thinking like God. If we look at what is happening today, it's the habit of many of us to be concerned about ourselves. If you see somebody who is possessed with the spirit of God, he/she doesn't think about himself, he thinks about how to be a blessing to other people.

It is easy to know the devil. The devil thinks about himself, so when he came to man, he started making him think about 'self.' The Bible made us to know that some people would lose their soul the day they start thinking of how to please themselves - *But God said unto him, Thou fool, this night thy soul shall be required of thee: then whose shall those things be, which thou hast provided?* – Luke 12:20.

When God clothed Adam and Eve with the animal skin, we would usually explain that gesture from God to them as the love of God. But I have thought it also to mean that actually, the moment Adam and Eve fell from grace, they took the form of animals in reasoning, as many animals use leaves as covering to hide from predators. So God only used the animal skin to explain who man had eventually become.

CHAPTER THREE

It is adequate to think that when man got into the field he started behaving like animals because he was no longer hearing from God; the wisdom of God was no longer in his heart. He had lost control from God, just as an aircraft would lose control from the airport control tower and would eventually crash-land. Man was no longer getting information from God and the only way he could get information was through the devices already masterminded by the devil – evil spirits now possessing idols, which was the only information, commonplace as instituted by the devil. Man would then have to contemplate in his reasoning – to know which voice was speaking to him, and often time would follow the devil, and would claim that God indeed spoke.

Now that the devil was with man all day in the field after man left the presence of God, let's see an instance of what kind of thoughts the devil would impregnate in their heart:

Devil (sowing a thought into man): 'You must be hungry - look at the monkey, it's eating a banana, try it.'

Adam (After reciting the devil's thought in his heart): 'Eve, we are hungry, let's do what the monkeys are doing.' In another instance, the devil could have asked Man to take a look at the lion killing another animal, and so on. So man started learning many things from the animals. Today, we have evidence to prove that man learnt from the animals. Then gradually, man intensified the thinking about 'self' again. If you look at the book of Genesis 11, Nimrod led the people who wanted to build a tower that would reach up to heaven so that they would make a name for themselves. That was after God had used Noah to start a new world which would have being devoid of evil.

The Works of the devil

That introduction made us to know that God had to dress man with animal skin so that he could cope in the new environment He was taking him into. And today man is still learning from animals. The aircraft is designed after birds. The submarine is after the fish, and most cars designs have an egg's streamlining characteristics. This is not supposed to be. That's why in the new heaven and earth, when God has redeemed those He's going to redeem, He will start talking to us in the spirit and then we will no longer be learning from animals. We will be instituting the values of heaven here on earth. That was why Jesus said: *let thy will be done in earth as it is done in heaven.* When the Kingdom of God takes over the earth in our consciousness, we will no longer learn from animals, we will be learning from heaven. The animal skin for Adam and Eve was a derogatory form of dressing because that was who man has become. So God had to dress the man like an animal, because that was who he was the moment he fell from grace. As we proposed earlier, he was no longer a living soul; because God said he would die if he ate the fruit of that tree, he died spiritually thereafter, and his heavenly citizenship was withdrawn with immediate effect, so he started living with the mind-set of animals. Many of us still live like that - having animal tendencies; hatred, backbiting, fighting, disorderliness etc.

How does the devil operate in our lives

Let's see what becomes of those Satan is in control of in their lives daily, by understanding Psalm 109:6-13:

CHAPTER THREE

6 Set a wicked man over him, And let an accuser stand at his right hand.

7 When he is judged, let him be found guilty, And let his prayer become sin.

8 Let his days be few, And let another take his office.

9 Let his children be fatherless, And his wife a widow.

10 Let his children continually be vagabonds, and beg; Let them seek their bread also from their desolate places.

11 Let the creditor seize all that he has, And let strangers plunder his labour.

12 Let there be none to extend mercy to him, Nor let there be any to favour his fatherless children.

13 Let his posterity be cut off, And in the generation following let their name be blotted out.

The wicked man and the accuser referred to in verse 6 above is Satan's agent whom he uses to achieve his objective of destruction of lives. Jesus is standing at the right hand of the father; sitting at the right side of God. God uses Jesus to actualize everything he has to do. That was why in John 1:1, the Bible made us to know that without Jesus nothing made that was made. In the same way, Satan uses his angels to actualize his works. Even as Christ has humans on earth who minister daily in His churches, so also is the devil having humans on his payroll who also minister falsehood in his name; and sometimes these agents will be disguised as servants of the God, just like their master, the devil also disguises in some instances as the angel of light – 2 Corinthians 11:14-15: *And no marvel; for Satan himself is transformed into an angel of light. Therefore it is no great thing if his ministers also be transformed as the ministers of righteousness; whose end shall be according to their works.*

What the Bible is making us to know in Psalm 109, as we read earlier, is that wicked people serve the devil's intent, meaning evil stands at the right hand of the wicked man. Now let's look into what the verses refer to above are saying:

1. Verse 7 of Psalm 109 explains that the devil brings condemnation because he's already condemned. That's why the Bible says in Romans 8:1: *there's now no more condemnation for those who are in Christ…* -

who are filled with the spirit of the Lord – who hears information from God and act exactly as God want rather than taking the wisdom of man to act. Children of God only hear from God and act. That was why Isaiah 30:21 says: *'Your ears shall hear a word behind you, saying, 'This is the way, walk in it,' Whenever you turn to the right hand or whenever you turn to the left.'* Not until one starts hearing that voice will one still be under condemnation. We really don't need to fight the devil. It is really of no use fighting someone who is already condemned, just as it will surely make no sense sending artillery to a warfront when you are already victorious – this is what Christ came to achieve for us, once and for all. All that is left is how we can walk ourselves into what the Kingdom of God has in stock for all faithful adherents. If you fight a criminal who is already condemned, the criminal does not have any pity on you. He will kill you because he is already condemned. So you really don't fight someone who is already condemned, you flee from him - you avoid him. You tell the devil – *'May the Lord rebuke you the more.'* Then you go away from him, avoiding anything he likes. If an insane person is sitting down where there is a dustbin or refuse dump, then you can't throw refuse there because you may be attacked. The devil has been defeated by the blood of Jesus, you only need to remind him where he belongs - condemned. You don't tangle or fight with him – never! Light and darkness have no part together. You just avoid him and love God, do the will of God and your life will be at peace. So when the devil comes into our lives, our prayers become sin before God, as they would become polluted with selfish desires to please men rather than God.

2. Verse 8-10 explains that, when the devil comes into people's lives, he takes away their good health and life of abundance. The Bible says in Exodus 23:26: *I will fulfil the number of your days.* But when the devil comes, he makes us curse God and the moment that happens, God withdraws, then the devil comes in and ends our life. That is what he does. Any time he comes into our life, he wants us to disappoint God. We have children in the street today who have become robbers and prostitutes. The Bible says, what can the righteous do when the foundation is destroyed. There are people who are eroding the foundation of good

morals every day. There are some people who have refused to learn wisdom from God so that their lives would showcase the presence of God, so these children come and mix with good children in school. Sometimes when one hears the kinds of things our children say, one wonders who taught them these. We labour to pay school fees for our children, only to send them into a devil-infested environment to be trained. Unless parents take up the responsibility of training their children in the love and way of God, we end up neglecting the great salvation that God offers in Christ. Many parents don't love God, nor even care about living an honest and pure life. If I had the opportunity, I would own a school to teach morals only. I can't imagine my children mingling with unrepentant vagabonds in society; someone under a curse.

We would remember that in the book of Hosea 4:6-7, God says He would reject the children of those who hate him and change their glory into shame, so there are many rejected children as a result of their parents' heartless behaviour in society who are friends to our children, for instance. They study in the same class, play together in the streets, and do things in common.

CHAPTER THREE

And as times goes on, as our children hears their evil communication, our hard labour and training will eventually give way to the intents of the devil. This is why we must work harder to teach everyone the ways of God. We are not going to stop until we tell people to embrace God, because if you don't do it, we can't have peace. We must know that if a cursed person mounts the seat of power, he will waste all the resources. That is what is happening to Nigeria and most economies the world over. Most of the politicians in power receive curses from the people because of their ill and selfish actions, depriving people the goodness of God in the land and because we have allowed them to be there, they will keep on wasting resources. The devil is a waster and those who dine with the devil are like him – wasting every resource that God gave to them, as the Israelites did when they gave their gold to Aaron to make an idol for them. These people waste their earnings on self-egoistic tendencies.

We are not going to give them that opportunity for too long. Every child of God who would want to rise up to authority in government, the Lord will give such

CHAPTER THREE

a one that position. That is my position; that children of God should go into decision-making positions of trust. The MD of your company cannot be an occult person - that is my stand – Amen! The government of the land cannot be an occult person. He will keep on wasting the resources of God. No company belongs to anybody. Every company belongs to the most-high God, because the Bible made me to know that the earth and the fullness belong to Him (Psalm 24:1). So we can't allow them to keep on damaging society for us. It is time to move up and take what belongs to us. That's why I am not happy when I hear servants of God buying jet planes. It is not time to buy jet planes yet. The money for them should be used to sponsor children of God for political positions, and gradually we would see that all the all night prayers for wealth and blessings would turn into praise nights in God's favour so that, instead of people living in heaviness, they would spend time thinking of better things and not lists of prayer points which only point to the fact that we have devil-induced people in leadership, who have left justice to seek for self-aggrandisement. We prayed that power must change hands, and now money is changing hands, and believers are gradually becoming wealthy; but when we don't know why the wealth came and use it to build a kingdom where peace and harmony will reign, the devil will take it away by trick.

The Parable of the Sower is recalled here, as wisdom for Christians, to understand every bit of favour we receive from God and use it for the advancement of His work here on earth. Christians are being favoured with contracts these days – no doubt about that. The Lord will only be seen as good when the poor have food and shelter. And so we have to kick against every form of waste. Private jets can be a waste of resources when they are really not the need at hand. Whether you use it or not, you must keep on maintaining it. What's the meaning of desolate places? Just as is happening right now in Nigeria and other nations, famine is gradually taking its toll on humanity. Is this not a desolate nation already? People are in pain daily. Many are begging to eat already. We are searching for food because the food is not there any more. And one other thing the Lord made me to know is that if we take a look at most of the currencies all over the world, most of the faces of the people there belong to the occult. Just like the coin carrying the head of Caesar, we would hear what Jesus says in Mark 12:17: 'Well, then,' Jesus said, 'give to Caesar what belongs to Caesar, and give to God what belongs to God.' And that is the same money you want to use to succeed in life? Things can never work this way. The very day we start taking up power, all these faces would become the cross of Jesus. We just have to know how the devil operates. The devil makes sure everything you are going to get access to is possessed by him. He has possessed your money with the faces of his agents of destruction who perpetuate themselves in power or are dead and suffering in hell. How can we have the face of someone in hell on our currency? Why won't the pains of hell be visited on our investments? Shall we just stay here looking at the devil's atrocities right before us? He has taken over our schools – lesbianism and all manner of immoral acts are now been perpetuated, to the extent that teachers influence our children into lesbianism, homosexuality and even cults. It's not going to be so for too long

3. Now, we go on to Verses 11-12: Extortionists are 419 people. If you don't have God in your life, you will put money in the stock market and that is when the market will collapse, because you will not hear the voice of God telling you: 'withdraw your money now.' When Joseph entered into the house of Potiphar, for his sake, Potiphar experienced increase. The stories of the exploits of the righteous are all there for us to learn from. I challenge anyone who claims to be a believer here to explain why he/she feels the anointing of the Lord upon one's life should not lift one higher in our human endeavours. When the devil enters into our lives, we begin to meet extortionists. They will be duping us, because the spirit of the Lord is not there to talk to us. Strangers would come in spoiling the fruits of our labour. People live a life of rejection when the anointing no longer speaks for them. The devil is after our soul. That was why King David rejoiced in Psalm 23: 'He restoreth my soul for his name sake.' Jesus also said in the book of Luke 1:19: 'In patience, you shall possess your soul.' The devil needs our soul because that's what we also need to connect to the realm of God, and the moment he locks our soul in

his den, we become ostracized, and would not have revelations from God again. Our dreams then would be filled with what happens in his kingdom – what we would refer to as frightening and bad dreams. But the moment our soul is restored (Hebrews 6:19-20), we will see ourselves praising God, happy, helping people, and preaching the gospel of Christ, because our soul is in the Kingdom of God. So our soul will be doing exactly what Jesus was doing while He was on Earth – this is the whole duty of man. And the Bible said wherever He went, He was going about doing 'good.' Not until we begin to do that, will our soul be free from the devil. So when our soul is restored, you will no longer see anybody hunting your life in your dreams – Light and darkness have no place together. A restored soul receives information from God.

4. Verse 13 implies: Let's take a look at the businesses in Nigeria, for instance, of all the business that are owned by Nigerians how many survive to the next generation of their children? The moment the initiators die, their posterity is cut off. The children come and fight over the estates and kill themselves in the process. The wealth of the ungodly will always develop wings and

fly. That is the way of the wicked. When the devil is in our investments, he cuts off our posterity and takes away our tomorrow. If he holds our today, he'll be promising us heaven on earth, meanwhile, when we get to where he is taking us to, we will not see anything promising. His trick is to keep on deceiving us. Posterity comes from God. If we don't want to lose all we had laboured for and let our children suffer, it is time we avoided the devil and his tricks.

❖

The Character of the Devil

❖

The Bible informed us in Genesis 3 that the serpent was the subtlest animal in the field. The devil is cunning and deceitful. Eve told God *'the serpent beguiles me.'* Jesus says we should be as wise as the serpent, so as to overcome him. Devil will only use what we say to judge us, and he is only waiting for what we will say because he doesn't have any information about our destiny. God has made it like that, that the devil should not have any information about us. The secret about our life is with God. What the devil does is to pick words from our mouths and use them as clues to what he expects our destiny to look like. This is why he accuses us with slandering tongues, so that eventually when we speak out in defence, he must have gotten all the information he is looking for so as to plot our downfall. Every sensible person will simply cast him out, or better still, ignore his antics. Sometimes too, he picks our heart desires from our prayer points. Then he would set frightening images before us in our dreams, expecting us to reveal them to someone. When he finally confirms that we did so, then he would use that person as his first agent of destiny murdering, in most cases. He will fill the person with much wisdom to deceive us. But if the person is filled with the presence of God, this would make us hate the person and then gradually he would link us to one of his agents of lies and darkness. Then we would be led into nights of fruitless prayers – as a form of distraction from the main solution, which would be connecting our soul back to God. This is his delaying tactics and before we know it, it is dark already and we begin to live in complaints. Once he can assure himself that our complaints would last for months to come, he will take his bag and depart until another season, when he will come with more deceits.

CHAPTER THREE

The secret things are of the Lord, which contains your future - Deuteronomy 29:29. The Bible says in 1 Corinthians 2:7, that JESUS is a mystery that was hidden from the world, even from the Devil. How would the devil know that calling the name JESUS would send him and his angels/cohorts bowing down? It is mind-boggling. This is how God works in our lives. If the devil had that wisdom, Jesus wouldn't have died for you and me. The devil would make sure no one betrays Him and that would have rendered that rescue mission futile. The hidden wisdom is what God gives to us. But the devil wants you to speak that hidden wisdom for him to hear. He knows the LOGOS; he knows the Bible very well, because men have being preaching the Bible over and over - but he does not know the Rhema, which God is about to release. This is the reason Jesus advised His disciples not to bother about what to say when they would be accosted, but to rely on the Holy Spirit who will minister to them at the point of their need – Matthew 10:19: *But when they arrest you, do not worry about what to say or how to say it. At that time you will be given what to say.* You don't rehearse what you will tell the devil; else the word will be filled with fleshly arguments filled with human wisdom of deceit instead of receiving the spirit of the Lord. Don't let us forget that it is the spirit that quickeneth – John 6:63. It is the spirit that brings the action of God concerning our lives, to pass.

King David went to the Altar of the Lord and prayed to hear the Rhema - Psalm 28:1-2. King David had the Bible and where the acts of the prophets are written, but he went to God, because he knows that God will reveal something concerning his situation. Who was the Oracle of God in his days? It was the Prophet Nathan.

When the devil does not have the Rhema which is the clue to your destiny, he cannot do anything to your life. This is why sometimes it's good to be quiet. If God is about to do something in your life, mind the kind of people you reveal it to. Mind the people who pray with you. It is not everybody that you should call and say 'let us agree together.' If you are a woman who is about to marry and you have a sister who is also about to marry and you tell the sister that someone is proposing to you, when the two of you pray a prayer of agreement together, she may go home and kick against it and the suitor might no longer be interested in marrying you. You have to be very careful, because what you release from your mouth is what the devil uses against you. Even when the police arrest you, it is advisable to be silent else anything said might be used against such a one in a law court. That's why the Lord keeps on releasing Rhema to you at the point of the need and not before the need. This is the reason you need to ask, else you won't receive. If you don't seek, you won't find.

The Devil's Power

Today the devil has invaded the church. How did he do it? Our answer would come from Matthew 4, of the tricks he used while trying to tempt Jesus. Materialism has entered into the heart of men and men now think of self instead of God. Whore fashion and ways of dressing are rampant, and God is asking who would tell them their wrongs so that they would repent. While many women think they are enticing their husbands with half naked clothing, those who designed those clothes, who were in most cases former prostitutes – as my internet research showed - who designed the clothes for their fellow whore

CHAPTER THREE

workers so that they could entice their prey, have found no reason to repent any longer, since the church now appreciates the product of their evil ingenuity.

We will now talk about the Devil's power. The Prophet in Ezekiel 28:14 says that the devil is an anointed cherub, meaning he is intelligent. There's no witch doctor that forgets spiritual things as easily as many of us claiming to have the spirit of God do. All witch doctors possess the anointing of the devil. This is why they ensure we pay every vow we make before their idol altars whenever we consult them as a means of binding our soul to the altar of the devil, from where we will be monitored remotely and controlled to act in ways that please the devil. Be informed that the devil is not one creature to play with. He remembers always the relationship we had with him or the covenant our grandparents entered with him in years past, because he is created after intelligence. God remembered the children of Israel because of the relationship he had with Abraham, Isaac and Jacob. It is the same thing with the devil. So now that we are about to become shiny stars, he comes in to destroy our destiny, as Herod in a deceitful manner, pretending to worship Jesus, wanted to end His life if not for God's intervention when He warned the magi in a dream. This is why at the point of our glory in life we should mind those who pretend to worship us with flattering in like manner. He can even cause the car we are in to have an accident only to discover that we didn't die, but many souls would have died as a result of that. The devil does not come when one is suffering; he comes into people's lives when they are at peace. The moment he enters into one's life, he sows seeds in the heart that would grow to become a tree of discontent, self-condemnation, blaming people for one's woes, etc. This is how he causes trouble in one's life.

By the time the tree start blossoming and bearing fruits of regret and sorrow, the devil is gone. What the devil does is to just visit, after destabilizing us; he leaves some demons behind to ensure that 'status quo' is maintained. So the demons help to maintain the status quo while he leaves for another place to cause more havoc. That is why he moves 'to and fro'. The moment one starts having problems, the angels of God come in, because God created this world to be in equilibrium, to experience 100% peace. The moment there's any disequilibrium, the angels are released immediately to the situation so as to return every vibrating matter into a state of equilibrium – a state of perfection. Hence Jesus admonished His disciples to proclaim peace into every house they entered – Luke 10:5-6. As long as you are not having peace, God is not having peace, because you were created after His person (Matthew 5:48).

There is something that belongs to God that is in your life and as long as you are crying, God is not having peace. If you come into His Altar to cry, or you are dedicated to His work, he knows when things are not all right with you. So when you are in trouble, don't think God is not intervening. He's intervening, but he just wants you to listen and hear, because he's about leading and directing you. This is where the power of the devil comes in – he will set distracting elements before you, to take away your attention from God. That is the only power he has – over our flesh, and not over our spirit. But we must learn to listen and hear God speak - if we don't hear we won't follow (John 10:27). That was why Jesus said 'those who have ears, let them hear,' because if we are not patient enough, the devil can lead us astray. The devil knows that God is about taking you high so he quickly wants to block it, and he needs your help to enable him succeed in hurting your life. But if you can give God your time, He will give you His attention.

❖

The Rhema defeats the Devil

❖

The devil is intelligent, as we understood earlier from Ezekiel 28:14, but over time we have seen that his magical powers could not compete with the power of God as shown in the story of Moses in Pharaoh's palace and that of Daniel in Babylon. Jesus says that He saw the devil fall like a star, because all power belongs to Him (Luke 10:18, Matthew 28:18). But you must be mindful of the fact that to overcome the devil, you must put on the full armour of Christ.

I would use this section to talk about some Prophetic Rhema in the Bible, how they overcame the devil:

1. The brazen serpent of Moses, which was a forerunner of the death of the Lord on the cross – John 3:14, healed the Israelites of snakebites, and further stopped the attack of snakes upon them. How could the devil had known that this act will defeat him?

2. The Elisha's new cruse of salt – 2 Kings 2:19-22, which he poured into the river, and the plague in the land stopped, is another spiritual Rhema. Who would have thought that a handful amount of salt in a cruse would avail much when used as healing Arm of the Lord? But it did work, because the prophet acted as he heard, and the people acted as he commanded, and the faith in their action resulted in the healing of the water. There is no way the devil would have thought of this action.

3. The water the Israelites fetched and poured out at Mizpeh in 1 Samuel 7:6, signifying that they had vowed to undergo a fast until peace returns to the land through the hand of God. Here Satan lost the loyalty which they had for the strange gods and Ashtaroth in their midst. And the moment they had gathered, the devil steered up the Philistines against them, but the servant of the Lord, Samuel, was entreated by the people to cry unto God on their behalf – 1 Samuel 7:8: *And the children of Israel said to Samuel, Cease not to cry unto the Lord our God for us, that he will save us out of the hand of the Philistines.* Once Samuel knew they regarded his office, he commenced action to

CHAPTER THREE

bring down the presence of the Lord – verse 9: *And Samuel took a sucking lamb, and offered it for a burnt offering wholly unto the Lord: and Samuel cried unto the Lord for Israel; and the Lord heard him.* And we saw later in that chapter how the Lord gave them the upper hand in that battle. Here, the water and the offering are all Rhema meant to bring down the Arm of the Lord at that material time, and may not be used in like manner in other situations.

4. The Holy Communion as a Rhema that will from time to time, based on the revelation of God, will always work to silence the antics of the devil. People have used the Communion for healing in several instances, with outstanding results. It has been used as an emblem of defence against armed robbers. The Communion blood sprinkled on the dead has resurrected life. My wife was having a miscarriage, and the Communion stopped the bleeding, even when the doctors have advised that we let go the baby. It all depends on the revelation, and the instruction of God concerning its usage at that material time.

CHAPTER THREE

The key spiritual verse that explains the importance of the Communion is - John 6:56,57: *He that eateth my flesh, and drinketh my blood, dwelleth in me, and I in him. As the living Father hath sent me, and I live by the Father: so he that eateth me, even he shall live by me.* To confirm this, Revelation 12:11: *And they overcame him by the blood of the Lamb, and by the word of their testimony; and they loved not their lives unto the death.* Implying that the Blood, our testimony of Christ and our steadfastness silenced the devil forever and ever.

The Devil is an Impostor – Be warned!

The trick of the devil is that he does not want anyone to receive the Rhema, the secret and hidden wisdom which we've just talked about. And this is vividly shown in the Parable of the Sower; those who did not have full understanding of the word they received loosed it to the devil's trick. The Bible went further to explain in Proverbs 16:22 that - *Understanding is a wellspring of life unto him that hath it.* This is why the Bible says that we should not give that which is holy unto dogs and cast our pearls before swine - Matthew 6:7, because these certainly lack understanding and would not make any value from what ever is Holy. Their carnal life will certainly deprive them of the glory of God. Now let's see some facts about his tricks on humans below:

- The devil persuades people not to accept the Rhema. He does not want you to receive it, and when you receive the word from the altar, he also persuades you not to accept it - John 6:53-60, 66 explains this better. He makes us doubt the Rhema, but will make one do something that will please him. For instance, the moment Jesus Christ told those who were around him about the Holy Communion, they ran away from him, save the twelve disciples (John 6:56-60). The devil will tell us 'this is wrong, don't take it'. This is because the Rhema is a hidden secret that is meant to defeat him at that instant. Revelation 2:17 calls it 'Hidden Manna' and the devil doesn't understand it, so he will deceive anyone not to accept it, making you to doubt the Rhema. The power of the Rhema is in our faith and trust in its power and purpose – Matthew 21:21: *Verily I say unto you, If ye have faith, and doubt not, ye shall not only do this which is done to the fig tree, but also if ye shall say unto this mountain, Be thou removed, and be thou cast into the sea; it shall be done.*

- He makes one blaspheme God. Remember what Job's wife said to Job in Job 2:9: 'curse God and die'? She knew that once Job cursed God, he was going to die, yet she insisted he should do so. To her death was the end of Job's suffering; she never knew that the moment Job curses God the punishment upon him will become severe without an opportunity for redemption of his soul, and the devil will then own Job's soul, because God had instructed the devil not to touch his soul (Job 1:12). The devil wants the soul of man, and the only way he gets the soul is when we curse or blaspheme God. The same reason why those in occult die at their prime age, so that the devil can lock up their souls and use them as his messengers of doom until their apportioned life expires and then he will have hold of them forever in hell. People are scared of contacting HIV or the dreaded Ebola Virus Disease (EVD), yet this is just a feeling of being in hell on earth, and not the real hell. Many times we've cursed God when things seem not to go well with us. And God is saying, 'testify against me'- Micah 6:3. Can we testify that God has been wicked to us? No! Of course – we still remember all His protective and caring gestures towards us.

CHAPTER THREE

- The devil causes disunity within the Kingdom of God. The devil knows that if we don't agree with God, He can't work with us - Amos 3:3. This fact is the reason why we should rather consider our ways when things seem not to work the way we expected. Ezra, in the Bible, determined to restore things in the house of God as recorded in the book of Ezra and in Haggai 1:5, God said we should consider our ways. The day I read Haggai 1, my life changed. I don't just blame the devil anyhow, but I usually ask myself if I am on good terms with God. This is because when you are on good terms with God, He will cover you with His wings. We should not forget that His name is a strong tower meant for the rescue of the righteous. That is why the Lord is calling everyone to be a gatherer and not one who scatters – Isaiah 60:21: *Thy people also shall be all righteous...* There's a difference between the Lord's commission and people just gathering to praise and worship the Lord. When someone is called to lead people to God - it is a commission. The call of a Servant of God in the New Testament era is more like what Samuel told Saul as he was been anointed - 1 Samuel 10:1: *Then Samuel took a vial of oil, and poured it upon his head, and kissed him, and said, Is it not because the Lord hath anointed thee to be captain*

CHAPTER THREE

over his inheritance? Just as Moses was called, such a person receives more prophetic Rhema, because he only need the Rhema to raise a church for God. Jesus said to Peter, when He informed him in the presence of the other disciples, *upon this rock I will build my church; and the gates of hell shall not prevail against it* - that upon this Rhema, which was the revelation Peter had of Him that the church would finally be established. After this statement, He promised to hand over the keys of heaven to Peter, which will give Peter unhindered access to the hidden Rhema in heaven – verse 19: *And I will give unto thee the keys of the Kingdom of heaven: and whatsoever thou shalt bind on earth shall be bound in heaven: and whatsoever thou shalt loose on earth shall be loosed in heaven.* So we would see that Peter's authority came from his knowledge of who Jesus is – the son of the living God. So when God calls somebody to lead you to him, he gives him 'Rhema,' and he uses those who have received Rhema to explain the Logos in the Holy Book of God. People should not just gather together to start a church. I didn't start like that, I was on my own in the street when the Lord called me that I should go and lead people to Him. He said to me that these people were in the church but they didn't know

CHAPTER THREE

where they were going. So responsibility is spelt out when one receives Rhema from the Lord for the preservation of souls unto His name. He said that to be able to do this work He was going to train me for six years, and as I write this line, the 1st day of September 2014, I am on my 6th year now. In my 1st year I didn't do well but he forgave me. In the 3rd year He told me, 'Write the books now, because the devil has set distractions in place for you.' He said to me, 'let them take Christianity to the extreme; Philip disappeared immediately the Eunuch was baptized.' We need a display of His power daily to overcome the devil's deceits.

The shadow of Peter healed the sick. He wants people who can overcome the devil. You don't overcome the devil with 'look at me, I look at you.' It is not a gazing contest; it is time for action, continually seeking the face of the Lord. The devil is commanded from above – with the power that sets things in place, this is only when he would respond and be defeated. All the devil wants is for us to curse God, and so he follows us until he makes us curse God. When we blaspheme the Holy Spirit, we have in effect cursed God. That was why Jesus Christ said to Peter -

CHAPTER THREE

Matthew 16:23: *Get thee behind me, Satan: thou art an offence unto me.* Though Jesus was talking to Peter physically, the reason behind why He addressed Peter that manner is contained in His final statement – *for thou savourest not the things that be of God, but those that be of men.* Peter is the same rock upon which God was going to build His church. This tells us that the devil is not looking for the hooligans or the vagabonds in the street; he is looking for the sane, so that he can make them insane. The devil is hunting those with the fruits of salvation to cast into his hell. The devil does not sleep in houses where people are crying, he sleeps in houses with air conditioners – the devil loves enjoyment. You can now see why those who are doing well and have wealth are also those who have more afflictions from the devil - and he wants to show anyone he possesses the beauty of the whole world; hence Jesus advised that riches comes with persecutions – Mark 10:30: *But he shall receive an hundredfold now in this time, houses, and brethren, and sisters, and mothers, and children, and lands,* **with persecutions.** However, if riches increase, set not your heart upon them - Psalm 62:10.

CHAPTER THREE

The devil is not in a slump as people would think; he left demons to mutilate the lives of those who drink to stupor, smoke Indian hemp, inhale cocaine, and all manner of devilish atrocities. The devil is in the house of those who make merry and will be waiting for an opportunity to strike whoever does not have the spirit of Christ. He likes enjoyment and he wants us to offend God in the midst of our merriment. The moment we do it he gives us some demons and walks away and goes to the next person he wants to devour.

So we now understand that he doesn't like dirt, and anywhere there is dirt, he is not there, but his demons are. God created this world to be in peace, so when there is chaos, the angels come down. So you must understand that when you are passing through pain, the angels are there to help you out, to help you know what to do. Therefore, instead of complaining when things seems not to be the way we want them to be, we should give thanks and praise to God, whose arm is already trying to put things in order, though we don't often recognise this. All we must do is to cast out the demons of the devil, the unclean and foul spirits, any time we sense his presence.

CHAPTER THREE

Names of the Devil and how they reflect his character

❖

- **Opposer of good works** - Matthew 16:23:

    The Devil opposes every good plan in your life. The moment you are planning for success and progress in your life, know that the devil is there. Saint Paul says – 1 Corinthians 16:8: *But I will tarry at Ephesus until Pentecost. For a great door and effectual is opened unto me, and there are many adversaries.* He opposes the restoration plan of God in our life by convincing us not to be active in church, study our bible, ask for forgiveness and pray for deliverance, pay our tithes, etc. He knows that once we do not pay our tithe, the doors of heaven will be locked, and once they are locked, we start struggling – Malachi 3:10-12: *Bring ye all the tithes into the storehouse, that there may be meat in mine house, and prove me now herewith, saith the Lord of hosts, if I will not open you the windows of heaven, and pour you out a blessing, that there shall not be room enough to receive it. And I will*

CHAPTER THREE

rebuke the devourer for your sakes, and he shall not destroy the fruits of your ground; neither shall your vine cast her fruit before the time in the field, saith the Lord of hosts. And all nations shall call you blessed: for ye shall be a delightsome land, saith the Lord of hosts. All these promises are too much for the devil to imagine, because when these happen to us, we would become controllers of the wealth upon the face of the earth, and what will he now use to deceive his adherents? The payment of a tenth of our income and proceeds unto the Altar of the Lord brings a curse upon him. And because he wouldn't want the curse from God, he would avoid whoever is paying tithe faithfully, implying further that the soul of such a person is untouchable by the devil and his cohorts. This is not palatable information to him, so all he would do is to ensure people treat tithes as mere physical gifts aimed at supporting the work of God. This idea has made many who haven't gotten a spiritual understanding of the purposes of tithe to err, thereby increasing their days of labour. In simple terms, tithe is Rhema, and being one of the judiciously guided secrets of possession, is meant to be a testimony of remembrance and commitment of the spiritual realm to our course here on earth. When he now discovers that the realm of God is not connected to our finance due to our negligence of fulfilling the tithing obligation, and that things are not working peacefully for us, the devil would then sow seeds of human wisdom of how to make ends meet, such as telling lies and cheating.

- **Slanderer - Job 1:11:**

   The devil said to God, thus challenging and finding fault in Job's righteous, life before God: *But put forth thine hand now, and touch all that he hath, and he will curse thee to thy face.* The devil libels us before God, as the accuser of the brethren – Revelation 12:10: ... *for the accuser of our brethren is cast down, which accused them before our God day and night.* We have people today who have this kind of character. They never see anything good in your righteous deeds. Even within the church, we see brothers and sisters who are unnecessarily angry over those who support the servant of God. I have heard people angry because a brother or sister takes food items to their pastor's house every month ending. And my question has always been, what is their own pain, if the brother or sister spends his/her items in the work of God? These sets of people have the spirit of those who murmur when Jesus was been honoured in Mark 14:4-5: *And there were some that had indignation within themselves, and said, Why was this waste of the ointment made? For it might have been sold for more than three hundred pence, and have been given to the poor. And they murmured against her.* Jesus' reply in verse 6 would confirm that though these sets of people are in the church and clapping hands, they are the tares of the devil and are working for him.

- **As an adversary - Revelation 2:9:**

  The devil discourages us from serving God. There are so many people who don't serve God again. They are serving pastors and pastors' wives, women leaders and men leaders, etc. They don't know God; they are just there to serve man. If we serve God with fear, we would also learn to honour those he is using to help us discover his ways. These people don't do the will of God; they don't always have time. Revelation 2:9 says - *I know thy works, and tribulation, and poverty, (but thou art rich) and I know the blasphemy of them which say they are Jews, and are not, but are the synagogue of Satan.* Are we undergoing tribulation and poverty because the adversary of God is operating in our midst as the synagogue of Satan? I was in a dream going for evangelism; all of a sudden we didn't see people to follow us. I was there with my wife; we were to enter into the dark to bring people out who were locked up. Because we were alone, we couldn't go into the dark, so we waited and later turned back, when we couldn't see more people to go with us. As we were returning, I saw a church; the surroundings of the church were dirty. And there were inscriptions on the church which said, 'Glory of God'. I thought to myself, how can this place be the glory of God, when the whole place is dirty with excreta all over the place? People were trooping into the church. And I told my wife I wanted to go inside and see what was happening, why such a dirty place would be used as a place of worship unto the Lord. Somehow her shoe got stuck in the ground, and she was trying to pull it out when we saw many people who wanted to go in. After my wife pulled her shoe

CHAPTER THREE

from the ground, I didn't bother to go inside but led the way out of the dirty and smelly environment onto a beautiful path of flowers. Many people who saw us leading the way out followed us. The people who were inside were mainly choir members and instrumentalists that day. Wonderful instruments, and sound of worship; one would not believe that such music of worship would come from such a dirty and smelly place. Yet it was, indeed, the synagogue of Satan. It points to the fact that many worship God in spiritual dirtiness. How can people have gathered in the church and over the years, they are still suffering from spiritual lack and want because those who have instituted the synagogue of Satan in our midst are blinding the sights of many, and making them to follow the call of the devil?

As an accuser, he tells God why he must not answer our prayers. We are informed that salvation came to Heaven the moment the devil was cast out - Revelation 12:10: *And I heard a loud voice saying in heaven, Now is come salvation, and strength, and the Kingdom of our God, and the power of his Christ: for the accuser of our brethren is cast down.* So we need to check our heart, in one accord we must achieve. You cannot be for God and the other person is for the devil, and you will expect peace. The Bible says that all of us must become righteous then we will inherit our inheritance – Isaiah 60:21: *Thy people also shall be all righteous: they shall inherit the land forever.* The synagogue of Satan is where you have people who don't have time for God, their presence in our midst is to gather and they cease our prayers from going up as incense unto God. So the fewer and more dedicated to the call of God, the better, so we can all work with ourselves and love ourselves so that the power and salvation of God can come down. Until this happens we are paying lip service to the call of God.

■ A rebel against God, Isaiah 14:12:

The devil is the father of rebellion and does not like the things of God or want anyone to give God glory; that's why when we are in a praise and worship session, the devil is busy making people walk up and down, to distract them so that they cannot give honour and glory unto God. He rebels against anything that has to do with God. The moment we

CHAPTER THREE

are about to go to church, he would come subtly and tell us, 'you don't need to move now, why don't you wait until the man mounts the pulpit?' Just then the phone will ring and it will be a business call you have been expecting. As you take the call, for instance, he will give you all the reasons why you have to see the caller, and finalize the deal. That is the end of service – the spirit of mammon is now in control. May you not pursue a contract again, in the name of Jesus – Amen! You are a city upon a mountain that commands attraction. Whatever is yours will definitely wait for you. The contracts will come when they come.

■ A tempter from the beginning - Matthew 4:

Matthew 4:3 say - *And when the tempter came to him...* Jesus was hungry and the devil came to tempt Him. What is the meaning of temptation? Temptation makes one operate with the word of God without understanding and seeking further advice from the Lord. If we look at the temptation of Adam and Eve, the devil used what the Lord told them and twisted it. Eve was quoting the word of God, though she added a stringent condition, but she wasn't aware that she

CHAPTER THREE

was dealing with an enemy of God who wanted to get her and her husband to blaspheme the word. This is why we have to be careful when we quote the word in the Bible, as many preachers have twisted the word of God to allow them do all manner of atrocities. This was why Jesus warned – Matthew 24:24: *For there shall arise false Christs, and false prophets, and shall shew great signs and wonders; insomuch that, if it were possible, they shall deceive the very elect.* The devil can only achieve this deceit by using these false Christ and Prophets to teach the Bible with *'mammonic'* intentions, embedded in the message that comes out of their mouth, which is referred to as frogs – Revelation 16:13-14: *And I saw three unclean spirits like frogs come out of the mouth of the dragon, and out of the mouth of the beast, and out of the mouth of the false prophet. For they are the spirits of devils, working miracles, which go forth unto the kings of the earth and of the whole world, to gather them to the battle of that great day of God Almighty.* Like the devil told Jesus to jump down from the top of a very high mountain that the angels of God would watch Him, and Jesus would let him know that such an act would result in tempting the Lord when it wasn't commanded by God, so he also went after Moses in the wilderness. When the Israelites cried for water, the first time, God instructed Moses to strike the rock and water came out – Exodus 17:6. The next time God said to Moses to speak to the rock for water to come out, the devil confused him with a prior experience and he struck the rock twice – Numbers 20:8-12. Though water came out, the devil had succeeded in making Moses defile the Lord's arm with him. And the moment he struck the rock, the devil had the opportunity to negotiate for his body - Jude 1:9. The anger of God in Numbers 20:12: *Because ye believed me not, to sanctify me in the eyes of the children of Israel ...,* explains the devil's utmost intention, which he had nursed while the Lord was working in Moses. So we would say that the devil followed Moses from Egypt, after he tried to set him up as a murderer and Moses had run for rescue, this time he made him to blaspheme God. Which one is easier? To strike or to speak? To 'speak' of course! Why did Moses take the harder way? The same reason why many are dying with the Old Testament practice of prophetic declarations, when greater than the temple lives among us. To this day, there are many believers who believe that their problem must be solved by multitudes of all-night prayers. The ways of the Lord are new every morning – the earlier we know it, the better for us, and our plight for a better life in the Lord. Imagine Moses with all he had done in the name of God, yet the devil could contest his soul. If the devil would bid for Jesus' life, he won't have to go far to get any soul he wants; he would present Paris before so many, and off they are getting flight tickets already. The devil will make us disobey God at every slight opportunity he has, especially when we are hungry. The devil is aware that God is perfect, and Jesus admonished us to be – Matthew 5:48, so all the devil does is to give anyone he catches a filthy garment of sin.

■ A known deceiver - 2 Corinthians 11:14-15:

The devil is all over the churches looking for people to deceive and lure into his den. This he does by simply transforming himself to an image that appears to be Christ. Saint Paul explains thus further – 2 Corinthians 11:14: *And no marvel; for Satan himself is transformed into an angel of light.* And many are worshipping him as if they are worshipping Jesus. To transform is to change form – meaning to adopt a character that can enable a particular action to be carried out. This will imply further that the devil is dynamic in character and action with one aim – to lure anyone he can with a false appearance, in order to take them out of the path of God. This further shows that the devil does not come as he is, else he would not win any soul into his kingdom. Hence, he is the supposed good man, who will later become evil. Many of those out there coming with the message of Christ may really not be representing Christ – they could come with the mind-set of helping us solve our problems through welfare, miracles, prophetic solutions, counselling, etc, but with time, with their wagging tongues, they would show who is behind them. Their major concern is how to get the crowd to accept them as working for Christ, and sooner they would turn them to the devil. That's why I am also very careful about who I mix with. As long as God has brought us into His commission, we should limit what we listen to and what we hear outside. We are in a journey; God cannot bring us this far and lead us astray. When I started off on this call, I was about to meet some servants of God whom I know, but I heard Him say to me – *'be careful, don't listen to them, they'll pollute you.'* And if I can stay these years without listening to any other person but to Jesus we can also do that, so that we don't begin to have contradicting doctrines and scriptures in our hearts that will drag us back. God is ready to lead us, and we must avoid those of the synagogue of Satan, those with whom the devil is working in their midst as angels of light. So it's not a new thing that people are performing miracles. A miracle is not a testimony to show that God is working in our midst. A miracle is likened to a senate decision to allow some students who wouldn't have graduated due to their academic performance to graduate. But that does not imply that such a graduate is top of class, or has actually understood the subjects taught. Our conscience must be alive to prove that Christ is our firm foundation.

❖

Where to find the Devil

■ **In our investment:**

What the devil will sow in our investment is tares. These tares are in the form of cheating customers, stealing from others, manipulating financial figures and the like. In life when we talk about investment it is not only business, our marriages too are an investment, even our salvation is an investment. Everything you do, the job, our employment, etc, is an investment. The devil wants to sow a seed inside, but I encourage you not to give him that opportunity. In whatever you are doing to earn a living, say the truth always. Don't cheat, don't lie. The moment you do that, you belong to him; he will arrest your soul, because he is after that soul. If your home is experiencing peace, the devil will come and sit down; sometimes he goes into the kitchen and messes up whatever is being cooked by blowing into the face of whoever is cooking, and the food gets burnt, or he sows the spirit of forgetfulness in the cook, and then things are messed up, just to ensure that there is quarrel in the home. So the devil comes to our homes when we are experiencing peace; he doesn't go to a place where there is quarrel. When the husband and wife are fighting, he's gone, he's not there any more. So many couples quarrel because the devil has sown the seed of lying, cheating, stealing, etc in the home.

In the church, he makes people praise the pastor, and the pastor praise himself, so as to disconnect the pastor from God, and he knows that once the shepherd is cut off from God, the sheep will scatter.

■ In our relaxation:

I learnt from the story of Noah – Genesis 9:20-25, who after he was saved from the flood, decided to plant a vineyard, and thereafter got himself drunk until he slept and became naked. And then, Noah cursed his grandson. Hasn't the devil succeeded? Of course he has! All his intention was to make Noah waste his inheritance, and he got him when he was relaxing and enjoying the fruits of his labour. Many homes that used to be in peace are now in pieces because the devil came in when they were elevated from want to a life of plenty. And again, we would see that all manner of people flock into a blossoming town, and there come with these multitudes armed robbers, murderers, prostitutes etc, all in a bid to make money from others through dubious means. The next time you are cooling off to enjoy yourself, watch your back, for the adversary is within.

CHAPTER THREE

❖

Avoiding the Devil

❖

As we discussed earlier, the devil enters into us through words and arguments. Once he possesses people and uses them for his glory, he will make them murmur, rebel and gossip the work of God. The first priority in avoiding the devil is to avoid foolish people - Proverbs 14:7: *Go from the presence of a foolish man, when thou perceivest not in him the lips of knowledge.* And we need to mind what we say, who we have discussions with, and what we desire. We need to also be careful not to worship in all manner of places because they sing praises as though they are worshipping God. There are many covens these days disguised as churches of Christ. I came across a pastor some time ago who claimed that he did spiritual cleansing through bathing pregnant women in his church every night, and that those that patronised him were the high class in the society, and that he was making so much money. He concluded that since people no longer patronise witch doctors in the forests and villages where they live, the witch doctors are now dressed in suits and have their own churches too. In his words, one can be a pastor for Jesus or for the devil, and that instead of being called a witch doctor, he prefers the name pastor.

❖

How to overcome the Devil

❖

We must have to make the Lord our habitation – Psalm 91:9-10: *Because thou hast made the Lord, … thy habitation; there shall no evil befall thee, neither shall any plague come nigh thy dwelling.* This is the only weapon to overcome the devil.

All we have been discussing in this chapter points to the fact that there do exist inter-kingdom wars – between good and evil, darkness and light. The purpose of the Kingdom of God on Earth is seen in the declaration of the Faith we bear in John 1:5: *And the light shineth in darkness; and the darkness comprehended it not.* This is our hope, and this is where we hinge our trust.

CHAPTER FOUR

THE KINGDOM OF GOD ON EARTH

As I began to write this chapter on the 9th of August 2013, the hymn 'All people that on Earth do dwell' came into my heart. We will sing the hymnal lines together now:

All people that on earth do dwell,
Sing to the Lord with cheerful voice.
Him serve with fear, His praise forth tell;
Come ye before Him and rejoice.

The Lord, ye know, is God indeed;
Without our aid He did us make;

CHAPTER FOUR

We are His folk, He doth us feed,
And for His sheep He doth us take.

O enter then His gates with praise;
Approach with joy His courts unto;
Praise, laud, and bless His Name always,
For it is seemly so to do.

For why? the Lord our God is good;
His mercy is for ever sure;
His truth at all times firmly stood,
And shall from age to age endure.

To Father, Son and Holy Ghost,
The God Whom Heaven and earth adore,
From men and from the angel host
Be praise and glory evermore.

Amen!

This Hymn is based on the words of Psalm 100:

1 Make a joyful noise unto the Lord, all ye lands.

CHAPTER FOUR

2 Serve the Lord with gladness: come before his presence with singing.

3 Know ye that the Lord he is God: it is he that hath made us, and not we ourselves; we are his people, and the sheep of his pasture.

4 Enter into his gates with thanksgiving, and into his courts with praise: be thankful unto him, and bless his name.

5 For the Lord is good; his mercy is everlasting; and his truth endureth to all generations.

Reading verse 1 through 4 would explain the whole essence of man on earth. The Kingdom of God on earth exists to render undiluted praise and worship unto God. This is why Christ came to earth to take away our burden of pain, and we are taught the principles of God's kingdom on earth, so that we would replicate heavenly character of praise and worship here on earth.

CHAPTER FOUR

❖

On the Creation of Heaven and Earth

❖

Once upon a time, there was neither heaven nor earth. A time came when heaven and earth had to be created by the movement of God – an example of what happens when God moves can be found in Exodus 20:18-19, Exodus 24:10,17, Revelation 4:5, 1 King 19:9-13. We would see what heralded His coming – strong wind, earthquakes, and then fire. This has to be because the Lord is landing on earth with His holy armies, worshippers, in chariots. This is why the earth is called 'His footstool'. We have heard vibrations on the earth when heavy equipment is transported on our roads before.

The movement of God that created the heavens and the earth is what scientist calls the big bang theory. That creation movement may have resulted in explosions as God moved, and this resulted in the formation of the stars, the planets (including the earth), moons, sun - and because they are spiritual entities which once existed as one big mass, they still maintain that space and distance from one another. Ever since then God has never stopped from moving - the winds, the clouds, the sun, the planets. Everything is set in motion because God is moving; He neither sleeps nor slumbers (Psalm 121:4). Genesis 1:2 captures all that when we are told - *And the Spirit of God moved…*

Now there is really no demarcation between heaven and earth, it is just for emphasis purpose because the earth is His footstool. So there is really no distinction. Hence He walked down to Adam in Eden. How did Adam know that God was in the garden? *And they heard the voice of the Lord God walking in the garden in the cool of the day* – Genesis 3:8. We just read of strong wind, earthquake and fire. No wonder Adam and his wife were hiding from Him. And how did God call out to them? With a thunderous voice, I guess! *And the Lord God called unto Adam, and said unto him, where art thou* – Genesis 3:9. The way Adam responded in fear explains the context we are trying to depict - *And he said, I heard thy voice in the garden, and I was afraid, because I was naked; and I hid myself* – Genesis 3:10. Was the garden a small garden? No, it was really large – rivers compassed a land mass made of beautiful trees. We have heard of UFOs and alien visits on earth. Could the UFOs be the chariots the Bible referred to? Could the aliens sighted be angels? Have angels refused to land on earth because of human hostilities? The purpose of this discussion is to enable us understand that the Kingdom of God on earth is made up of both physical and spiritual entities. Without the spiritual there is no physical. The physical is a manifestation of the spiritual among us. The Bible rightly pointed out that the Kingdom of God on earth is only possible under the *'Immanuel'* cloud, when the enemy will no longer have power over the children of God - *Take counsel together, and it shall come to nought; speak the word, and it shall not stand: for God is with us* – Isaiah 8:10. Have we felt the presence of God on earth through the signs we have explained – wind, earthquake, and fire? We have heard of attacks on churches worldwide – is God still with us? Have we not read that - *When the enemy shall come in like a flood, the Spirit of the Lord shall lift up a standard against him* – Isaiah 59:19. We must as a matter of fact live a life of sanctity and adherence to the holy statues of God, so that we will experience the *Immanuel* cloud on earth. That *Immanuel Cloud* is the evidence of the Kingdom of God on earth.

Many of us think that God and the angels are far up there - there is no demarcation between us and them, once the Kingdom cloud is in our midst. That is why they are spirits, not controlled by physical boundaries. We share the same road, the same car, the same room, etc. That is why we talk of His presence. The heavenly beings are more than earthly beings. If they were all physical, there would be real chaos on earth. So the spiritual perfects all things and our physical senses just put the spiritual the way we can see them with our eyes. The same things you see in your dreams are as real as they are and would manifest in the physical someday. The kingdom in the spirit has to be duplicated on earth for humans to have a feel of what eternity is like, so that when we become fully spiritual after our death, we won't really perceive and experience much difference, and there won't be much to learn about. So the spiritual is the same as the physical, except that one is tangible within the physical sense and the other is intangible within the spiritual sense, but both harmonize one another. The imperfection in this harmony is the reason why Jesus came to earth to set the foundation for the take-off of a like-for-like platform where heavenly values would be learned by the human race. This platform is the Kingdom of the Lord, which He has put in the care of those we call 'Servants of God' worldwide. It is a pitiable scene to see Servants of God running after earthly leaders to be favoured, thereby allow infiltration of worldly human wisdom into the doctrine of heaven they were supposed to uphold. The prophet Isaiah says - *For the Lord spake thus to me with a strong hand, and instructed me that I should not walk in the way of this people, saying, Say ye not, A confederacy, to all them to whom this people shall say, A confederacy; neither fear ye their fear, nor be afraid. Sanctify the Lord of hosts himself; and let him be your fear, and let him be your dread. And he shall be for a sanctuary* – Isaiah 8:11-14. The Lord says – Say 'NO' to coalition of thoughts against the precepts of God. Many a pastor today would rather join the multitude to wash down the standard handed down to them by God, just to have multitudes that would give offerings and tithes in their churches. The last portion we just read says that if we sanctify the Lord of hosts – meaning if we uplift His name through our acts of holiness and sanctity - then the *Lord shall be for a sanctuary*. The moment the Sanctuary of the Lord is present in our midst, we would have the *Immanuel cloud* circumscribing the Kingdom, and we won't have to fear the enemy. Our all-night prayers of fears will give way to worship in His sanctuary. The Kingdom of God is still far from being a reality in our present day gathering because we have flirted with the heathen idols. Christianity as we have it today has an infusion of idolatry, which has enabled all manner of persons to gather together supposedly believing they are in God's presence, whereas they have only gathered together as a mixed multitude with varied intentions, and as such, the sanctuary of the Lord, which is the seat of the King of kings is not set in order. Hence Christ says of the will of God being done as it is in the spiritual - heaven.

Take a look at your neighbour and see how wonderful he or she is. If you can't see that, there is no way you will understand what the angels are set to do in your life when you are in the Kingdom.

Now why did God create the earth? Just say, as His investment, as we also do. He created all for His enjoyment. After the heavens were created, God raised angels from the elements around Him. Jesus talked about God being able to raise worshippers from stones – Luke

19:40. And so, when Earth was also created, God raised man from the dust and all living creatures came to be from the earth.

This is the only difference between man and angels – one is made with a fully spiritual substance, while the other is a mixture of both spiritual and earthly substance, but both function to ensure the Kingdom of God is establish forever. Our heart operates as the human timer on earth. The human spirit is supposed to be compatible with the spirit of God – mind of God. When we die the human spirit returns to God – Genesis 6:3, to be united with Him, but if it bears iniquity from the sins we committed then it will not be received into God and it is judged as a rebelling spirit after the devil. Hence the Bible says that after death there is judgement. The time of judgement is when the spirit is supposed to be united with God. Whatsoever came from earth will go back to the earth. But to be wholly assimilated into the God spirit, from whence our spirit came, we have to love one another in unity with the purpose of God. This is another reason for a secluded gathering of people on earth in a kingdom life, where we are taught the values that are accepted in heaven, so that as we live to practise them, we become fully integrated into the heavenly life. Our spirits carry our thoughts, and once our thoughts are dissimilar from those of God, there is a repelling force that pushes our spirit away as we try to come into the light of God. We need the word of God through fellowship with His spirit to receive the light that will light our world - *The Lord sent a word into Jacob, and it hath lighted upon Israel* – Isaiah 9:8. Let's look at the verse carefully – the word was sent *into* Jacob. Which means, the word was fused into the heart of Jacob by His encounter with God, and the indwelling light lighted the whole of Israel. No wonder Christ told His disciples that they are the light of the world. How did they finally become this light? They were with Jesus learning about the values and life of heaven in obedience to Jesus' command - *Take my yoke upon you, and learn of me; for I am meek and lowly in heart: and ye shall find rest unto your souls. For my yoke is easy, and my burden is light* – Matthew 11:29-30.

We cannot understand what the Kingdom entails until we can digest the words and terms of the agreement between God and Moses in Exodus 20:1-17, which became the Ten Commandments. The word of God to Moses explains the fact that God wants a kingdom of people who bear His name, living in peace and harmony, governed by certain rules and regulations that will make every citizen of that kingdom revere Him as their King and God. To do this, He would require the service of some people whom He will fuse with His spirit so that they can reason like Him, not rebelling against His commands, but will from time to time honour His reign in their midst. Moses was used in his time. Various prophets existed after then. Jesus found the disciples and then many servants of God now living and more to come. The people of Sodom did see angels with Lot but regarded them as terrestrial visitors. Saint Paul argued that many have entertained angels as visitors. Even in our world today, it would be reasonable to argue that angels are in our midst carrying out the will of God. I once had an accident with a motorcyclist. The moment I came down, I saw three soldiers approaching me. Even as people gathered and tried to cause trouble, these soldiers knew the cyclist had ridden wrongly and was at fault. The moment they came to the scene, they told me to enter the car and leave. That was all I saw of them and as I looked into the mirror behind, they were gone. Who were they? So, the presence of God, and hence His kingdom is with us if we would understand.

Now we will be explaining the Kingdom of God from the revelation of Daniel. We will also explore the pattern of design, which Moses was commanded to use for the tabernacles. We will then explore further what Jesus likened the Kingdom of God to in His teachings. At the end of these expositions, we will be well informed what God expects in His kingdom here on Earth.

In the book of Daniel, the Kingdom of God on earth was revealed in Daniel 7:27 - *And the Kingdom and dominion, and the greatness of the Kingdom under the whole heaven, shall be given to the people of the saints of the most High, whose kingdom is an everlasting kingdom, and all dominions shall serve and obey him.* This points to the fact that the Kingdom of the earth shall be handed over to the saints of God, who will now oversee these kingdoms as under shepherd kings to ensure that the whole world and dominions *shall serve and obey* Him.

The book of Lamentation 4:5 - *They that did* **feed delicately** *are desolate in the streets: they that were* **brought up in scarlet** *embrace dunghills.* The Kingdom of God on earth is a home of royalty, where the people eat like kings and queens, princes and princesses, and dress in royal apparel. These are marks of honour and respect, accorded to everyone in the Kingdom. Anything that negates this attribute is not permissible under the rules that govern the Kingdom – Exodus 32:21 says: *And ye shall be holy men unto me: neither shall ye **eat any flesh that is torn of beasts in the field**; ye shall cast it to the dogs,* and in like manner, Matthew 22:11-14 says: *And when the king came in to see the guests, he saw there a man **which had not on a wedding garment**:... Then said the king to the servants, Bind him hand and foot, and take him away, and cast him into outer darkness;.. For many are called, but few are chosen.* Those in His kingdom must exhibit the character of decency and holiness. The kingdom is filled with the glory of eternity. One may gaze into the skies and see the beautiful arrays of stars. Anyone desiring heaven must understand what it takes to live in the glory of God.

No one kingdom has it all. Each of these kingdoms, like the characters of the disciples of Jesus, are unique and one kingdom's values would not be seen totally replicated in another, but the Lord who created them knows the calling upon His servants and the values and mysteries He would want them to showcase. This is why

St. Paul says, be ye followers of me. It is dangerous to compare kingdoms. We see this also clearly shown in Revelation 2. Severally, in the book of Matthew Jesus explains the patterns of these kingdoms. Let's see some of these verses for us to be able to understand what God requires from His children. The more the children of God are taught kingdom values and they learn to live as one family with respect and order, the more they will overcome the devil – Colossians 1:13, through power (1 Corinthians 4:20) and wisdom.

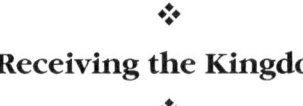

Receiving the Kingdom

Belonging to the Kingdom of God starts by receiving the word of the Kingdom. The word comes with peace. The kingdom has been instituted here on earth - Matthew 16:28: *Verily I say unto you, There be some standing here, which shall not taste of death, till they see the Son of man coming in his kingdom.* The disciples did experience the beauty of His kingdom, and we are now living in His kingdom, with miracles, signs and wonders as some of the evidence of His presence. The revelation of spiritual

CHAPTER FOUR

secrets has never been as rampant as it is today. Of a truth, the Kingdom of God is live with us.

You cannot enter into the Kingdom of God until you receive it with your heart. This is why you cannot grow and increase in life when you don't receive Jesus and then those God has called to be His servant, who will lead you to Him. In effect, you must have received the Servant of God before you can receive Jesus: Matthew 10:40 – *He that receiveth you receiveth me, and he that receiveth me receiveth him that sent me*; because the servant bears the gospel in his lips.

This Kingdom of God is only within you when the servant of God, the bearer of the anointing of God, is in your midst to teach you the ways of heaven – Luke 17:21: *And when he was demanded of the Pharisees, when the Kingdom of God should come, he answered them and said, The Kingdom of God cometh not with observation: Neither shall they say, Lo here! or, lo there! for, behold,* **the Kingdom of God is within you**.

Many disregard servants of God and would see them as one who reaps where he has not sown (Luke 19:21-22). Every day you come in contact with God's servants, either through physical contact or through their books or messages, they have given you the talent to invest and you must make profit with what you have received. When I listen to messages from God's servant, God instructs me to sow a seed in some cases because that message had borne fruit in my life. When we reject the bearers of the gospel, how shall we be saved from desolation? Jesus referred to this in Luke 13:35: *Behold, your house is left unto you desolate: and verily I say unto you, Ye shall not see me, until the time come when ye shall say, Blessed is he that cometh in the name of the Lord.* To receive from the Kingdom of God one must first receive one sent by the Lord. This is how you receive the Kingdom of God. Jesus says that anyone who rejects His servants, who oversees His kingdom on earth, and therefore acts as kings over His estates on earth, has likewise rejected Him. They should be treated with honour as long as they bear the gospel and the anointing from the Melchizedek Order, and anyone who rejects them is doomed - Luke 10:16 *'Whoever listens to you listens to me; whoever rejects you rejects me; but whoever rejects me rejects him who sent me.'* It is not about the servant of God, it is about the anointing He carries. If you

CHAPTER FOUR

retort back at him, you retorts back at Jesus, and then God. You must learn to receive God's servants with love, and treat them with honour. Your pastor cannot wear rags and you are dressed in colourful clothing. They bear rule over you with the anointing upon them. Let them stretch that staff towards you and your life will never experience stagnation again. The anointing flows from the source to the receiver through respect and loyalty. For the oil to flow from the head to the toe, the legs and toe must stand still. To stand still is to submit. Submission comes with humility - Luke 14:11: *For whosoever exalteth himself shall be abased; and he that humbleth himself shall be exalted.*

Jesus has been given the authority to oversee His kingdom both in heaven and on earth (Matthew 28:18). And this kingdom, He has divided into smaller kingdoms and handed over to His servants so that they will bear rule in their respective kingdoms (Luke 19:12-13), through the staff of office contained in the anointing (1 John 2:27). Now anyone who want to be in any of this kingdom must first have the heart of a child – Luke 18:17: *Verily I say unto you, Whosoever shall not receive the Kingdom of God as a little child shall in no wise enter therein.* Who is a child? Children demonstrate the beauty of the Kingdom of God. They are eager to learn. This is what anyone coming into the Kingdom of God should expect. Jesus says their life explains what the Kingdom of God represents Luke 18:16: *But Jesus called them unto him, and said, Suffer little children to come unto me, and forbid them not: for of such is the Kingdom of God.* I will also recommend that you study my book *Gifted and Anointed* for an understanding of this also. We all must press our thoughts on what is preached so that we would be stamped by it. This implies that our entire lives would be like a paper document, or certificate of a sort, carrying the stamp of the Kingdom as a sign of approval. Jesus says in Luke 16:16-17: *The law and the prophets were until John: since that time the Kingdom of God is preached, and every man presseth into it. And it is easier for heaven and earth to pass, than one tittle of the law to fail.* It is not about seeking miracles and running around like sheep without a shepherd. God works through His shepherds. This is why when Christ saw them running about for miracles, He knew they had no shepherd – Matthew 9:37… *The harvest truly is plenteous, but the labourers are few.* You cannot belong to the fold of one of His shepherds and you will be in want. From the portion we just read, it is clear that you must receive every instruction from God and act on them because *it is easier for heaven and earth to pass, than one tittle of the law to fail.* And these are the standards we would be judged by. If we don't receive the messengers of the gospel, how do we expect the move of God? We are told in Luke10: 8-9: *And into whatsoever city ye enter, and they receive you, eat such things as are set before you: And heal the sick that are therein, and say unto them, The Kingdom of God is come nigh unto you.* Implying that it is only after the disciples were welcomed and received that they could heal those who were sick. Accept the servant of God, and the anointing in him shall work and speak for you; *He that receiveth a prophet in the name of a prophet shall receive a prophet's reward; and he that receiveth a righteous man in the name of a righteous man shall receive a righteous man's* reward – Matthew 10:41.

Every servant of God oversees a kingdom in the large Kingdom of God. This is why Jesus says in that house, there are mansions – the house is the Kingdom of God, the mansions are the individual realms or kingdoms which have now become the domains of the faithful servants who overcame while on earth. God told Moses about the people he had brought – this is how it is in God's Kingdom. Your pastor bears responsibility for how much of God you know, and how far you will grow in Him.

❖

Roles of Angels in the Kingdom

❖

Until God created heaven and earth there were no angels; He only existed alone as God. There was no reason for their existence. God is a planner. Everything He does falls in place, in due time and season. Just like men and women, a time comes when you feel like getting married, and then having children. Then other things in life come as necessity warrants. This is why we say that necessity is the mother of invention.

The angel that announced the birth of Jesus to the shepherds in the field in Luke 2:10 reminds us of something - *And the angel said unto them, Fear not: for, behold, I bring you good tidings of great joy, which shall be to all people. For unto you is born this day in the city of David a Saviour, which is* **Christ the Lord**. The message was given to Shepherds first, and the purpose of the Kingdom is good tidings of great joy to every nation who accepts the message and work to earn this assurance.

The Birth of Jesus indeed shows the roles that angels would play henceforth to ensure that the Kingdom of God is established on earth. And later, the Lord would inform us that the angels will play a major role in the establishment of the new heaven and the new earth.

Matthew 13:41, 49: *The Son of man shall send forth his angels, and they shall gather out of his **kingdom** all things that offend, and them which do iniquity; so shall it be at the end of the world: the angels shall come forth, and sever the wicked from among the just.*

Then John recounted in his vision later in Revelation 14:18-19: *And another angel came out from the altar, which had power over fire; and cried with a loud cry to him that had the sharp sickle, saying, Thrust in thy sharp sickle, and gather the clusters of the vine of the earth; for her grapes are fully ripe. And the angel thrust in his sickle into the earth, and gathered the vine of the earth, and cast it into the great winepress of the wrath of God.*

CHAPTER FOUR

Angels work closely with servants of God to ensure the people are fed with spiritual milk and meat unto maturity. Abraham referred to this in Luke 16:29: *Abraham saith unto him, They have Moses and the prophets; let them hear them.* So all those who refused to hear the servants of God are those who will offend God, and will be doomed after death.

When we translate unto eternal glory – angels also would come to lead us home - *And it came to pass, that the beggar died, and was carried by the angels into Abraham's bosom…* Luke 16:22. This shows that any Kingdom of God on earth must operate with the leading of God's angels – Exodus 23:20: *Behold, I send an Angel before thee, to keep thee in the way, and to bring thee into the place which I have prepared.* Moses understood the ways of God and knew when the angel would be around. So they pitched their tent and moved it under the command and leading of the angel, appearing like a cloud upon the tabernacle, with the message from God. Elijah in, 1 Kings 19, also recognised the angels. This is the duty of the servant of God in the Kingdom. He knows when God is around because he maintains an allegiance with the authorities from heaven.

CHAPTER FOUR

Now we may see the importance of angels in the Kingdom:

1. God used them to plant Eden

2. They ministered to Jesus after He defeated the Devil in Matthew 4. Remember Jesus was hungry, which means they must have provided food for Him. To minister is to go on errands. The Bible says that we shall judge angels.

3. An angel gave Elijah food

4. They present prayers to God

5. They lead the way to your inheritance

6. The Holy Spirit talks to you when the Angel is ahead – Exodus 23:20, Isaiah 30:21.

The plots of the enemy daily do not consume us because there are angels around us. We must have this at the back of our mind. No angels, no blessings, protection or provision. Since they dwell in Holy sites such as altars, Hebrews 12:22, they take prayers made there as incense and present them before God in heaven - Revelation 8:3. God will use the angels to actualise His purpose for the new heaven and earth - 1 Thessalonians 4:16.

CHAPTER FOUR

God created angels for Himself in heaven as messengers and man on earth to manage the earth. Angels are His spiritual employees while we are His physical employees, with one purpose – to tender His creations. Just as He demands reports from us, so also He is demanding reports from them. To ensure they respond to our needs, we are made their judge - 1 Corinthians 6:3, and any complain of suffering we give in our prayers to God will be investigated and if an angel is found guilty, he will pay dearly for it, and this will include demotion. Hence God says testify against Him - Micah 6:3. The Psalmist recognise this in his confession of the working ways of God in Psalm 34:7: *The angel of the Lord encampeth round about them that fear him, and delivereth them.* Meaning that the angels build their camps around anyone who is controlled by the spirit of the Lord. This implies further that the habitation of the servant of God is a kingdom of God. And Daniel says - *My God hath sent his angel, and hath shut the lions 'mouths, that they have not hurt me* – Daniel 6:22.This was possible for Daniel because he was connected to the heavenly Jerusalem.

So, we can see that we are our own problem, and not God. All provisions have been made to see that we

CHAPTER FOUR

succeed. Why are we not getting results when we are in need?

Angels are Holy, and they only hear holy prayers. Hence if we can have Christ in us, then we can be heard. This is why we use 'in Jesus Name,' because of our imperfection. When we call Jesus, the angles know that these are they whom the Lamb died for.

God is able to raise worshippers from the stones if we fail to honour the Lord. How are you not sure that the scientists who invented many of the things we are using today were not angels. So you can understand that God created angles to carry out specific duties. How are you sure that there are angels sitting with you now? Angels are here to beautify your life and they will not sleep until your desires are met except you are out of tune with God. You are here to be peaceful. In the beginning, the earth had no peace, but God intervened.

People complained against Sodom and God sent down angels. I want to let you know that angels are here. They are seated with you. You can't see them because they are spirits, but they are here. This is why in Ecclesiastes 5:1-2, the Bible says when you enter into the house of God, be quiet. Angels don't like noise. They understand your heart, though they can also hear your language, but they read your thoughts more.

Our individual responsibilities in the Kingdom

This will be further discussed later. Here I would want us to give this a thought – that we have our individual responsibilities in ensuring that the Kingdom of God benefits the whole earth. We are informed in John 10:10 that we must have life in us and have it more abundantly, as long as we are in the Kingdom. We can see the manifestation of greatness when the serpent of Aaron swallowed that of the magicians in Egypt. Daniel was declared ten times better than his peers. The order of sustainable progress in the Kingdom of God is *'Forward and Upward.'* We would now explain this:

Forward sustainable progression: This involves mostly gaining learning experience through the acquisition of specific knowledge, understanding and wisdom.

CHAPTER FOUR

Upward sustainable progression: Supernatural upliftment and development in spiritual things. We must desire and love the things of the spirit to achieve this growth pattern.

Both progress patterns gives rise to a linear growth. The non-sustained progress is the one that is vertical. The first pattern is likened to a waiting period, when one matures in exercising the learning gained in the Kingdom through exercising the gift acquired thereto. When this learning is not there, it becomes difficult to sustain linear growth.

When we know our responsibilities we will experience the beauty of the Kingdom. For instance, a wife is a help to the husband and not the one to champion the course of sustaining the home. A husband is the head of the family and not a beater. Some men cannot function as the head without beating their wives. I am a pastor - one who feeds God's children with knowledge and understanding. Micah 4:2 explains that what is most needed is how God would teach us His ways and our duty would be to walk in His paths: *And many nations shall come, and say, Come, and let us go up to the mountain of the Lord, and to the house of the God of Jacob; and he will teach us of his ways, and we will walk in his paths*

CHAPTER FOUR

All I believe is that people have a physical problem, which needs both spiritual and physical intervention. And this would require them undergoing a training to upgrade their knowledge and understanding, in physical and spiritual matters. For instance, somebody who does not know how to acknowledge people or talk in public should not expect to have a good job - if such a person is employed, the likelihood that he will sustain the job is thin. Someone with an attitude problem is a time bomb in marriage, as there will be no peace in the home. So I will spend time to teach you first before praying with you. I know my God and I know what He hates.

As we prepare to leave this chapter, I will want us to go back to basics, as recorded in the book of Genesis:

1. God created heaven, earth, all we see today and made Man after His thinking to manage the earth, and to give Him status report whenever He came visiting

2. He gave him a woman as an embodiment of wisdom, to help him survive the Eden environment

3. The woman left her responsibility and began to gossip and argue the information the husband gave to her.

CHAPTER FOUR

4. The husband didn't challenged the evil that was going on and both of them altered the spiritual and physical order in the garden.

5. By this singular act, all the spiritual laws that govern heaven were altered - animals would begin to eat animals, man would become obese, sickness would come, death would come, hatred, competition and survival tricks - which the devil had learnt after leaving heaven into earth. Man was going to change his new life to be able to survive - he would look for comfort and peace without finding it, he would smoke, drink and womanise in search for happiness and peace.

6. It was going to cause God so much to put in place what man had destroyed. His angels would have to frequent the earth to put things right. He drove man out to secure the tree of life from their reach, else they would have lived in evil forever.

7. He found Abraham, then Jacob.

8. He separated the children of Adam born in sin, from the children of the covenant (Deuteronomy 32:8).

9. The only way for rescue is to be linked to the Jacob root - Isaiah 27:6, John 4:22.

CHAPTER FOUR

10. Forgiveness of sin was due to the sacrifice upon the brazen altar in the Old Testament Tabernacle.

11. Meaning anyone who would be saved from all nations would have to go the Jerusalem with animals for sacrifices. We all know that it would have been only the rich who could afford that; there would be no hope for the poor.

12. The plan to set up a spiritual Jerusalem was hatched -Hebrews 12:22

13. For this to happen, the brazen altar has to become null and void – because it represents the law.

14. Meaning the brazen altar must bear a sacrifice that is compelling enough to make God reject every other animal sacrifice, which would not by any standard meet the sacrifice earlier made, just as you won't want to eat soured food after eating a delicious meal.

15. This would only be possible if the sacrifice is as perfect and holy as God Himself.

16. Jesus became that lamb.

17. But we need to believe in Him to be a partaker of the brazen altar sacrifice - the altar in Golgotha.

18. After believing, baptising, we can now be admitted into the Kingdom of God, to learn about His ways - Micah 4:2.

Instinctively, one would think that to annihilate and regain the initiative earlier depicted in His plan for Eden will not be possible, but here we are; God regained control of the lost man without any form of air assault, as the Kingdom of this world would do to gain control. As the years goes by, so also God's control is felt everywhere the head turns. One of the ways of knowing the works of God in our lives is our ability to understand the duties of angels in the Kingdom.

CHAPTER FIVE

THE PURPOSE OF THE KINGDOM

It was on the 19th of January 2013 when the Lord said to me – 'Life is made up of people on a race to nowhere and as such they would always need someone to take them somewhere.'

We can affirm this from Daniel 12:3,10 - *And they that be wise shall shine as the brightness of the firmament; and they that turn many to righteousness as the stars forever and ever. Many shall be purified, and made white...* We have the duty of each kingdom administered by the saints of God clearly written here, which is to feed people with the wisdom of God, and turn many to righteousness. This is what Jesus meant in Matthew 28:20 – *Teaching every citizen of the Kingdom to observe all things that Jesus commanded.* Leading souls to Christ is more than just preaching and teaching, it involves mentoring and providing spiritual guidance. This implies therefore that we all must have the true knowledge of what the Kingdom of God is all about, rather than running with our individual vision, which in most cases leads to self-righteousness and condemnation. Hence Jesus said –Luke 13:27: ... *I know you not whence ye are; depart from me, all ye workers of iniquity.* How did they become workers of iniquity? They certainly healed and worked miracles in Jesus' name. So what went wrong in their service before the Lord?

It is the responsibility of the king in a Kingdom to put in place what it takes to lead people to God – so that they would store their treasures in heaven. Anyone who accepts the terms and conditions of the Kingdom, and exercises same, is visited by the King of kings with favour and blessings. No one has ever come to God who has not been blessed by Him (Hebrews 11:6, Isaiah 45:1-3, 14). Unto God shall every knee bow and every tongue shall swear (Isaiah 45:23), because He is the reason for their living. The purpose of the Kingdom of God on earth is to encourage people all over the earth to come unto the Lord of hosts, hence the miracles – so that the word of God can strike through the heart of the stout-hearted sinner and make him submit with God. What the Lord does is explained better in Ezekiel 16:9-14: *Then washed I thee with water; yea, I throughly washed away thy blood (Sin) from thee, and I anointed thee with oil. I clothed thee also with broidered work, and shod thee with badgers 'skin, and I girded thee about with fine linen, and I covered thee with silk. I decked thee also with ornaments, and I put bracelets upon thy hands, and a chain on thy neck. And I put a jewel on thy forehead, and earrings in thine ears, and a beautiful crown upon thine head. Thus wast thou decked with gold and silver; and thy raiment was of fine linen, and silk, and broidered work; thou didst eat fine flour, and honey, and oil: and thou wast exceeding beautiful, and thou didst prosper into a kingdom. And thy renown went forth among the heathen for thy beauty: for it was perfect through my comeliness, which I had put upon thee, saith the Lord God.* The Lord beautifies whoever submits to Him and dwells in His kingdom. What we read above is indeed the height of beauty. The book of Isaiah 61:10 summarises it this way

CHAPTER FIVE

- I will greatly rejoice in the Lord, my soul shall be joyful in my God; for he hath clothed me with the garments of salvation, he hath covered me with the robe of righteousness, as a bridegroom decketh himself with ornaments, and as a bride adorneth herself with her jewels.

The Kingdom of God is aimed at adding value to our lives and making us more beautiful and accepted than the way we used to be. To experience this, we ought to live the values of God's kingdom here on earth, as stated earlier. The King of kings raises kings who are called servants of the Lord, who also are Lords in their area of jurisdiction because Jesus is the Lord of Lords. Each of these servants of Jesus acts as a 'Lord.' Hannah referred to Eli, in 1 Samuel 1:26, as 'Lord.' These Lords have the capacity to make rules, and to punish offenders – 1 Samuel 7:15:*And Samuel judged Israel all the days of his life.* The Servant of God also has the power to forgive sins once He operates with the power of the spirit of God, John 20:23: *If you forgive the sins of any, they are forgiven them; if you withhold forgiveness from any, it is withheld.* God raises His servants to be able to conquer territories and then preserve them. God raises men of God to set up kingdoms for Him – the name, 'Abraham' literally means the 'father of many nations'. Before God called Him, he was Abram – exalted father. After the call, he became the father of many nations.

In Revelation 3:8-12, the Lord says: *I know thy works: behold, I have set before thee an open door, and no man can shut it: for thou hast a little strength, and hast kept my word, and hast not denied my name. Behold, I will make them of the synagogue of Satan, which say they are Jews, and are not, but do lie; behold, I will make them to come and worship before thy feet, and to know that I have loved thee.* Here, we understand that the servant of God is a person of honour, as unbelievers begin to see the manifestation of God in his life and would come to worship at his feet. It is this honour that many have misinterpreted as if the servant of God is being worshipped rather than worship God.

A servant of God has the knowledge to equip people so that they can overcome the temptations of the devil, and at the end of the day receive the reward of the Lord. His duty is to teach and preach Christ to them so that in that repented form, they would receive the word of sanctification from God - John 17:17. The servant of God is also raised to pray for the people, for the mercy of the Lord upon them as seen in the life of Samuel - 1 Samuel 12:23: *Moreover as for me, God forbid that I should sin against the Lord in ceasing to pray for you: but I will teach you the good and the right way.* I have often told people that there is no fake servant of God. He is either a servant of God or a servant of the devil.

The purpose of the Kingdom of God here on earth can be seen in the light of raising a *Holy Nation* unto God who will worship and minister before the Lord in His sanctuary.

The purpose of the Kingdom is explicitly explained in Revelation 11: 15-18: *And the seventh angel sounded; and there were great voices in heaven, saying,* **The kingdoms of this world are become the Kingdoms of our Lord, and of his Christ;** *and he shall reign for ever and ever. And the four and twenty elders, which sat before God on their seats, fell upon their faces, and worshipped God, Saying, We give thee thanks, O Lord God Almighty, which art, and wast, and art to come;* **because thou hast taken to thee thy great power, and hast reigned.** *And* *the nations were angry, and thy wrath is come, and the time of the dead, that they should be judged, and that thou shouldest* **give reward unto thy servants the prophets, and to the saints, and them that fear thy name, small and great;** *and shouldest destroy them which destroy the earth.*

Let us do some justice to what we just read:

- Verse 15 - **The kingdoms of this world are become the Kingdoms of our Lord, and of his Christ:** We are to take over control, occupying the whole earth till He comes.

- Verse 17 - **because thou hast taken to thee thy great power, and hast reigned:** At the end, at the commencement of the reign of Christ, He will receive back His Holy Spirit which He released to enable us do His will when He says in John 16:7: 'Nevertheless I tell you the truth; It is expedient for you that I go away: for if I go not away, the Comforter will not come unto you; but if I depart, I will send him unto you.' The Holy Spirit is now given to us as a loan.

- Verse 18 - ***give reward unto thy servants the prophets, and to the saints, and them that fear thy name, small and great:*** Those in the Kingdom are Servants, the prophets, the Saints, and the multitude of righteous people who supported the servants of God in the calling (fear thy name, small and great). We are all working towards a reward (Hebrew 11:6). We are working toward sanctity. The vision of the Royal Diamonds International Church is to build a kingdom of Saints – the church of the firstborn, whose name is written in heaven; the church that overcometh.

Daniel saw a great revelation confirming what we read above in Daniel 7:9: *I beheld till the thrones were cast down, and the Ancient of days did sit, whose garment was white as snow, and the hair of his head like the pure wool: his throne was like the fiery flame, and his wheels as burning fire.* And from this throne He has also make His ministers a *flaming fire*– Psalm 104:4.

The reason why God established His Kingdom on earth is to enable Him to sanctify His children and keep them in that separated form, from the world of sin. For the purpose of clarity, I want to throw some light on what sanctification is all about.

The Kingdom is centred on 'sanctification.' Without sanctification, the Sanctuary of the Lord cannot be established in our midst – Ezekiel 37:27-28: *My tabernacle also shall be with them: yea, I will be their God, and they shall be my people. And the heathen shall know that I the Lord do* **sanctify** *Israel, when my* **sanctuary** *shall be in the midst of them for evermore.* This is why it took the centre stage of Jesus' recommendation of the acts of the disciples before God in John 17:17 – 19: *Sanctify them through thy truth: thy word is truth. As thou hast sent me into the world, even so have I also sent them into the world. And for their sakes I sanctify myself, that they also might be sanctified through the truth.* To sanctify is to make clean for the use of God. It is purity unto holiness. Jesus says - *Now ye are clean through the word, which I have spoken unto you. Abide in me, and I in you. As the branch cannot bear fruit of itself, except it abide in the vine; no more can ye, except ye abide in me* – John 15:3-4. Until they were clean, they couldn't have been invited to abide in Him. Speaking in tongues while still in sin and ignorant of the word of the Kingdom is simply' demonic illusion.' King David knew that sanctification is about receiving a clean heart from God, which now becomes a home for a steadfast spirit - Psalm 51:10: *Create in me a clean heart, O God; and renew a right spirit within me.* The Lord cannot set the *Immanuel cloud* around us until we are sanctified. In the book of 2 Chronicles 7:16, the Lord says: *For now have I chosen and sanctified this house, that my name may be there for ever: and mine eyes and mine heart shall be there perpetually.* It is only when God has sanctified a place that His eyes and heart will be there. When this happens the citizens will experience humility because of the presence of the Lord - *...thou shalt no more be haughty because of my holy mountain* – Zephaniah 3:11. And this has a lot to do with the transformation of the citizens of the Kingdom, to such an extent that they will begin to speak the language of heaven - *For then will I turn to the people a pure language, that they may all call upon the name of the Lord, to serve him with one consent* – Zephaniah 3:9.

The basis for sanctification can be seen from the following light:

■ **Prayers:** For our prayers to receive answers, the

Angels of God have to present them to God as incense – Revelation 8:3. Before the Angels can do this, Jesus has to recommend us to them. And He can only do this if we confessed Him before men through publicly declaring for Him, and championing the course of preaching and teaching about the Kingdom of God. We must learn to ensure that our words are few, so that we can communicate more with our hearts, and learn to listen to God. Those who speak volumes are those who murmur, complain and gossip. And these characteristics will never allow us to build with God; rather they will make us scatter what God is building.

- **Praise:** Praise is possible when we have a clean heart. We are admonished to worship Him from the beauty of Holiness. This is because God is Holy.

- **Protection**: Many of us want God to protect us. The question is, are we standing on the side of the Lord? Jesus complained of this fact in Luke 18:8: *I tell you that he (God) will avenge them speedily. Nevertheless when the Son of man cometh, shall he find faith on the earth.* God can only avenge those who are upright in Him. This is where our sanctification comes in.

- **Provision:** The earth and its fullness belong to Him – Psalm 24:1. Saint Paul says of this fact – Philippians 4:19: *But my God shall supply all your need according to his riches in glory by Christ Jesus.* This is why He is called Jehovah Jireh.

- **Promotion:** The Lord is a rewarder of those who diligently seek Him – Hebrews 11:6. Saint Paul was sure of this when he said that he was expecting a crown of righteousness from the Lord at the end of the day – 2 Timothy 4:8.

I refer to these as the 5Ps of basis for sanctification. This relates to the fact that it is for our own benefit, and to ensure that we are still covered by the *Immanuel Cloud*.

As I was praying one morning I heard the word *'maccaddeschem.'* This word would be found in Exodus 31:13 and Leviticus 20:8: a Hebrew word which means 'sanctifier.' Gradually it dawn on me that God wants to see people who are dedicated in holiness and sanctity unto His name. This act of sanctification will enable the name of the Lord to rest upon us (2 Chronicles 7:14, Psalm 23:3). Hence we are told in the Bible that the name of the Lord is a strong tower for the righteous (Proverbs 18:10).

Sanctification refers to spiritual cleansing. In Ezekiel 36:25-29, we are brought into the understanding of a mystery about the effect of sanctification: *Then will I sprinkle clean water upon you, and ye shall be clean: from all your filthiness, and from all your idols, will I cleanse you. A new heart also will I give you, and a new spirit will I put within you: and I will take away the stony heart out of your flesh, and I will give you an heart of flesh. And I will put my spirit within you, and cause you to walk in my statutes, and ye shall keep my judgments, and do them. And ye shall dwell in the land that I gave to your fathers; and ye shall be my people, and I will be your God. I will also save you from all your uncleannesses: and I will call for the corn, and will increase it, and lay no famine upon you.*

What does water represent spiritually? It represents the word of God. Water is used for bathing, before we anoint our body with cream. This is what the Lord is referring to here. Once we are spiritually clean, the Lord's anointing will now come upon us, like the dove that came upon Jesus. So as water cleanses, so also the word of God cleanses us. Without the Lord sanctifying us the Lord's blessing cannot take effect in our lives, as we read from the above verses.

But lack of the understanding of the purpose of sanctification was the reason the Israelites where suffering. God works with symbols and words, as we can see in the Bible portion above. The water in Exodus 36:25 is the sanctification symbol, just as the Holy Communion is for consecration.

The truth Jesus referred to in John 17:17, is the fullness of the knowledge of God, which is the perfection of sanctification (Matthew 5:48). This is why we are implored to seek the knowledge of God - Hosea 4:6.

To help us out, the Lord goes symbolic sometimes. But we need the word to sustain it - Luke 10:40-42. The word is what gives us a perfect understanding of what repentance is all about. The Lord is taking a quick fix to get us up to speed, and regain all we might have lost while we were not in tune with Him. This is the number one purpose of God establishing us in His kingdom. But we need to sustain it through your dedication to His service - Isaiah 55:6: *Seek ye the Lord while he may be found, call ye upon him while he is near.*

The Lord releases oracles in due season in order to help us overcome the antics of the devil. Sanctification brings the blessings of the Lord into your spirit. As long as we are ready to develop and imbibe the character that sustains our sanctification. The purpose of the Kingdom of God on earth is to ensure God has His way in the affairs of men. A last word on the purpose of the Kingdom of God within us is seen in Zephaniah 3:15: *The Lord hath **taken away thy judgments**, he hath **cast out thine enemy**: the king of Israel, even the Lord, is in the midst of thee: **thou shalt not see evil any more***. As long as we are in the Kingdom the Lord will keep on holding back His judgement against us by forgiving us our sins, protecting us from enemies' plots so we are continually safeguarded from evil. The Kingdom of God is the *Immanuel* cloud over us.

CHAPTER SIX

BUILDING KINGDOM RELATIONSHIPS

Now that we know the purpose of the Kingdom of God on earth to be the establishment of the **Immanuel cloud** over us so that the Lord's arm will continually hold back the enemy from attacking us, we will now talk about how we can build relationship among ourselves to further enhance our stay in this kingdom. If we don't endure loving and caring relationships between us, the sanctuary of the Lord will not stay among us. In the Ten Commandments, the Lord instructed Moses that His children must love one another. Jesus reiterated this fact as the reason why heaven is at peace.

God values those who serve Him – (Exodus 12:3, Isaiah

65, Isaiah 61:6). He keeps all the goodies for those who serve Him. Hence the Lord says: *Therefore thus saith the Lord God, Behold, my servants shall eat, but ye shall be hungry: behold, my servants shall drink, but ye shall be thirsty: behold, my servants shall rejoice, but ye shall be ashamed* – Isaiah 65:13. Kingdom life is about interaction with one another as way of demonstrating the love and care from God.

I have learnt over the years that what God is really interested in is how we can build a relationship with Him. We are given a standard in the Bible for what we should do when we are trying to build a relationship – we must love God with our hearts, mind and soul, then love our neighbours as we love ourselves. This is the rule that will ensure there is no breakdown of law and order in the Kingdom.

Building a relationship with God

The Kingdom of God is set in place in the Order of Melchizedek, which makes it a priestly kingdom. Why do we build relationships? Why do we get attached to some people to the extent that we are willing to die to defend their beliefs? It is because of the attachment a relationship brings; it takes the whole of your emotions to the extent that you are willing to relinquish control to the authority you are building a relationship with. I have learnt over the last five years that what God is really interested in is how we can build a relationship with Him.

The Biblical standard is spelt out in Mark 10:29: *And Jesus answered and said, Verily I say unto you, There is no man that hath left house, or brethren, or sisters, or father, or mother, or wife, or children, or lands, for my sake, and the gospel's.* Our relationship with God is also likened to a marriage relationship – we must be committed to Him who has become the husband to the church, in an intercourse between our spirit and His Spirit, as obtainable during the marriage consummation night. This is when *deep calleth unto deep* – Psalm 42:7. We cannot build a relationship with God until we are sold out to the gospel. Jesus gives us the clue on what we should do– Luke 2:49: *And he said unto them, How is it that ye sought me? wist ye not that I must be about my Father's business.* Even when His mother came looking for Him He says –

CHAPTER SIX

Matthew 12:48-50: *But he answered and said unto him that told him, Who is my mother? and who are my brethren? And he stretched forth his hand toward his disciples, and said, behold my mother and my brethren! For whosoever shall do the will of my Father, which is in heaven, the same is my brother, and sister, and mother.* In another instance, He reiterated this fact when He said – Luke 9:62: *And Jesus said unto him, No man, having put his hand to the plough, and looking back, is fit for the Kingdom of God.* What do we use the plough for? To till the soil in wait for seed sowing, so that when the rain comes, the seed will germinate, grow to maturity and bear fruits for the vine owner's delight. Our relationship with God can be seen from this context as being labourers in His vineyard, with ploughs to work. In another context, Saint Paul added erecting building blocks on an existing foundation to our tasks –1 Corinthians 3:11-15:*For other foundation can no man lay than that is laid, which is Jesus Christ. Now if any man build upon this foundation gold, silver, precious stones, wood, hay, stubble; Every man's work shall be made manifest: for the day shall declare it, because it shall be revealed by fire; and the fire shall try every man's work of what sort it is. If any man's work abide which he hath built thereupon, he shall receive a reward. If any man's work shall be burned, he shall suffer loss: but he himself shall be saved; yet so as by fire.* To ensure that we are able to do this work in such a way that God will be pleased with us, Saint Paul gave a clue in verse 16 - *Know ye not that ye are the temple of God, and that the Spirit of God dwelleth in you.* Suffice it to say that only when God dwells in us can we be seen as having a relationship with Him. This will be confirmed with the evidence in Galatians 4:6-7: *And because ye are sons, God hath sent forth the Spirit of his Son into your hearts, crying, Abba, Father. Wherefore thou art no more a servant, but a son; and if a son, then an heir of God through Christ.* So, in simple terms, we can relate the facts that explain our duties –

■ Jesus acquires a vineyard (Matthew 13:14),

■ He looks around for anyone idle and He employs them (Matthew 20:1-16),

■ He makes then to Plough (Luke 9:62), Plant and Water the vineyard (1 Corinthians 3:6),

■ He comes to give the increase (1 Corinthians 3:6).

CHAPTER SIX

This explains the fact that working in His vineyard is the only way we grow in this relationship with God, and when we do this, the more we inherit sonship trust from God, and He will reveal secrets to us –Matthew 13:35: *… I will utter things which have been kept secret from the foundation of the world.* It is these secrets that establish and distinguish anyone in the Kingdom because the path to life is made up of secret revelations, and only few find it – Matthew 7:14. The secrets are revealed to enable us to endure our work in the vineyard – such as in agricultural terms, knowing when to plough, what seeds to sow, what fertilizers to apply, when to harvest, pest treatment, storage methods, etc, then our fruits will abide. John 15:5 says - *…He that abideth in me, and I in him, the same bringeth forth much fruit…*

We are told in the Bible what we should do when we are trying to build a relationship with God – we must love Him with our heart, mind and soul.

Our growth and maturity in the Christian faith is hinged on how well we build this heavenly kingdom relationship – nurturing our feelings for the things of God, seeking to mature the anointing we bear of Him, dedicating time for

Him and being secluded from the world in order to appreciate Him. How can these things happen? It all boils down to the basic facts of receiving instructions, working them out and abiding within the tenets of the Kingdom.

Our focus here would be on knowing God. If we know Him, we will know how to build a relationship of trust, mutual dependence, sincerity, respect, and acknowledgement with Him.

- **To Know God:** My spiritual eyes and understanding opened the day I came across Daniel 11:32: *And such as do wickedly against the covenant shall he corrupt by flatteries: but the people that do know their God shall be strong, and do exploits* **for the Kingdom of God** *(emphasis mine)*. We would break this verse into two parts; the first part explains the fact that building a relationship with God have to do with entering into a covenant with Him, and failure to fulfil this on our part will lead to eternal destruction as Satan would seduce us with *flattery* – whereby they will begin to praise self and give glory to other gods outside God. The second part says that apart from entering into a covenant with God, we must endeavour to know Him; only then will we receive strength to work with Him. When people read the part b of this verse, they often explain it to mean wealth – especially for prosperity preachers. The verse talks about defending our faith, by not falling into the devil's tricks of deceit and helping other to stand firm in the Lord – Daniel 12:3: *...and they that turn many to righteousness.* We must turn many to righteousness – this is the Exploits we would do in the name of the Lord.

- **To build trust in God:** Knowing God is about building trust in the Lord – without doubting the working power of the received word. The Bible says in Proverbs 3:5-6: *Trust in the Lord with all thine heart; and lean not unto thine own understanding. In all thy ways acknowledge him, and he shall direct thy paths.* What will breach this trust is when we begin to lean on our own understanding – when we begin to apply human wisdom to lead us into taking decisions to live daily. We are admonished to recognise His importance and seek His guidance before we do anything on earth. Failure to do this is a breach of the covenant we entered with the Lord the day we gave our life to Christ. The more we grow in this trust, the more our relationship with God grows warm. And as a display of His trust, He will apportion unto us His estates for us to manage on His behalf – Matthew 24:45: *Who then is a faithful and wise servant, whom his Lord hath made ruler over his household, to give them meat in due season.* When we trust in the Lord, we shall wait for Him to come and attend to our needs and wants – Isaiah 40:31: *But they that wait upon the Lord shall renew their strength; they shall mount up with wings as eagles; they shall run, and not be weary; and they shall walk, and not faint.* Today we see many hoping for scientific developments to solve their problems of childlessness and barrenness. Many even buy children because they have exhausted their patience. Jeremiah 17:7 say also: *Blessed is the man that trusteth in the Lord, and whose hope the Lord is.* Impatience is the result of our inability to build an enduring relationship with God.

- **To create spiritual warmth:** We are informed of this fact in the book of Revelation 3:20: *Behold, I stand at the door, and knock: if any man hear my voice, and open the door, I will come in to him, and will sup with him, and he with me.* Warmth is created when we live in the Lord and He in us. Jesus says to the Father in John 17:1 – ...*the hour is come; glorify thy Son, that thy Son also may glorify thee.*

- **Help to discipline us:** Because we have Him guiding us, He will also chastise us when we go wrong, as a way of making us perfect as He is.

- **So that the Lord is present in your Situation:** we have read the popular story of how Shadrach, Meshach, and Abednego were delivered by the Lord.

- **To merit eternity:** So that Jesus can welcome us into His glory in heaven on the day our souls shall depart this earth.

Many are called, few are chosen. The few are those who build relationships. Saint Paul said, 'Follow me even as I follow Christ'. How will you know a man is following Christ when you don't know Him? If you read the Bible, can you know who Christ is?

Dos of the relationship

- Sincerity, honesty and integrity
- Dedication and time consciousness

- Financial commitment and prudence
- Humility and long suffering for the work of God
- Presence management: We must contribute our own quota to ensure the relationship works in line with the agreed covenant through our presence whenever the Lord calls. For He said - John 10:27: My sheep hear my voice, and I know them, and they follow me.
- Studying the word to grow in His wisdom
- Evangelism and Soul winning
- Prayer and Holy Communion
- Receiving and exercising the Holy Spirit
- Sanctification, consecration and righteousness unto Holiness
- Building faith through spiritual consciousness

Don'ts of the relationship

- We cannot have two masters - Mark 10:29.
- The Lord should come first in all we do
- We must kill pride by imitating Jesus, who went about doing good

- Avoiding bad association, even if the person is a blood relation

- We should not demand too much from tomorrow.

If God is thinking about we, why not we think about Him? This is how a relationship starts.

Building a relationship with the servant of God

Why build a relationship with the servant of God in our midst? Jesus handed over the disciples to Peter (John 20:17), when He told him to feed His sheep. The servant of God is holding a secret, that you need to walk down the strait and narrow path that leads to life (Jeremiah 3:15, Matthew 7:14). Your relationship with the servant of God will help you find the secret to life on time rather than meeting those who will take you through the path of deceit through human wisdom and philosophies, as Jesus went further to explain in Matthew 7:15. Many who disregard the servant of God in their midst are those who misunderstand the spiritual relevance of the veil which tore into two when Jesus gave up the ghost. They have explained that because the veil tore into two, they can as well offer their prayers to God without the need of the servant. While we can offer individual prayers unto God, such prayers often have limitations. To conclude the prayer cycle, God would usually lead us to His servants – Paul was led to Ananias, Cornelius was led to Peter, and severally, the disciples would call on Peter to minister the Holy Spirit to new converts. God values His servants, especially when they do His will -... *for the Lord God shall ... call his servants by another name* – Isaiah 65:15. This is exactly what God did to Abram – when He changed his name from Abram to Abraham. Jesus asked a very relevant question about what building a relationship with your pastor is all about – it is about leading. He asked: *can the blind lead the blind?* Why this question, one might ask – the Israelites were being led by those who were spiritually blind, and as such, they were being engulfed in the nest of the devil. But even when light came, what did they do? They simply ignored it and continued in their 'used to' life – the life in darkness because their ways were evil (John 3:17). As I pondered over this session, of why a believer need to also build a relationship with his/her pastor, I received this illumination; the Pastor has publicly declared for Christ, which made him one on the battlefield against the works of darkness – and he would be taking guidance from God, to survive in the battle field. His experiences are needed by his congregation to remain in the faith. No wonder St. Paul admonished them to follow him even as he follows Christ. The fact remains, that many haven't know Christ hence they would follow anybody they see, as their Pastor, who may be blind. If you know Christ, you will hear His voice, and then follow Him. If this is done, it will be easy for you to know those whom He has raised to be in charge over you to give account of their stewardship in the vineyard.

We have discussed how we can build a relationship with God, so that we would know the things to do and not to do. When we do the right things as commanded by God, we become in good standing with Him, and we are covered with a garment of righteousness by the hosts of heaven. This garment will eventually announce us and give us favour in the sight of God, and men. This was what established Jesus (Luke 2:40,52). We will learn how to build a relationship with the arm of the Lord on Earth, those He has called to carry on His work of restoration,

CHAPTER SIX

so that all men shall be drawn unto Him. In simple terms, the servant of God in your midst is one who is the physical mouthpiece of God, who has been appointed to oversee a portion of the Lord's estate here on earth. We will learn today that knowing the servant of God can help many out of their predicaments. The servant of God is already at the war front, and as long as he is surviving, you too will survive – it all depends on how you relate with the instructions the Lord is giving to you through His servant. Often times people tend to compare pastors – this is not possible. The disciples of Jesus were people with varied characters. Peter was harsh, so was James and John. Matthew was in their midst, but calm (he wrote the Gospel of Matthew). Philip was there, deeply spiritual. Thomas was there, with a doubting character. Luke was one of His disciples too, though not among the twelve, a successful medical doctor, and a writer (wrote the Gospel of Luke and Acts). We are all different but needed by the same God. The Lord leads you to a pastor that understands you, and has what it takes to help you to know Him more. People often want to know who is a genuine servant of God. There is no fake servant of God; one is either a servant of God, or a servant of the Devil. If you listen well to the voice of God, you will know where He needs you to serve Him.

CHAPTER SIX

Some examples of how some persons built relationship:

- Samuel and Saul: Until Saul disobeyed God, He was always meeting Samuel to know the way forward
- Moses and Joshua: Joshua ministered unto Moses
- Elijah and Elisha: Elisha observed Elijah using the mantle on the river Jordan, and when it was his turn to cross, he did likewise. When we observe the servant of God, we also learn to overcome situations.
- Jesus and Nicodemus: Admired Jesus' wisdom and came seeking Him in the night.

We can build this relationship through:

- Supporting him in the call of God upon him – as he administers the Kingdom daily. Everyone must know the task before the servant of God, and the vision he is driving. After understanding the vision, it is also necessary to understand the mission statement, and then what is required to ensure the mission statement is fulfilled to the letter. This is the burden the servant of God bears for the Lord. We can also support every request he makes from the altar, as it relates to the vision of winning souls into the Kingdom.

CHAPTER SIX

- Providing for his needs as Marta did in providing for Jesus. Severally in the Bible we read of how Jesus ate meals in the houses of others. He even advised the disciples to stay only in the houses of those who were worthy – and to explain this, we would see that He advised them not to take along with them what they will wear, meaning that it is the responsibility of those they minister to clothe them.

- Praying for him.

- Going out to give testimonies of what the Lord is doing through him to others so that they too can be saved.

❖

Building a relationship with other believers

❖

The citizens of the Kingdom are called believers. Wherever you belong, to put your hand on the plough to till for the Lord, be it choir, usher, etc, you must understand why you are in that function. For instance, if you are in the choir your relationship will only bear fruit when you grow your praise and worship gifts. As an usher, you must have the character of the Kingdom – well

CHAPTER SIX

dressed at all times in service for the wedding union between you and Jesus. Any time there is service, it is time for union with Him, a fresh consummation takes place as He forgives your sins again and takes you back home, as typified in the case of Gomer and Hosea.

Jesus said in Mark 10:29 that we should leave all to follow His leading. What He meant here is that we should work on our emotions, because for us to confront evil, we have to undermine whatever emotional ties with have with people.

The gathering of God's children cannot be complete until they join together in one accord, lifting up Holy hands unto the King of Kings. The Bible says that believers are like a crown unto to Lord – they are Royal Diadems (Isaiah 62:3). We are a holy people, and the redeemed of the Lord (Isaiah 62:12). Most times, believers just gather together without being aware that their gathering is primarily to host the Lord Jesus in their midst. And because of this ignorance on their own path, many join in fellowship with fellow brethren with divided attention, making the entire fellowship effort fruitless. In the book of Acts 2:1, we were informed that while they were there, in the upper room, in fellowship together, they received the guest of honour from heaven, the Holy Ghost, and their entire lives transformed into a supernatural form.

Why were they there in one accord? It is because they had built a relationship with one and another. This is the subject of this discussion. It is my prayer that at the end of this, you will find the reason to be among the gathering of God's children in the vineyard, where your works will be accounted for. One obvious reason why people don't build relationships with fellow believers is because they haven't understood the purpose of the Kingdom of God on earth yet, and as such, many compare the gatherings of God's children and would want to attend a gathering where their immediate physical needs are met, in neglect of their spiritual growth. And over time, many have become spiritual prostitutes, moving from one gathering to the other without a pastor over them – no one takes responsibility for their spiritual wellbeing. These sets of believers will eventually die, and may still not find their way to heaven.

CHAPTER SIX

The role of children in the Kingdom

❖

We come across several portions of the Bible as we study the book, on the importance of children in the Kingdom of God. A very striking one is found in Mark 10:14-15 - *Suffer the little children to come unto me, and forbid them not: for of such is the Kingdom of God. Verily I say unto you, whosoever shall not receive the Kingdom of God as a little child, he shall not enter therein.* In another portion of the Bible, Matthew 18:10, He says that children have angels who are always with God, interceding on their behalf. The role of children in building a virile kingdom for God here on earth cannot be overemphasised. We would also see this importance attached to children in Genesis 18:19 - *For I know him, that he will command his children and his household after him, and they shall keep the way of the Lord, to do justice and judgment; that the Lord may bring upon Abraham that which he hath spoken of him.* This is where we get the responsibilities of parents before God, and God expects that every child should obey his/her parents as these parents help them

CHAPTER SIX

to know Him (Exodus 20:12). When a child is brought up in the fear of the Lord, then the child will bring glory unto the name of the Lord – Matthew 5:16. And the evidence will show for all to see – the child will begin to grow into both spiritual and physical maturity, and find favour with God and everyone (Luke 2:40,52). In Titus 2:3, the older women were told to train the younger ones. This is our duty before God as elders – teaching children the truth about God, and making them to know Him, and having a personal relationship with God early in life. As this is done, the church and society will reap a multiplying effect of godly qualities – humility, sanctity, respect, integrity, forthrightness - and all we are complaining about now; corruption, armed robbery, nonchalant attitudes among youths, etc., will become a thing of the past (Psalms 37:2).

In all we must learn to interact positively among ourselves, live a life that will bless others and us and maintain peace and tranquillity before the Lord, who has called us to serve Him in sanctity.

CHAPTER SEVEN

OPERATIONS OF THE KINGDOM

We would start this important chapter and discussion of the manner of operations that is permitted in the Kingdom from the book of Romans 14:17: *For the Kingdom of God is not meat and drink; but righteousness, and peace, and joy in the Holy Ghost.* We have seen all over the world how many believers desire food and drink more than what the Kingdom of God stands for – **Righteousness**, **Peace** and **Joy in the Holy Ghost**. And this has driven many into untold hardship, as they are unable to stand firm in the faith while looking for food and drink to keep them living. Even as we have come to appreciate the message of great wealth as a panacea for our spiritual emptiness, it is still not certain that when Christ returns, he will find many of us occupying the estates He left for us to manage. It is certain that He would have to drive out money changers, those selling holy water and mantles, and many who have turned His kingdom into wealth-making seminars and workshop arenas. Our focus here is how can we administer the activities of the Kingdom in such a way that God becomes our focus, and we would store our treasures in heaven.

One great enemy of the Kingdom of God is impatience. Many of us have become what and who we are today as a result of impatience – we married out of impatience, we had children out of impatience, we are in the job we do today out of impatience, many have become pastors out of impatience, etc, and with time we would begin to complain and become a distraction to the operations of the Kingdom. Set your heart on the things above and your reward will be from above. The greater love attracts, which means we are drawn towards the direction where our love and affection is greater. Love is a force of attraction, which is more in the direction of our desire. Many women are unable to ascend to heaven, not because of sins, but because their affection is on earthly things. When a country or a university wants to honour an individual, you usually go there to receive the honour. So it is with God; if God found favour in you here on earth, you will ascend unto heaven to receive the reward, hence we are admonished to be quiet in the spirit – Isaiah 30:15.

Blessings are dispatched from the King of kings to each of His kingdoms; it is left for the king in that kingdom to bless his kingdom. And this he does during service, when he prays for his congregation. Angels are dispatched to protect each of these kings in the spiritual. And in the physical, the king raises men to protect the Kingdom from infiltration of other cultures that will affect the stability of the Kingdom. As the people makes their prayers daily, the onus is upon the king to attend to them, as his delay will also cause the delay of answered prayers. He may wake up in the morning and make proclamations and then connect to his citizens, in his prayers and beg the King of kings to look upon their afflictions. David prayed that the Lord should withhold his anger against the people but, rather take his own life – 2 Samuel 24:17:*And David spake unto the Lord when he saw the angel that smote the people, and said, Lo, I have sinned, and I have done wickedly: but these sheep, what have they done? let thine hand, I pray thee, be against me, and against my father's house.* He finally raised an altar unto the Lord as he was commanded, and the Lord withhold His anger.

Again, we would see how Moses interceded too –Exodus 32:9-12: *And the Lord said unto Moses, I have seen this people, and, behold, it is a stiffnecked people: Now therefore let me alone, that my wrath may wax hot against them, and that I may consume them: and I will make of thee a great nation. And Moses besought the Lord his God, and said, Lord, why doth thy wrath wax hot against thy people, which thou hast brought forth out of the land of Egypt with great power, and with a mighty hand? Wherefore should the Egyptians speak, and say, for mischief did he bring them out, to slay them in the mountains, and to consume them from the face of the earth? Turn from thy fierce wrath, and repent of this evil against thy people.* If it were some of our pastors today, they would have rejoiced that God was going to establish only them and their families, out of lack of understanding.

From this premise, we would now discuss how the Kingdom of God is operated here on earth. The kingdom is operated on a theocratic pattern. The problem we have in most churches of God today is the infiltration of a worldly governance system into the church. The kingdom is not to be operated with the opinion of the people, but of God. Severally in the Bible, and from the verses we read earlier in this chapter, we would see that the calamities that befell or were to come upon the people were a result of them accepting the opinion of the people. The Israelites had compared their lives in the wilderness with what they had in Egypt – Numbers 11:5: *We remember the fish, which we did eat in Egypt freely; the cucumbers, and the melons, and the leeks, and the onions, and the garlick.*

The servant of God must have a leadership character that puts God first in all that he does – 2 Samuel 23:3: *…He that ruleth over men must be just, ruling in the fear of God.*

We have heard of acclaimed servants of God worldwide preaching a prosperity message that has made many put their lives at risk to make money for the use of these churches. Is that how a kingdom should be operated? There is a lesson to learn from King David – 2 Samuel 23:15-17: *And David longed, and said, Oh that one would give me drink of the water of the well of Bethlehem, which is by the gate! And the three mighty men brake through the host of the Philistines, and drew water out of the well of Bethlehem, that was by the gate, and took it, and brought it to David: nevertheless he would not drink thereof, but poured it out unto the Lord. And he said, Be it far from me, O Lord, that I should do this: is not this the blood of the men that went in jeopardy of their lives? Therefore he would not drink it.* To operate a kingdom of God, we must ensure that the lives of the citizens are not endangered. This is the number one duty of the king as he reports daily to the King of kings. Before we go further, we would take learning from Jesus –John 18:8: *Jesus answered, I have told you that I am he: if therefore ye seek me, let these go their way.* And, again we would see the operations in the Kingdom becoming clearer. It is mainly for the propagation of the culture of heaven on earth, and since humans are needed to establish the Kingdom, and to propagate the culture of heaven, it would be to the interest of God and of the servant of God, the king in the Kingdom, reporting to the King of kings, to put in place, activities and processes that would preserve people unto God. The Lord said in Exodus 22:31

CHAPTER SEVEN

- *And ye shall be holy men unto me.* We now proceed to define within the context we have explained above, the operations of the Kingdom of God on earth.

In every kingdom, the king raises subjects to work with him. The absence of this made Moses cry unto God, until his father-in-law advised him– Exodus 18:20-21: *And thou shalt teach them ordinances and laws, and shalt shew them the way wherein they must walk, and the work that they must do. Moreover thou shalt provide out of all the people able men, such as fear God, men of truth, hating covetousness...* Though the father-in-law was talking from experience, it shows how a kingdom is run, and there was nowhere in the Bible where we were told that God was angry at the idea posited by his in-law. As Moses obeyed the in-law and raised men he had trained, and appointed them to work with him there, had time to commune more with God, and later in Exodus 19:6 God showed His approval - *And ye shall be unto me a kingdom of priests, and an holy nation.* There were more priests now, and that would establish the Kingdom as a holy nation. After this God anointed seventy elders through him. For the first time, Moses knew that what the people needed to work with him was the anointing he was bearing, which would make the others his clone. This finally set the order for him to find and institute a successor who became Joshua, whom he transferred his anointing upon by laying his hands upon him – Deuteronomy 34:9: *And Joshua the son of Nun was full of the spirit of wisdom; for Moses had laid his hands upon him: and the children of Israel hearkened unto him, and did as the Lord commanded Moses.* Elisha served Elijah and would later desire the anointing to the extent of risking his life, and this made him a prophet after the stead of Elijah. Jesus breathed the Holy Spirit upon His disciples before His crucifixion.

❖

The office of the Queen in the Kingdom

❖

Two areas spell her duty out clearly. One is of intercession on behalf of the citizens – John 2:3-5: *And when they wanted wine, the mother of Jesus saith unto him, They have no wine. Jesus saith unto her, Woman, what have I to do with thee? mine hour is not yet come. His mother saith unto the servants, Whatsoever he saith unto you, do it.* Here we would borrow a duty for the queen – despite Jesus' unwillingness she still went ahead to command the servants to be expectant. The reason is because she knows and understands the anointing and the working power behind the king. She knows what the king can do and what he cannot do. The second one is that of care – John 19:26: *… he (Jesus) saith unto his mother, Woman, behold thy son.* She is a mother to the Kingdom, supporting the call of God upon the servant through the provision of food, and often guiding the young ones – children and youths. Many of those who end up benefiting from the anointing upon the servant of God come through the wife. We would see how Jesus even took the trouble to heal Peter's mother in-law – Matthew 8:13: *And when Jesus was come into Peter's house, he saw his wife's mother laid, and sick of a fever.* A key verse of the Bible that would mean that her role in maintaining stability in the Kingdom cannot be overemphasised is Proverbs 14:1: *Every wise woman buildeth her house: but the foolish plucketh it down with her hands.* When we search through the Bible, we would see various righteous roles that women played throughout history to uphold sanctity, and these roles are much needed in the Kingdom.

CHAPTER SEVEN

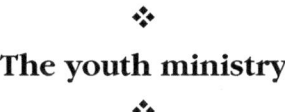

The youth ministry

I decided to talk about youth after the queen, because of what Jesus did at the cross – handing over John to His mother, and vice versa. What makes the youth ministry very important is simply that they are the lifeblood of every growing society. They are strong and fearless. They are often those who enrol in the army in every growing society, and this applies to the Kingdom. The importance of the youth age is why the angels are immortal – a never-grow-old life. The posterity of the Kingdom lies in the zeal the youth puts into the activities of the Kingdom – Psalms 127:4: *As arrows are in the hand of a mighty man; so are children of the youth. Happy is the man that hath his quiver full of them: they shall not be ashamed, but they shall speak with the enemies in the gate.* They defend the doctrines they hear and learn from the servant of God, as many haven't been corrupted yet by the quest for material wealth, and haven't made irreparable mistakes which is associated with many of old age, as Nicodemus complained to Jesus – John 3:4. *How can a man be born when he is old*, so it is easy to teach them how to store their treasure in heaven. They are still within the age of correction, and because they are younger than the servant of God, they would treat Him with respect, and obey his instructions. They would also do it to the elders. They are still fresh wine bottles that can be filled with fresh wine. They are mostly those who will occupy the singing ministry, and the pastors in training. Their lifestyles possess an issue to holiness, as many do swim inside lust and carnal sins. In the midst of this, though, there are still possibilities of raising a God fearing Kingdom from, and through them. However, young people are vulnerable and delicate, because what they learn at this age is what will either establish or destroy them. This is all the more reason why even the devil is so much interested in youths. And sometimes, the church has erred here because they haven't gotten the wisdom to retain them.

Marriage committee

I have decided to treat the marriage committee next, because this is another part of the lifeblood of every successful kingdom. The importance of marriage to the success of the Kingdom is the reason God warned the children of Israel not to marry people from certain nations. Marriage gives birth to sustainability. It is the foundation of the next generation of believers, who would continue from where this generation will stop. It is true that there is little people can do in the choice of the wives and husbands that the young people of nowadays eventually choose to live with, but good doctrinal teaching on time would set things right. The Bible says – Proverbs 22:6: *Train up a child in the way he should go: and when he is old, he will not depart from it.* Training has to do with attestable evidence that would stand the test of time. And for us in the Kingdom, the evidence of the training would be when there is widespread fear of God. Those who would become members of this committee must be proven without reasonable doubt to be people who are faithful to the vision of the Kingdom. They must also have enjoyed considerable peace in their marriages, with long-standing evidence of the rule of God in their homes. Their children must not dress like harlots; the women in the committee must have a sense of moral decorum, without obscene appearance. The men must rule their houses well enough to command the respect of all and sundry. Anyone who would function in this committee must have the heart of posterity. The rules that must be applied would be as agreed to be scripturally and morally sound. Any brother proposing to marry a sister, for instance, must have to seek permission from the pastor first, who is the custodian on behalf of Christ, before approaching the sister; anything outside this is a misrepresentation of the order. It is after the pastor has given his approval that he can talk with the sister, and then see the parents. In all these both will have to be faithful in prayers, and abstain from premarital sexual sin. I have started a Singles Seeking Marriage Fellowship (SSMF), in the church for the purpose of enlightening young people on the importance of marriage and the rules that set it in place. The fellowship meets every Monday at 5:30 pm.

Kingdom women's ministry

The next important ministry in the order of vulnerability is the women's fellowship. I have seen within these years of my service in the vineyard that women are one set of people that are easily deceived as a result of their low emotional tolerance level. Many also are not willing to make a deep study of the scriptures and revelation from God. Many of them are under the influence of familiar spirits which manipulate them, and as a result of this, many have gifts of visions and revelations from the devil, and they would use this ill-gotten gift to derail the church. They visit all manner of prophets, as experience has shown, all in a bid to secure their marriages with the fear that another woman would soon chase them out of their marriage. So, while the servant of God is busy teaching the secrets of the Kingdom, they are busy thinking about how to secure their marriages. When the servant of God is not their favourite, they would cook up stories and lead their husband and children to another church. Some are even afraid to allow their husband to serve God in a church with beautiful sisters. Their meetings are often visited with rancour, backbiting, murmuring and heightened rebellion, which tends in most cases to destabilise the church. And at the centre of this is the hatred they have for the wife of the servant of God in their midst. Factions often brew up, and their meeting days would end with frowning faces. Often, their meeting and prayers are geared towards the vision they have for their homes – securing the homes from intruding ladies, and not for the cause of evangelism. Then they would meet to buy special wrappers during church anniversary celebration, but you won't see many on evangelism days. In the midst of these, the women ministry have a power to propagate the Kingdom, if their weaknesses are harnessed and turned into roles that would make them useful. For, instance, the women can be used to function in ministering to first timers – and they would set the values of the Kingdom right before the new initiate. Their jealous acts would put the young sisters in check, and make them dress responsibly. Their monitoring eyes would be the first to sight a sister and a brother engaged in immoral acts, and that would bring sanity to the Kingdom. In the event of celebrating a feast in the Kingdom, their ministering gift will ensure that every visitor is well taken care of. Their smiles can be yet another soul-winning bait. Who should be in this ministry? It is certainly not for all women, but those who have the fear of God, and willing to follow Jesus all the days of their lives. My preferred women's mentor is Anna – Luke 2:36-37, the prophetess who was dedicated to the service of God in the temple, despite being a widow, and would not depart from the presence of the Lord. The Bible says of her - *which departed not from the temple, but served God with fastings and prayers night and day.* This is the woman who should teach the younger ones – Titus 2:3-5: *The aged women likewise, that they be in behaviour as becometh holiness, not false accusers, not given to much wine, teachers of good things; That they may teach the young women to be sober, to love their husbands, to love their children, To be discreet, chaste, keepers at home, good, obedient to their own husbands, that the word of God be not blasphemed.* I encourage the women to be steadfast in the Lord, and earn a successful life in their chosen career, as agreed by their husbands. They should avoid murmuring and gossip, and learn to seek the face of the Lord, concerning their family, putting them into the hands of God, sustaining the fear of the Lord in their homes. That they should not dress as whores, with the excuse of trying to seduce their husbands in public, but be modest, as representing the mother of Jesus here on earth, and as examples of purity unto all generations.

CHAPTER SEVEN

Kingdom men's ministry

If there has been any group that have proven to be difficult for me to work with, it has been the men's fellowship. Why? Many have made several mistakes, which has led to their inability to manage their families financially and morally. In some cases, many have married stubborn women who have turned their homes into the abode of the devil. Some also have bad companies of friends who are drunkards and womanizers, and as such it has been difficult for them to adapt to the teachings the Lord is giving to me. They are aware the Lord is working in my life, but they just feel that the process of indoctrination set in place by the Lord is not meant for them because they are older believers. This hasn't set the right example for the young people I am trying to bring up. Some have been accused of having extra marital affairs with the ladies in the church. Yet in the midst of these, there are still men who prefer to live their lives to please the Lord. They are faithful to their commitments of tithe paying and serving as advisers of repute to the young ones. The main function of the men in the Kingdom is seen from the fact that they run the homes, and would put to play the values of the Kingdom, if they understand it well. Naturally, what we learn is what we live. What qualities are expected of the men? – Titus 2:2: *That the aged men be sober, grave, temperate, sound in faith, in charity, in patience.* And as time goes on, they would take up roles of trust in the Kingdom, when proven to have satisfied Christ and the Spirit of the Lord now certifies them, as bearers of salvation.

Kingdom Children ministry

❖

These sets of Kingdom adherents are too delicate to handle because of the value the Lord placed on them. He once said – Matthew 19:14-15: *But Jesus said, Suffer little children, and forbid them not, to come unto me: for of such is the Kingdom of heaven. And he laid his hands on them, and departed thence.* It is a well understood fact that laying of hands means to commission the works of the Lord. In this portion we just read, it could be adjudged that Jesus had commissioned these children for

His works. Another verse of the Bible that would come to bear is – Matthew 18:3,10: *I say unto you, Except ye be converted, and become as little children ... Take heed that ye despise not one of these little ones; for I say unto you, That in heaven their angels do always behold the face of my Father which is in heaven.* This last portion is the reason why I always pray with little children, because I know that the Lord loves them and hears them when they pray. If the children's ministry is adequately taken care of, and they are taught the principles of Christ on time, then no sooner than we expect, the Spirit of Christ will start leading them as live conscience – Galatians 4:6, and they will abhor evil, leading to the building of a society that fears the Lord.

Outreach Ministry

Reaching out to the world with our testimonies helps to enlarge the Kingdom and brings the altar close to the people. This principle is derived from the story of how Obededom opened his house for the Ark of God. The Gospel is the Ark of God in our midst. This was what

Christ referred to when He said that the Kingdom of God is within us. A crusade is just the right opportunity to announce the faith we believe to the world. I encourage every Kingdom adherent to be part of a crusade. I don't believe that crusades have to be expensive to be successful. This well said, venues have to be rented – the place would be adequately lighted, involves mass publicity, journals and books have to be shared, musical equipment will be rented, and in some cases commuting means have to be employed, and all these require funds. In all the Lord is capable of providing for His work because the earth and the fullness belongs to Him. Our outreach ministry is Giant Strides World Outreach Crusades (GSWOC).

Finance management

Many kingdoms have been torn apart because of money. The recent level of fraudulent practices in churches worldwide calls for concern. There have been high levels of embezzlement, while most of the citizens whom the Lord have brought into the Kingdom are living in abject poverty. Kingdom adherents are taught how to manage waste and convert it to profit. How is fund generated in the Kingdom? The servant of God, through the doctrine he received from the Lord, teaches prudence, and encourages the Kingdom adherents to take their works of life seriously, but should avoid whatever works are suspected of being the devil's apple of deceit, which would lure them out of the truth they received of the Lord, which they also minister.

❖

Purpose of the Welfare Ministry

❖

Severally we have read how God wants the poor to be cared for. A key verse in the Bible that will set us starting is Exodus 22:25: *If thou lend money to any of my people that is poor by thee, thou shalt not be to him as an usurer, neither shalt thou lay upon him usury.* The category of people that merit this welfare care are clearly stated here - *any of my people.* They are not just everybody, but those in the Kingdom. Welfare is linked to the show of Love. Welfare is also linked to hospitality, especially in the care for well-meaning strangers – Hebrews 13:2: *Do not neglect to show hospitality to strangers, for thereby some have entertained angels unawares* (ESV). Many have argued that Christ commanded that charity be provided to people who are hungry and in the prison, quoting Matthew 25:34: *For I was an hungred, and ye gave me meat: I was thirsty, and ye gave me drink: I was a stranger, and ye took me in: Naked, and ye clothed me: I was sick, and ye visited me: I was in prison, and ye came unto me*. A careful reading through this chapter of the Bible clearly explains that Jesus was referring to those suffering for the sake of the gospel. A confirmation of this would be seen in John 17:9,20: *I pray for them: I pray not for the world, but for them which thou hast given me; for they are thine. Neither pray I for these alone, but for them also which shall believe on me through their word.* I have seen some servants of God taking food and clothing out to people in the streets, who have not yet received Christ while under the full coverage of television, as a show of charity, and when these people come into the church, all they would be expecting is provision. In these churches too one would see real poverty in their midst, but the servant of God is out there receiving fame for the works of charity, and often times the government would confer on them national honours. A good working welfare ministry should be administered by deacons and deaconesses, with outstanding qualities that sets them apart from mere carnal men and women – Acts 6:3: *...of good repute, full of the Spirit and of wisdom* (ESV).

❖

Educating the minds of the citizens

❖

The book of 2 Timothy 2:15 says - *Study to shew thyself approved unto God, a workman that needeth not to be ashamed, rightly dividing the word of truth.* The purpose is to save us from ungodliness. The more we learn of Christ, the more we yield to His bidding. There is so much wisdom in circulation all over the world. This is why we are admonished – Romans 12:2: *... be not conformed to this world: but be ye transformed by the renewing of your mind, that ye may prove what is that good, and acceptable, and perfect, will of God.* Severally many Kingdoms have lost their adherents to the world because the world seems to be faster in disseminating information that would eventually corrupt their minds in various social network platforms – Facebook, twitter, 2go,

CHAPTER SEVEN

YouTube, BBM etc. Various singles dating sites have made matters worse, as many unsuspecting young ladies have lost their lives. Cohabiting couples are on the increase also as a result of these, leading to more single parents and abandoned children in orphanages. We would see that people called by God to serve Him in His Kingdom wrote the Bible. The more they wrote the more the people would have materials to relate to, and this information ended up making them understand the ways of the Lord better, though many didn't still adhere to His ways. I support believers attaining a high academic standard, with the intention of using what they learn to beautify the Kingdom of God, and to become a voice in the committee of nations, where they would advocate good moral upbringing as a panacea for national growth and stability.

In our kingdom, we have the School of Ministry courses developed into three stages – Certificate, Advanced and Diploma, with the aim of developing believers to become steadfast in the Lord, sets of beliefs and codes of conduct, which are put in place to fulfil the three cardinal responsibilities of Recruit, Train and Spiritually empowerment (RTS). These responsibilities will be achieved through the following three ministerial commitments: The Word, Raising Leaders and Building a Kingdom of saints. It is our belief that 'The Word' yields 'Leaders,' and 'Leaders' yields 'Saints.' These trainings answers the demand placed on the ministry by God in Isaiah 42:6,9,16 and 22.

❖

Dedication of Children and properties to God

❖

To dedicate something simply means to hand over ownership to the beneficiary. What we dedicate to God becomes His own and hence we have lost the right of ownership to whatsoever is dedicated to God. The most we can do is act as custodians on behalf of God. When we dedicate children, we should take learning from the story of Samuel, whom the mother handed over to God. Jesus was dedicated at the temple, and later in His years he was all about doing the work of God. I met a young lady one morning and I was led to pray with her. When I demanded what her request was, to my amazement, she said – 'I want my children to serve the Lord.' And I was so glad to pray with her, unlike many that would say they need money to train the children. If we give children to God, he is faithful to take care of His own – the children can even gain scholarships. Honestly speaking, whatsoever is dedicated to God can be given to someone else to oversee, on behalf of God, except the person wants to redeem it from the Lord; for instance Numbers 18:16 says … *shalt thou redeem, according to thine estimation.* Exodus 13:13 also says … *And every firstling of an ass thou shalt redeem with a lamb.* Right from the moment of dedication, we only become custodians. It is somewhat more stringent with the dedication and sanctifying a house unto the Lord – Leviticus 27:14: *And when a man shall sanctify his house to be holy unto the Lord, then the priest shall estimate it, whether it be good or bad: as the priest shall estimate it, so shall it stand. And if he that sanctified it will redeem his house, then he shall add the fifth part of the money of thy estimation unto it, and it shall be his.* For houses, those who have this understanding have volunteered and supported the works of evangelism to the tune of the cost of the house plus 1/5th of the estimated amount. This same practice is inclusive of any material possession dedicated and sanctified unto God – cars, machinery etc., but not loans. There are some believers who have this understanding

CHAPTER SEVEN

and would never dedicate whatever God blessed them with. Dedication is vow taking before the Lord – Deuteronomy 23:21: *When thou shalt vow a vow unto the Lord thy God, thou shalt not slack to pay it: for the Lord thy God will surely require it of thee; and it would be sin in thee.* It is not a sin to dedicate your possessions unto the Lord for sanctification; one can just give the testimony and that suffices. But dedication ensures additional protection and multiplication from God. If you dedicate any possession and sanctify it unto God, and not fail to redeem it in accordance to what is explained above, then God will grant you the grace to acquire more material possessions, and His hand will continually be upon you. Jesus even added a more stringent rule, when He told the rich man to sell all he had and give to the poor – Matthew 19:21, as an act of perfection. So, which one is easier, dedicating and redeeming it, or forfeiting it to the poor? In Luke 9:23, He says - *If any man will come after me, let him deny himself, and take up his cross daily, and follow me.* The standard of this followership would be understood by what happened in Acts 4:34-35: *Neither was there any among them that lacked: for as many as were possessors of lands or houses sold them, and brought the prices of the things that were sold, And laid them down at the apostles' feet: and distribution was made unto every man according as he had need.* The more we dedicate our possessions to God, the more we gain. This is the principle that is blessing my family and me; giving it brings me my pleasure for the work of the gospel. The understanding of this is the essence of the money believers usually put in an envelope, though many do not understand this. But with this knowledge, they should discuss an estimated value with whatever they dedicate to God and present a free will offering as the price to redeem whatever they dedicate to God. Many times we make vows, which we often fail to fulfil. Vows, like dedications are taken very seriously in the sight of God – Deuteronomy 23:21: *When thou shalt vow a vow unto the Lord thy God, thou shalt not slack to pay it: for the Lord thy God will surely require it of thee; and it would be sin in thee.*

❖

Judiciary system in the Kingdom

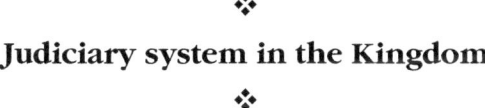

The purpose of the judiciary system is to ensure sanctity and sanity, because the name of the Lord is involved. To ensure disputes are genuinely investigated we are warned

CHAPTER SEVEN

not to judge anyone until the matter is well attested to by eyewitnesses – Matthew 7:1,18:16. We are also warned not to judge the servant of God except when proven beyond reasonable doubt by trustworthy witnesses – 1 Timothy 5:19. The Lord can rebuke His own – He did it to Peter twice (Matthew 16:23, Matthew 26:52). He also warned Peter of an impending temptation that was set ahead of him – Luke 22:32. If your Pastor is called of God, the Lord will definitely rebuke him of his wrongdoings, except we wish to do the work of the Lord. This manner of issues resolution is set in place because the devil's weapon is slandering and lying tongues, which he would set against the work of Christ, and therefore against everyone championing the course. I have often wondered why people can easily gossip the servant of God and yet leave witch doctors alone. Even the way many government officials go away with scandalous remarks said against them is baffling, yet all unfounded scandals against the servants of God have wrought havoc in their lives and those of their families – no wonder Jesus says – Matthew 10:25: *If they have called the master of the house Beelzebub, how much more shall they call them of his household.* This does not make anyone above judgement, but for the purpose of peace, is here set in place by the rule of forgiveness and mercy. We should forgive those who offend us seventy times seventy times, to enable us obtain God's everlasting mercy. We are also admonished to show mercy to fellow adherents so that we would obtain the mercy of the Lord – Matthew 5:7. We are also to settle with one another whatever we might have against each other before coming to present our gifts before the altar of the Lord – Matthew 5:24. The servants of God have the approval of the King of kings to forgive sins, so that the devil will not take it against them and cause them to sin more as a result of hatred that will grow unabated. Zechariah 7:9-10 - *Thus speaketh the Lord of hosts, saying, Execute true judgment, and shew mercy and compassions every man to his brother: And oppress not the widow, nor the fatherless, the stranger, nor the poor; and let none of you imagine evil against his brother in your heart.*

Finally, to conclude this section, the Bible says – Matthew 5:7-9: *Blessed are the merciful: for they shall obtain mercy. Blessed are the pure in heart: for they shall see God. Blessed are the peacemakers: for they shall be called the children of God.* Those who make peace receive the blessings of the Lord. But to do this, our hearts must be pure from hatred, and unforgiveness.

CHAPTER EIGHT

PROSPERITY IN THE KINGDOM

It is the expectation of God that His Kingdom on earth prospers beyond the proclivity of human wisdom and understanding. But, how can this be? The Bible tells us that it is through righteousness - Isaiah 60:21-22: *Thy people also shall be all righteous: they shall inherit the land for ever, the branch of my planting, the work of my hands, that I may be glorified. A little one shall become a thousand, and a small one a strong nation: I the Lord will hasten it in his time.* I am on a mandate to raise fifty righteous men for the Lord. The number seems small, but are people willing to endure what it takes to live a righteous life? We may claim all the numbers that come to Sunday service as evidence that the Kingdom has indeed prospered, or the numbers of high-tech cars parked outside as confirmation that we are doing well for the Lord. Is this prosperity? From what we just read, righteousness is the basis for our inheritance, and then we would grow from little to a thousand and from a small kingdom to a strong kingdom. We know that the word of God doesn't lie. If we accept this as it has always been, how then are we going to judge the churches worldwide that swim in material prosperity in the midst of unrighteousness? Someone of the order of the spiritual who tries to disguise himself in the name of the Lord must be involved in this deceit. Who could this be? 2 Corinthians 11:14 has a clue to our question: *And no marvel; for Satan himself is transformed into an angel of light*. I was in a church service some time ago. A brother came to give a wonderful testimony, then I hadn't been called into the vineyard, or maybe I wasn't aware that God was calling me to work for Him; when he was done, I heard a voice - 'he is lying, it was not I that blessed him.' I was overcome with shock, and I expected the servant of God to rebuke him as Jesus would have done, but that paved the way for this preacher to announce the

CHAPTER EIGHT

power of God in his church. My heart was bleeding, because of the high level of spiritual chaos and insincerity in the house of God.

The word of the Lord says in Zechariah 1:17 - *My cities through prosperity shall yet be spread abroad.* The Psalmist says in Psalm 34:9-10: *O taste and see that the Lord is good: blessed is the man that trusteth in him. O fear the Lord, ye his saints: for there is no want to them that fear him. The young lions do lack, and suffer hunger:* **but they that seek the Lord shall not want any good thing.** This is because they understood the importance of prosperity to the establishment of the Kingdom of God on earth. Prosperity brings announcement, but righteousness establishes our prosperity and would make it smell sweet savour unto God all the days of our lives.

The Lord is happy when we prosper - The gifts and the talents the Lord gave to us are to be employed to grow His kingdom and not to serve His enemy, the devil. We would take a look at the Garden of Eden and all its beauty – Adam was to explore and tender the garden. We are told the gold of the land was good. Of what use is such good gold if it is not used to enhance our worship of God? This is fact – and in the wilderness altar, gold showed as an instrument of decoration for the altar – the children of Israel also put some on themselves for beauty. If the altar was decorated with gold, we too must look on beauty in gold as a show of His glory in us. Romans 8:19 says - *For the earnest expectation of the creature waiteth for the manifestation of the sons of God.* The kingdom manifests the glory of God. The Lord spoke to me some time ago in the month of June 2014 during a one-month revival program we held in the church, saying, *'You shall manifest the beauty of my Glory.'* The statement took me aback – but now I understand better. And so like Paul said in Romans 8:18 - *For I reckon that the sufferings of this present time are not worthy to be compared with the glory which shall be revealed in us.* The glory ahead, which is the reward for those who submitted to God's will (Hebrew 11:6), is worth labouring for.

What are talents used for? We are told of how in Exodus 31:1, God informed Moses of someone filled with wisdom to work on the tabernacle. After Bezaleel built the tabernacle, what would he be doing with this special gift? To feed himself and to raise income for the nation of Israel – growing her GDP. So our talents are to be employed to yield prosperity.

CHAPTER EIGHT

The operation of any Kingdom of God here on Earth is tied to a situation of need, as the people throng to God daily to cry for Him to intervene. Jesus explained this when He said they should pray for labourers. These labourers become the servants of God, who would now become the shepherds. This need is also captured in Isaiah 42:22. Elihu, Job's friend, in counselling Job, had this to say about the working power of God for those who favour His righteous course – Job 36:3 - *He withdraweth not his eyes from the righteous: but with kings are they on the throne; yea, he doth establish them for ever, and they are exalted.* This statement about God establishing those that serve Him and make them reign with kings could be confirmed in the lives of Joseph, Moses, Esther, Daniel, and many others in the Bible. The people can only rejoice when the righteous have a say in the government of the people. Establishment brings prosperity. It brings consolation. This is what God intends for all who would follow Him. Prosperity brings confidence of authority and command – this is what David meant in Psalm 30:6 - *And in my prosperity I said, I shall never be moved.*

The live wire of the Kingdom of God on earth is prosperity. This is what brings the announcement, and the world would want to surrender to God. Even when the Israelites were leaving the land of Egypt, God favoured them with gold, silver and various precious items from their Egyptian neighbours. It is God's desire to bless and favour His people, who are in His Kingdom. Salvation is directly linked to prosperity, as this becomes the evidence that the Lord has indeed visited His children. Hence, David also, having a perfect understanding of the influence prosperity has on the perception of victory by heathen nation, cried unto the Lord – Psalm 118:25- *Save now, I beseech thee, O Lord: O Lord, I beseech thee, send now prosperity.*

Now that we understand how prosperity affects the Kingdom of God on earth, we will reflect on what the Kingdom needs to do in order to ensure prosperity floods the land. Our first point of discussion would be the utilization of the wisdom residing in the Kingdom. Our attention would go straight to Jesus Christ and what He taught and lived for, which is the establishment of the Kingdom of God on earth. The book of Colossians 1:10-13 says: *That ye might walk worthy of the Lord unto all pleasing, being fruitful in every good work, and increasing in the knowledge of God; Strengthened with all might, according to his glorious power, unto all patience and longsuffering with joyfulness; Giving thanks unto the Father, which hath made us meet to be partakers of the inheritance of the saints in light: Who hath delivered us from the power of darkness, and hath translated us into the Kingdom of his dear Son*

- Fruitful in every work.
- Increasing in the knowledge of God.
- Strengthened with all might: Saint Paul referred to this when he attested to the fact that the reason he was succeeding was because Christ was strengthening him – Philippians 4:13.
- Receive glorious power.
- Be patient, enduring longsuffering with joyfulness.

And the reward of that from the Bible portion we read says:

- Inheritance of the Kingdom of light: We prosper in whatever we do now as we live on earth.
- Deliverance from the power of darkness: No evil force can manipulate our existence.
- Translated into the Kingdom of Jesus Christ when we depart this earth, to enjoy eternal bliss.

CHAPTER EIGHT

❖
Behold the Lamb of God
❖

The book of John 1:29 opened up with a thought-provoking message - *Behold the Lamb of God, which taketh away the sin of the world.* What was eating up the prosperity of the children of God was sin, and since there was one who would bear this burden of sin, and lead the world to God, there would be a flourishing prosperity all over the Kingdom. To do this, the Lamb would have to transform everyone who agrees to be led into the Kingdom of prosperity through baptism with the Holy Ghost and fire. Behold the Lamb of God! It was a feeling of exhalation - a sign of relief. The Messiah is here to tell them all things. The Israelites and the world at large have been experiencing pain without knowing the reason why.

The story of their depravity was so pathetic that they had come from everywhere to meet John the Baptist to enquire if he was the coming help of God. In the days of David, he prayed for God to send prosperity - Psalm 118:25, and he knew that a messenger was going to come from heaven with prosperity in His arms (Psalm 118:26)

CHAPTER EIGHT

- *Blessed be he that cometh in the name of the Lord.* There was desolation and pain everywhere. The prosperity of the Lord was far from being a reality. Would help ever come? Was God still going to fulfil His own part of the agreement? Their hopes were being dashed. Herod had killed all their sons, for fear of being overthrown when he heard about the birth of Jesus. People thought the king too must have died in that inferno. Evil was multiplying. The Pharisees and Sadducees were muzzling the oxen. The people were subjected to deprivation. There was no faith anywhere. Love had died. God was no longer in their midst. Just like the manna stopped falling, God's mercy was leaving them by the day. They wanted to be free from the claws of Satan. They wanted to have life and have it more abundantly. They prayed without watching. Then the Lamb came in disguise, only to be announced on that fateful day by John the Baptist. How many people were there? Did they believe in John's announcement? No! No!! No!!! Jesus confirmed in John 5 that they did not believe in John's message of Him. John knew what Easter celebration is all about, when we experience the new birth in Christ, and would carry a new heart - the heart of flesh. We will become children instead of dogs who have no regard for holy things.

So many of us today are unable to appreciate this sacrifice because we haven't really experienced the kind of pain the Israelites were going through. We need to continually see the need to expect freedom and deliverance. If we are not there to receive it, there is no way we can be free.

Why do children cry once they are born? Because of the change of environment. Right from the day when man changed his original environment from Eden, we have all being crying like new-born babies.

Prosperity comes from acknowledging Jesus as the Son of God. If we have done this, then we have received a blessing that will sustain us through life.

We would now look into the downfall of man, and how man started living the life of want. We will just pick out the main ideas needed for our discussion from Genesis 3:

- Verse 6: Eve's desire wasn't wrong but she was acting against the will of God. Her giving the fruit to her husband wasn't wrong, but she was acting against God's instruction and plan.

- Verse 7-9: Their discovery of nakedness wasn't wrong but they were not supposed to think of 'self,' but of God. It was their running away from God that offended

Him. Making God to now look for them, and calling out to Adam. If caring for yourself cannot make you face God, then something is wrong.

- Verse 12: The man blaming the wife wasn't wrong but he was supposed to save the situation. And if that had happened there wouldn't have being any need for prayers today.

- Verse 13: Eve blaming the serpent was foolishness. She shouldn't have listened to a creature that was not human - this is wisdom. We mind from whom we take advice, and to know what wisdom is in them.

- Verse 14: God didn't allow the serpent to defend itself. Well, God knows that the serpent is culpable always, and going about spoiling His investments. We would see that God loves us – even when He knew the truth, He still gave Adam and Eve the benefit of doubt to be able to defend themselves. Even today, the Lord is doing this on our behalf.

Let's investigate the curses and how the salvation of Christ has nullified them, if only we believe in Him to give us that abundant life – the prosperity of the Father in heaven.

- Verse 15: Because children are very vulnerable and could be hunted by the devil, to put an end to their destiny, the Lord made it in such a way that their angel would behold the face of God always, interceding on their behalf even before the coming of Christ to earth - Matthew 18:10.

- Verse 16: Many women want a man to appreciate them always. They dress to attract men. Such an attitude is for an unsaved woman and such a woman sees her living as people's responsibility with no wisdom in her. Proverbs 31:10-31 and Job 28:18 explain that a virtuous woman is sought after always. So instead of prostituting and dressing to seduce men, a saved woman seeks after wisdom, and her prosperity will come.

- Verse 17-19: Any man in Christ would not experience the cursed upon the Land. It was greed that made them eat the fruit. So as a saved person, greed dies in you. You have the kind of wisdom that will stop you from struggling. You now possess leadership qualities that will make you run enterprises and people working under your leadership. Since man fell for Satan's trick, we have been under satanic influence, as can be seen in businesses worldwide. The ruling class today is made up mostly of those who submit to these evil practices. But now that we are restored, there is no way they can rule over us any more.

Now that we are free from the curses that were laid as a burden upon mankind as a result of Satan's deceit, I would encourage us to examine our lives to see if the curses are still affecting our prosperity now that we claim to be in Christ. A candid approach would be to understand the words of Psalm 23:1: *The Lord is my shepherd; I shall not want.* What follows after verse 1 are the beauty of prosperity. So quickly we would now follow through the evidence of prosperity as captured in Psalm 23:2-6:

- Verse 2: We are placed in positions where we would have more than enough to sustain us. Even for those who don't have, the Lord brings them in contact with those who can meet their needs in the Kingdom – Acts 4:34: *Neither was there any among them that lacked: for as many as were possessors of lands or houses sold them, and brought the prices of the things that were sold.*

- Verse 3: Our souls are restored back to the Kingdom of light. It shows that we have been delivered from the oppression of the enemy. We now have the strength to succeed. Hence Saint Paul said – Philippians 4:13: *I can do all things through Christ which strengtheneth me.* The more we are able to do more things, the more we would prosper.

- Verse 4: We are protected by His arm, in all situations. His rod corrects us – meaning we apply the right wisdom at all times. We also put up good attitudes as He disciplines us unto good characters. And because we now have good manners, whatever we do will also attract the attention of people who will come to patronize our business. For those of us in paid employment, we are favoured and promoted as a result of our enterprising qualities.

- Verse 5: We always have enough as a result of God lavishing His blessings upon us, even when we live in the midst of devourers who uses their tongues to try to pull us down.

- Verse 6: As a result of the death of Christ on the cross, we now experience the prosperity of the Lord in the land, because the enemy no longer has power over our reasoning. Our testimonies of the Lord's faithfulness are the reason why we would dwell in His house forever and ever.

Restoration is about re-evaluation of the old status quo. As we begin to discover ourselves, our worth and value before people also increase. Wisdom is more than rubies. And if we want to be valued above rubies, above what money can buy, we need the wisdom to know what we need to succeed in life. This is why we must pray. So prayer is about tightening the nuts that have loosened in our lives. We have royal blood and therefore we are priceless and unique. As we pray today we need to take back what we have lost.

To ensure that we imbibe the spirit of prosperity on time we need to plan our lives on time. This is the reason why we are educated in school early. This is done to so that we are not in a hurry in life. Most of our struggles for prosperity and wealth are because we started late in life to start the life planning process.

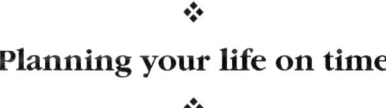

Planning your life on time

Life involves learning and unlearning. While I was developing this subject I received a word of wisdom, that planning involves **Prospects, Purpose** and **People.**

CHAPTER EIGHT

Prospects are available opportunities staring at our face waiting to be explored. For us to know which of these prospects we should be interested in, we would have to understand the purpose of the life we intend to live. Once this is done we would also need to know who would be of value to us. But if the plan is to succeed, then the hand of God must be in it. If God is in our marriage it will blossom. If God is in our job we will see increase. So we must bring God into our plan. For each of the people we have listed, after bringing God's purpose into the plan, we need a character to attract them, and such a character must be approved by God, else we will find ourselves experiencing pain after a while. Know those who are ready to work with you. Many of those we see as Christians are lazy, and they see the house of God as a place where they will come to cry for help. So when they see you calling them, they see you as the help they have been expecting, and when you try to engage their thinking, you will see them rebelling. We should not forget that King Solomon had finished the temple before calling on the Levites and the house of Israel for the dedication. He used servants and men from Lebanon to hew timbers; the gold and silver were donated by

CHAPTER EIGHT

foreigners. Only few of those you call today as Christians yield to building for God, and this is one reason why they don't increase financially, and the Kingdom is lacking in want – Haggai 1.

Planning is all about wisdom and we all know that wisdom is the beauty of life - Proverbs 9:10-11. Wisdom teaches us to fear God. How do we fear God? By given regard to all that concerns Him. Let's see what David did - Psalms 132:2-5: *… and vowed unto the mighty God of Jacob; Surely I will not come into the tabernacle of my house, nor go up into my bed; I will not give sleep to mine eyes, or slumber to mine eyelids, Until I find out a place for the Lord, an habitation for the mighty God of Jacob.* David vowed to build a house unto the Lord. Yet today we see many calling themselves Christians who are the ones destroying what the Lord is building. We must Love Him with everything in our life - Mark 12:30. There is no way we will commit our ways to the Lord that He will not prosper us. I am a living testimony today.

We must be ready to serve Him in His altar. Why do we think God raises His servants and they raise altars? God's servants create a sacred environment, patterned after

CHAPTER EIGHT

what is in Heaven, where faithful worshippers would gather to bless the name of the Lord. Since God inhabits His sacred altars, our dedication to such a place of worship will attract His showers of blessings upon our plans - Psalms 133:3. It was this understanding that convinced David that when God dwells among humans, there will be a multiplication of blessings, hence an abundance of prosperity. This implies that to see prosperity, we must belong to a household of God. The reason Zion was so important was because King David brought the Ark of God there. Hence in Hebrews 11:22-23 we are told that angels are there. Angels inhabit every altar of the Lord, set in place by those He calls to do His work. These altars are likened to base stations and repeater stations. When we worship in His house it shows that we have accepted the Ark of the Lord. It is evidence that we desire the Lord, and as we take responsibilities in His house, opening our home for fellowship, and respecting the servant of the Lord in your midst (Luke 13:35), because they have a role to play in your blessings as seen in Numbers 6:23-27. Why will you respect the servants of God? It is because the Lord hears him often, since He is on a message for Him. And we heard when Jesus was talking to Peter that the gates of hell shall not stand against His decree. This is our strength, and our hope.

❖

How to sustain our Prosperity

❖

We must desire the anointing of the Lord always. Any time there is an anointing service is an opportunity to be earmarked for greatness. This is an opportunity for the servant of God to be a blessing to anyone who desires the Lord. Saint Paul says in Ephesians 3:2-5: *Assuming that you have heard of the stewardship of God's grace that was given to me for you, how the mystery was made known to me by revelation, as I have written briefly. When you read this, you can perceive my insight into the mystery of Christ, which was not made known to the sons of men in other generations as it has now been revealed to his holy apostles and prophets by the Spirit* (ESV). This implies that the blessing of the Lord is a respecter of no man – it is for all those who wish to come to the Lord. The message the Lord is given me to you may not have been preached by another before now, but the times we are in now demand that God has to release secrets from the

Melchizedek Order unto you so that your knees don't stay too long on the floor. Saint Paul's message was how the Gentiles might be partakers of the grace of God. It is no news and mystery now that the Gentiles are partakers of the grace of God in Christ Jesus. What is needful now is the truth about the character God wants us to exhibit. We cannot be like any other commission, else there is no need for a calling. The Lord spoke to me that He is about using me to build the largest church ever. How will this be if we do everything as others do? The Lord had spoken to me, that the people He is sending me to, are in the church but they don't know where they are going. This kind of information demands some form of secret that hasn't been known before.

The evidence of the anointing is not far-fetched. If you have the secrets of God in your hands, you don't need to ask for too long before you hear God speak. Isaac only decided to move out and he heard God – Genesis 26. I live a life filled with the evidence of the Lord's presence and if it is not affecting the church yet, it means the church is rebelling. The secret to sustaining your increase is obedience. The Lord is waiting for me to raise people who can stand with me. A servant of God is in charge, as the centurion rightly said, and carries out his operation in most cases, without consulting anybody but the Lord who kept Him as an overseer. We can sustain our physical increase when we listen to God's servants, and carry out the instructions from God aimed to better our lives. A word of advice lies here in wait in the book of Zechariah 7:11-14 -*But they refused to hearken, and pulled away the shoulder, and stopped their ears, that they should not hear. Yea, they made their hearts as an adamant stone, lest they should hear the law, and the words, which the Lord of hosts hath sent in his spirit by the former prophets: therefore came a great wrath from the Lord of hosts. Therefore it is come to pass, that as he cried, and they would not hear; so they cried, and I would not hear, saith the Lord of hosts: But I scattered them with a whirlwind among all the nations whom they knew not.*

God wants us to be perfect - Matthew 5:48, so He raises pastors for us - Jeremiah 3:15, to teach and train us unto perfection - 2 Timothy 3:16-17, and that we will also teach and train others, until our habitation will be filled with the word and wisdom of God – Jeremiah 31:31-34. The Lord tells me severally that I don't need prayers before He would come to my aid if I do His will. From the story of creation, prayer isn't one of the things He commanded man to observe. Man invented it as a means to get in touch with Him, after the devil had taken over the consciousness of humans. God wants our body to be His temple so that our heart will be His dwelling place, and all our thoughts will receive spiritual illumination, and then we would live as He wants.

Thoughts are like magnets. What we think daily is what draws the world to us so that we can have what we have desire. Our thoughts carry our faith. And our faith is a manifestation of the spirit that is in charge of our bodies. When the Lord is in us, our thoughts will be holy and would draw His blessings and favour to us. The teacher is accountable for a student's failure in an exam, until it is proven that the teacher indeed taught the student the complete syllabus, and that it was the student's fault to have failed. This is how it will be on the judgement day. Your pastor is the first to receive the blame of not nurturing you with the word of God, until proven otherwise by the record of your own life.

A young lady met me one day and she said – 'Teach me about God. I have been watching you and I can see God.

CHAPTER EIGHT

You don't behave like the pastors I have seen, but you are simple and progressing in life.'

And I said to her – 'God is in you. Behave like God. People meet God for different reasons. Make yourself available without feeling you are better than your neighbour. Kill pride, and people will see God in you. Humility to the voice of God is all you need and not fasting and prayer.' She marvelled and smiled. The House of God is a house of Prayer because people come there to repent so that they will live as God intends. But if we can walk away from sin, we don't need all that prayer. We only decree things, and see them establish. The Bible says – Psalms 37:4 *Delight thyself also in the Lord; and he shall give thee the desires of thine heart.* You don't sustain your prosperity with, 'O, Lord fight the devil!' Obedience is better than sacrifice.

I have seen that most of those who claim to be prayer warriors are the most disobedient to the move of God, because often times they don't hear God and because they don't, but still want to maintain their relevance, they will say the Lord has not spoken. Many of them eat their tithes and challenge the pastor, always causing others to err. They over time will start an intercessory prayer band meeting, as if God is interested in people crying to be heard. If we see Genesis 11:6: *And the Lord said, Behold, the people is one, and they have all one language; and this they begin to do: and now nothing will be restrained from them, which they have imagined to do the Lord said,* we would see that these people erred by trying to push their selfish ambition against the command of God to fill the earth.

As I have seen from the Bible, Melchizedek blessed Abraham, Abraham blessed Isaac, Isaac blessed Jacob - they all received only from the one higher. Samuel anointed David. All we need is the anointing.

Look around the world today. Sin is multiplying and the church is praying for prosperity or to sustain what they have, instead of confronting the evil with our voices to tell people to stop sinning. It is the multiplication of sins that is eating up our increase. Sin is a devourer and no sinner should think of prosperity until he/she repents to follow the ways of the Lord.

This is what God is interested in now. If a brother does wrong, rebuke him. I don't have time to call people who have erred for special discussion. If the wrong was done in public, the correction should be in public so that others will learn from it. When the earth opened to swallow those who rebelled in the wilderness, it was in public. When Christ rebuked Peter, it was in public, right where he erred. When companies sack their employees for misconduct, other employees are informed, and in some cases the faces of such staff are published in the papers. Many of us are too proud to be used by God.

As a servant of God I have the grace of God upon me that is enabling me to succeed, and I want to transfer this too so that people's knees are lifting from the floor, but many who also come close have always desired to take the wrong route of continuously hiding and crying to God.

We should do the needful. God did not create prayer. He created us to see and hear Him, not to be shouting and crying in our prayers. We should walk our way back through repentance and obedience. And our prayers won't be to ask for increase, but as a means of adoring Him in our hearts.

Now that you have read up to this point, I would oblige

you to obey the following instructions and you will see the results by the end of the month:

- Do not pray or asking for anything from God for one week. Just praise and worship Him and that will suffice.
- Just think and write down all you have been thinking - thoughts of increase, for yourself and the work of God.
- Continue with this book until you have finished studying the entire book. Do not read another book, so as not to mix thoughts. When we mix thoughts we affect our spiritual receptive power.
- Do not miss church services, including midweek meetings, where you are sure the word of God would be studied.
- Think good of your pastor and all that concerns him, including his wife and children, and wish them well.
- Do not eat your offering and tithes.
- Learn to greet people with a smile on your face.
- Treat people with respect, as you would treat God.

CHAPTER EIGHT

■ Keep your surroundings clean.

And see what will happen to all that you have been thinking.

CHAPTER NINE

DEVELOPING KINGDOM CHARACTER

Nicodemus met Jesus, and Jesus told him that to be saved one has to be born again, and then born of water and of the spirit - John 3:3,5. John the Baptist explain that Jesus would baptise everyone that came to Him with fire and the Holy Spirit - Matthew 3:11. Jesus says for this to happen one has to learn of Him – Matthew 11:29. The reason for all this is because humans have a soul that can be easily affected by forces and energies. On earth we have electromagnetic waves and the force of gravity, and both affect our lives here on earth, and how we perceive things and events that happen around us. Many have accepted the characters presented to them in horoscopes as to who they are and always will be, without need to change their personality. Even psychologists have prescribed behavioural patterns based on some observable traits, and have concluded that humans are who they are, as an explanation to their lifestyle. And all this points to the fact that we have to allow people to live as they want in order to create a non-homogenous behavioural environment and society where we all must learn to accept each other the way we are. Does the Bible believe this too? I don't think so, as there is evidence to prove that God wants His children to develop Kingdom characteristics, and learn to live by them. Adam lived by the character of heaven before his sin, and since then time and season, planetary motions and the rays of the sun affect every human born into the earth. The actions of celestial bodies, as they cause day and night, the months and then the years, force humans to think and reason in similar patterns as they try to make ends meet. During this process, as humans go about their daily activities, spiritual clouds are generated in response to the demands of the flesh – comfort, warmth, cooling, relationship, habitation, etc - and the human soul with time adapts to these needs. The soul of every child born within a certain season of the year, under the control of celestial bodies, would adapt to the habits of the people. And as the child grows, the character prevalent in the month he/she was born will be reflected in his/her life. This is what is call horoscope prediction. It is a false way of determining the life of believers. This character predicted by the horoscope is the life of the Adamic nature we carry, which has come short of the glory of God (Romans 3:23). It is this inputted character carried by our soul that gives way once we are born of the spirit and of water. How would proponents of horoscope explain change in behaviour when one encounters Christ? I will quickly want to shed some light on how one can determine one's Adamic character. Let's take a child born in the month of January, for instance. There are 12 hours in a day and another 12 hours in the night. We will only use the daytime, because night depicts death. Daytime is seen as life spiritually. Now, to predict the Adamic character that the soul of a child born in January has inherited, we would look at the prevalent activities of people in the month of January – people tend to be spiritual, trying to figure out what the new year holds for them, there is a high level of expectation everywhere, etc.

Then we would match the first month with the first hour of the day – 6 am. Now what happens at 6 am? People are in a hurry to get to work. So the soul of a child born in January will be inputted with these qualities of humans in the environment, and that would become the attitude of the child overtime, until the Lord takes over the soul with His character. If we treat the month of December and match it with 6 pm, we would see that these people like gathering and keeping safe, tidying up the environment, cooking their own meals, festivities etc, because these were the characteristics the soul inherited from the environment when the child was born. Most of the traits exhibited by our children are not unto godliness. It is our duty to lead them to Christ to be baptised with fire and the Holy Spirit, so that the soul would become free to learn the character of heaven.

In the Kingdom we have 'Kingdom Character' and 'Heaven First' principles, as a way of life. The Bible says of Daniel in the book of Daniel 5:12: *Forasmuch as an excellent spirit, and knowledge, and understanding, interpreting of dreams, and shewing of hard sentences, and dissolving of doubts, were found in the same Daniel* And we would see this in the book of Joel 2:28 - *And it shall come to pass afterward, that I will pour out my spirit upon all flesh; and your sons and your daughters shall prophesy, your old men shall dream dreams, your young men shall see visions.* Saint Paul further explains – 1 Corinthians 12:4-11: *Now there are diversities of gifts, but the same Spirit. And there are differences of administrations, but the same Lord. And there are diversities of operations, but it is the same God which worketh all in all. But the manifestation of the Spirit is given to every man to profit withal. For to one is given by the Spirit the word of wisdom; to another the word of knowledge by the same Spirit; To another faith by the same Spirit; to another the gifts of healing by the same Spirit; To another the working of miracles; to another prophecy; to another discerning of spirits; to another divers kinds of tongues; to another the interpretation of tongues: But all these worketh that one and the self-same Spirit, dividing to every man severally as he will.* We see that the Kingdom is filled with people with diverse occupation to serve the Lord and function in various works of life with the aim of making society a better place:

1. The manifestation of the spirit of uniqueness in all we do. This is the excellent spirit upon Daniel, which

comes through seeking knowledge, understanding and wisdom.

2. Ability to dream, prophesy and see visions, and to discern the interpretation thereof.

3. The gift of working miracles, and healing

The following are what is needed to develop these characters:

Spiritual hearing

Spiritual hearing is a skill needed to hear what the spirit says. Jesus says in John 5:30: *I can of mine own self do nothing:* ***as I hear***, *I judge and my judgment is just; because I seek not mine own will, but the will of the Father which hath sent me.* Implying that to be able to hear, we must develop the habit of 'deep listening.' The qualities we mentioned above include the ability to prophesy and interpret visions. In both, we need to hear. Hence the angels would inform John in his Revelation that only those who have ears would hear what the spirit says, as revealed to him. How does one develop the ability to hear? One enemy to our ability to hear deeply is lack of trust in the Lord's ability to save us from our situations of sorrow – Matthew 13:15. What we hear is useless without the gift of understanding – Matthew 13:19: *When anyone heareth the word of the Kingdom, and understandeth it not, then cometh the wicked one, and catcheth away that which was sown in his heart.* This is what actually distinguishes everyone in His Kingdom. We all have a different depth of understanding of the released Rhema. How many times has God revealed Himself to us in our dreams, and how many times has God spoken to us through His servants, yet we would push it aside? This is why some are able to employ the services of the agents of the Lord, while others are still finding clues to what they should do. Jesus says – Matthew 13:16: *But blessed are your eyes, for they see: and your ears, for they hear.* Now that we have developed our ability to hear, we must ensure we avoid the following, else what we hear will not yield benefits to us:

- Not putting what we have heard of the Lord into practice is living a life of shadows and falsehood. If we have obeyed the commands of the Lord since we gave our lives to the Lord, we won't be where we are today – Matthew 7:24: *Therefore whosoever heareth these sayings of mine, and doeth them, I will liken him unto a wise man, which built his house upon a rock.* Our salvation will only profit us and lead to our promotion in life, and enable us to exhibit the gift of the Lord in our lives when we apply what we heard from the Lord as precautionary measures against the deceitful leading of the devil. Hence the book of Romans 2:13 says - *For not the hearers of the law are just before God, but the doers of the law shall be justified.* It is not enough to sit before the pulpit on Sunday to hear, we must go home and to our workplaces to apply them as qualities expected of people of a royal priesthood order. Those who fail in life, after giving their lives to God, are those who thereafter did not practise what the Spirit says – James 1:23: *For if any be a hearer of the word, and not a doer, he is like unto a man beholding his natural face in a glass.* Beholding our natural face in a glass is living a life of deceit. It is a life lived by those who sit on the fence waiting for others to take decisions. They are the 'it doesn't concern me' set of people. The reason why we hear is so that we would take decisions. Many believers are just too lazy to even study their Bibles –

their desire is for someone to bring bread for them to eat. Many attend new churches every year-end seeking those who will provide their needs. To them, Christianity is all about welfare.

- Slow to speak: before we say what we have heard, let's allow time for meditation, as the sheep will graze, and later lie down to ruminate the food. It is from our meditation that we would begin to understand what we have heard, and then set actions in place to ensure that we carry out every instruction, as it is pleasing unto the Lord. The Bible says in James 1:19: *Wherefore, my beloved brethren, let every man be swift to hear, slow to speak, slow to wrath.*

- Covetousness is a habit that destroys our ability to hear deeply, because it is an act that breed enmity among brethren. It is one characteristic that is against the gains of unity, and with time what those who are involved in this act hears are the cries of sorrows and pains that they have caused others. God hates covetousness and would not want it mentioned in the midst of His children. Yet, is this not the character of many acclaimed servants of God? Are many not greedy and working after the character of the devil? Jesus referred to the devil as a thief. A covetous person is a thief and judging by the words of Christ in John 10:10: *The thief cometh not, but for to steal, and to kill, and to destroy,* we would say that covetousness breed mass killings and destruction of lives in the Kingdom. Anyone with such character can never be of God.

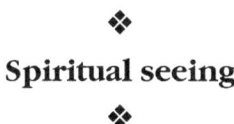

Spiritual seeing

Closely related to hearing is seeing. Jesus made a remark in Matthew 13:16 - But **blessed are your eyes, for they see.** What kind of seeing was He referring to? Is it this same seeing we see with our physical eyes? Let's find out – Matthew 6:22: *The light of the body is the eye: if therefore thine eye be single, thy whole body shall be full of light.* Among all the human rational faculties which we refer to as the human senses, the one that has the ability to process information from a distance is the eye. Its inability to process information would mean deadness to the human body. Does this send a thought into our thinking consciousness, that even as the eye is important in the physical so also it is needed for us to receive spiritual wholeness? Severally we read how the prophets were questioned about what they saw. For instance, in Jeremiah 1:11 we may see what God asked him - *Moreover the word of the Lord came unto me, saying, Jeremiah, what seest thou? And I said, I see a rod of an almond tree. Then said the Lord unto me, Thou hast well seen. ...* This is the height of spiritual sensitivity. Imagine if Jeremiah hadn't seen well, the Lord wouldn't have been happy with him. Our Kingdom identity is in what we see God showing to us. It is not about mere surface dreams of seeing ourselves eating, swimming in water, dancing or being pursued, as many have claimed to be the evidence that God is using them. In Numbers 12:6-7; the Lord says He reveals Himself to His prophets through a vision and dream. Spiritual seeing is a character that will enhance your stay and well-being in the Kingdom. Without this, then the devil will always have his way in our lives. In Isaiah 42:9 the Lord says - *... and new things do I declare: before they spring forth I tell you of them*. He will tell us about what is about to happen to us in a vision and in our dreams.

CHAPTER NINE

❖

Extreme Humility

❖

While on a search for people who will work with me, and what simple criteria I will use to know them, I was led into this deep insight. On that fateful morning, the 2nd day of March 2013, at about 8:36am, I received a word of knowledge – 'Extreme Humility' and 'Availability.' As I recited these words, it dawned on me that these were the qualities of people that must work with me in the vineyard of the Lord. I was so happy. We will treat Extreme Humility now. Jesus opened my understanding to what it is all about in Matthew 11:28-30: *Come unto me, all ye that labour and are heavy laden, and I will give you rest. Take my yoke upon you, and learn of me; for I am meek and lowly in heart: and ye shall find rest unto your souls. For my yoke is easy, and my burden is light.* We would now bring out the character of Extreme Humility embedded in what we just read:

- ■ It is about bearing a burden on behalf of someone, so that he/she can have rest.

- ■ It is about taken the yoke of the Lord upon us.

CHAPTER NINE

- It is about learning His ways.

- And the character that makes this possible is meekness and lowliness.

The key character there is that Jesus is meek and lowly – this is humility at work. To be meek means to submit under an authority, and Jesus proved this attribute of submissiveness to the will of God concerning the establishment of the Kingdom when He said – John 10:17: *Therefore doth my Father love me, because I lay down my life, that I might take it again.* In John 9:4 Jesus also says - *I must work the works of him that sent me, while it is day: the night cometh, when no man can work.* These verses are proof that He submitted to the will of the Father. And to prove that He is lowly, which means to be modest in character, we may see how He was described in Acts 10:38: *How God anointed Jesus of Nazareth with the Holy Ghost and with power: who went about doing good, and healing all that were oppressed of the devil; for God was with him.* Service demands humility, obedience and loyalty, to the vision enshrined in the calling. We would also see what Extreme Humility is from the relationship between Elisha and Elijah – 2 Kings 2:14: *Where is the Lord God of Elijah? and when he also had smitten the waters, they parted hither and thither.* Why would Elisha call the name of Elijah? It was humility and loyalty. If He had called the God of Israel, the river would still have parted for him to walk through. A display of his extreme humility would be seen as the people who saw him daily with Elijah recounted – 2 Kings 3:11 … *Here is Elisha the son of Shaphat, which poured water on the hands of Elijah.* One problem many Kingdom adherents are having is pride, and this is affecting the growth of the Kingdom, and the enemy is plundering our habitation because of our disunity.

Availability

The next characteristic I heard was 'Availability.' The Disciples followed Jesus the moment He called them, because they made themselves available. They all had one thing or the other doing before following Jesus. A confirmation that they indeed left their precious vocation to follow the Lord is seen in Mark 10:28: *Then Peter began to say unto him, Lo, we have left all, and have followed thee.* This is availability at work. Again, we would see that when Elijah threw his mantle on Elisha, he was busy in the farm helping his family – 1 Kings 19:19-20: *So he departed thence, and found Elisha the son of Shaphat, who was plowing with twelve yoke of oxen before him, and he with the twelfth: and Elijah passed by him, and cast his mantle upon him. And he left the oxen, and ran after Elijah...* Is this how available we are to answer the Lord? The Lord wants those who are willing to follow Him wherever He wants them to go, to champion the course of the gospel.

Emotional maturity

Everything we do as humans has an emotional tone attached to it. Our life in the Kingdom of God depends on how we work on our emotions. Frail emotions grow fears. This is one reason we need the infilling of the Holy Spirit. Here we would be discussing how we could enhance our emotional maturity, because of the important role our emotions play in our spiritual growth. People who don't have the fear of God cause most of the emotional triggers, so if we limit our associations with such people, we would have limited emotional triggers. How many of us will accept a brother who is passing through temptations of the flesh? Even Jesus had an angel to strengthen Him because He was made a little lower than angels, to suffer death. The moment a man drops from the level of spiritual grace, temptation is inevitable, but the ability to overcome it resides in the grace of God. What then is emotional maturity? Is it the ability to overcome pain and suffering? It is the ability to keep Christ in view as the reason for our sacrifices in His Kingdom. Emotion cannot be hidden; it is the first expression someone will notice in us, and it is the fruit that often gives us the name people would know us by. You may have heard people being referred to as – 'he/she is always angry,' 'he/she does not laugh,' etc. We are admonished to always rejoice – 1 Thessalonians 5:16. The following is some advice from the Bible to help us mature our emotions:

- **Matthew 5:39-40:** … *'but whosoever shall smite thee on thy right cheek, turn to him the other also. And if any man will sue thee at the law, and take away thy coat, let him have thy cloke also. And whosoever shall compel thee to go a mile, go with him twain.'*

CHAPTER NINE

- **Philippians 4:6:** *'Be careful for nothing; but in every thing by prayer and supplication with thanksgiving let your requests be made known unto God.'*

- **Matthew 24:13:** *'But he that shall endure unto the end, the same shall be saved.'*

- **Matthew 5:43-44:** *'Ye have heard that it hath been said, Thou shalt love thy neighbour, and hate thine enemy. But I say unto you, Love your enemies, bless them that curse you, do good to them that hate you, and pray for them which despitefully use you, and persecute you.'*

❖

Discipleship Character

❖

Let's take learning from the disciples of Jesus and how they exercise their calling to serve God in His Kingdom here on earth:

Peter's profile:

- **Occupation:** Fisherman – Matthew 4:18
- **Calling:** Fishers of men – Matthew 4:19

- **Marital Status before his calling**: Married – Matthew 8:14
- **Fulfilment of Calling:** Apostle and Evangelist – Matthew 16:19, Acts 1:13
- **Height of ministry:** Ministers the Holy Spirit, His shadow healed the sick.
- **Weakness:** Often falling into temptation

Philip's profile:

- **Occupation:** Not mentioned
- **Calling: Follow me** – John 1:43
- **Marital Status** – not mentioned
- **Fulfilment of Calling:** Brings Nathaniel to Jesus (John 1:45-50), Assisted in caring for the over 5000 fed by Jesus (John 6:5-7), brings people to Jesus who wanted to see Him (John 12:20-22), ask Jesus to show them the Father (John 14:8-13), baptised the Ethiopian Eunuch and departed to Azotus and the only disciple reported to have been caught to another city by the Holy Spirit (Acts 8).
- **Weakness:** None recorded

So also the other disciples performed their own calling to the pleasing of the Lord. Even Judas has to betray Jesus for the scriptures to be fulfilled.

To mature our Kingdom character we can also take learning from Galatians 5:16-26: 'This I say then, walk in the Spirit, and ye shall not fulfil the lust of the flesh. For the flesh lusteth against the Spirit, and the Spirit against the flesh: and these are contrary the one to the other: so that ye cannot do the things that ye would. But if ye be led of the Spirit, ye are not under the law."

'Now the works of the flesh are manifest, which are these; Adultery, fornication, uncleanness, lasciviousness, Idolatry, witchcraft, hatred, variance, emulations, wrath, strife, seditions, heresies, Envyings, murders, drunkenness, revellings, and such like: of the which I tell you before, as I have also told you in time past, that they which do such things shall not inherit the Kingdom of God.

'But the fruit of the Spirit is love, joy, peace, longsuffering, gentleness, goodness, faith, meekness, temperance.'

CHAPTER NINE

Hindrances to the institution of Kingdom character

The only reason why many believers fail to develop Kingdom characters is an unrepentant heart due to ignorance, occasioned by lack of individual spiritual intelligence – Matthew 13:15 - *For this people's heart is waxed gross, and their ears are dull of hearing, and their eyes they have closed; lest at any time they should see with their eyes, and hear with their ears, and should understand with their heart, and should be converted, and I should heal them.*

CHAPTER TEN

ALLEGIANCE TO THE KINGDOM

On the 28th of November 2013, the Lord spoke to me: 'You are doing well, do not mind what people may say, just keep on doing the good.' This gave me joy. Prior to this dream, on the 21st of November 2013, I was given a scroll and I was also very glad, because the scroll contains the secrets I had been waiting to receive from the Lord. Why will the Lord acknowledge our exploits in the Kingdom – Acts 23:11: … *the Lord stood by him, and said, Be of good cheer, Paul: for as thou hast testified of me in Jerusalem, so must thou bear witness also at Rome.* When we demonstrate allegiance to the call of the Lord, He will recommend us before the holy angels, and these will connect us to our sources of help.

CHAPTER TEN

Our allegiance to the Kingdom of God is non-debatable, for the singular reason that He has purchased us with His blood – Exodus 15:17: *till the people …, which thou hast purchased. Thou shalt bring them in, and plant them in the mountain of thine inheritance, in the place, O Lord, which thou hast made for thee to dwell in, in the Sanctuary, O Lord, which thy hands have established.* So we would look into what is requested of us as heir of the Kingdom; first, we are purchased with a price, which makes us God's inheritance, and as such He has every right over what we own and over us. Secondly, He is taking us from a path we used to know into a new path where He would lead us - Isaiah 42:16, so that we are planted on His mountain, to become a city set upon a mountain – Matthew 5:14, so that from thence, we will bring forth light out of His sanctuary – Matthew 5:16. Now we must be convinced that the sanctuary where we are worshipping is established by the hand of God, before we can shine forth as His people, hence Saint John advised that we must test all spirits, whether they be of God. How can we tell the spirit that is of God? The spirit of God does not preach the message of mammon, or show the children of God the beauty in the Kingdom of the world to entice them into money making venture - it was only the devil in Matthew 4:8-9 that did this - *Again, the devil taketh him up into an exceeding high mountain, and sheweth him all the Kingdoms of the world, and the glory of them; ...* The first message of Jesus to the world is on repentance – Matthew 4:17: *From that time Jesus began to preach, and to say, Repent: for the Kingdom of heaven is at hand.* And, again we are told that the angel of the Lord have the everlasting gospel to preach in Revelation 14:6-7: *And I saw another angel fly in the midst of heaven, having the everlasting gospel to preach unto them that dwell on the earth, and to every nation, and kindred, and tongue, and people, Saying with a loud voice, Fear God, and give glory to him...* The act of whitewashing the message to please people so that they would spend their money for the work of God is not the Kingdom message. Christ would have told Nicodemus the night he met him to invest his money so that he would go to heaven – John 3:1-5. And so we would be careful not to mix worldliness with the recipe of heaven. This is how we may measure allegiance to the works of the Kingdom. The doctrine of the Kingdom must not be corrupted with another message because we are trying to please men. We must keep the standard of righteousness that Christ preached and died for. The Bible says in Leviticus 19:19: *Thou shalt not let thy cattle gender with a diverse kind: thou shalt not sow thy field with mingled seed: neither shall a garment mingled of linen and woollen come upon thee.* We are also informed that evil communication corrupts good manners – 1 Corinthians 15:33. Where did the corruption come from? It came from co-mingling. This is the effect of mingling every the doctrine of righteousness with the doctrine of wealth acquisition. The doctrine of righteousness is very easy and simple - *But let your communication be, Yea, yea; Nay, nay: for whatsoever is more than these cometh of evil.* Which is to say we should not involve ourselves in arguments – implying further that we should not allow unhealthy co-mingling that will affect our walk with God.

If we believe that among the disciples of Jesus there was a devil in their midst – John 6:70, and that in heaven, out of the anointed cherubs there was a devil who left with one-third of the angels in heaven down to the earth, and that out of the spies Moses sent to the land of Canaan, that five-sixth of the twelve rebelled and sowed a seed of discord among the Israelites in the wilderness, thus undermining the authority of God upon Moses, we would be set to confront opposition in the Kingdom. The antonym of opposition is allegiance. Jesus carefully explained this in the parable of the tares – Matthew 13:25, to make us know that in every gathering in his name, there are some gatherings for the devil in their midst.

Now let's see how we measure allegiance to the Kingdom:

1. In the leadership team, there is every tendency that out of every twelve, there is a rebel.

2. Out of the congregation, who are the citizens of the Kingdom, there is the probability that one-third are rebels.

3. To every idea the servant of God is hatching, there is the possibility of five-sixth who will instigate the congregation against their shepherd, and try to discourage them from moving with the plan.

4. It is also a possibility that those older than the servant of God, as family members or in the congregation will try to challenge the anointing he carries.

CHAPTER TEN

From above, if we take as the average the first three realities of the possibility of rebellion, we would come out with a figure of one-fifth. Simply put, that 1/5ᵗ of those around the leader may rebel against the vision he is driving for God.

The 'Odd Reality'

Jesus first used this word in John 6:70: *Jesus answered them, Have not I chosen you twelve, and one of you is a devil?* This is a fact, that there is always an odd person out there who is against all we stand for. As a guide for a rational care of selection, from what we have discussed earlier and knowing that 1/5 is an odd fraction, we now have to discuss a phenomenon which I would like to call the 'odd reality.' I submit that: 'In every gathering of five persons or groups, aimed at pursuing a common purpose, there is the tendency that one-fifth of those gathered will disagree with the purpose of the gathering – some will speak out, to air their views, others will keep silent, only to go behind and recruit more voices to counter the plan at hand.'

CHAPTER TEN

With these realities, how can we measure allegiance? The Bible gives us a clue –1 Chronicles 12:18: *Then the spirit came upon Amasai, who was chief of the captains, and he said, Thine are we, David, and on thy side, thou son of Jesse...* When the people demonstrate allegiance, they also confess it with their mouths. They also bring food and other items, even from far into the home of their leader, so that he can have enough to take care of those working with him to keep the Kingdom healthy and defend it against infiltration from the outside with unhealthy cultures and beliefs – 1 Chronicles 12:40: *Moreover they that were nigh them, even unto Issachar and Zebulun and Naphtali, brought bread on asses, and on camels, and on mules, and on oxen, and meat, meal, cakes of figs, and bunches of raisins, and wine, and oil, and oxen, and sheep abundantly: for there was joy in Israel.* The joy that was in Israel was because they demonstrated allegiance to the anointing upon David, so they were ready to support him to bring peace to the land. In a church where there is a high level of disloyalty to their shepherd, it is difficult to see joy in their hearts because what the Lord will be doing during the period of rebellion is to vent his anger upon the congregation, and what we would see is a high level of sickness, poverty, stagnation, hunger etc. I have tried to measure the level of allegiance I receive from my congregation by fixing impromptu meetings, and what I receive is always a far cry from what one would call loyalty. It has always been the young people who will respond. The married and older people would stay at home, and this supports the instruction I received of the Lord, as if implying – *Go after the youths, the older ones will not obey you, they will feel you are too young to instruct them on what to do – some will even claim to know more than you.* One of the congregation members looked into the 'Dedication' page of one of my books and asked me, 'why did you dedicate the book to your wife instead of to God?' It wasn't long before she and her husband followed the path of rebellion. One day in the workers' meeting I told them to wear a suit as the dress code for our Sunday service, and one challenged me right there, saying she would not. This is how a leader measures allegiance. After careful analysis, I discovered that those showing allegiance were the young people, and I have to throw my weight behind them so that we can succeed together. This led to me carrying out a restructuring of my team, and I had no choice but to take out everyone who showed rebellion acts. This was how the Kingdom became united again as one loving entity. I wasn't bothered as long as the anointing of the Lord was speaking for me – many felt the church would not grow again, but they were wrong. The Lord told me to intensify efforts in mass publicity – I had a recorded music album, and we were playing the video on air. We carried out a crusade within the neighbourhood. I got the services of people outside the church to share the flyers carrying the church program after discovering that many who take the flyers would go home and hide them without giving them out. I encouraged my wife to come out with a musical video and that was also on air. I got the services of a specialist who mounted billboards to announce the church activities. Then the Lord breathed upon our efforts, and the people started coming in to worship the Lord. Shame came upon all those who had rebelled, and many started packing out of the vicinity. If I had given in to their rebellion threats, I would have lost the Kingdom to their opinion rather than the opinion of God. My sermons, according to them, were centred on righteousness and change of characters. I had pointed them to the Bible that we must not be hearers only, but doers of what we learn, and that Jesus says we must learn of His meek and lowly character. They wanted a prosperity message, and I would always refer them to churches preaching prosperity, and say that my calling is different – it is a response to the voice I heard: *who shall go before me as Moses and Elijah did, to tell these people their sins so that they would repent?* I cannot be alive and God is looking for Moses and Elijah to do His work here on earth. The Bible says in Daniel 12:3 that we should turn many to righteousness. This is the rock upon which I stand. What was affecting me was that I had people working with me who were taking instructions from the books of other pastors they were reading. They loved to listen to their messages, and would criticise ours. They would, in some occasion bring those messages to me. Those in my visitation team would go out to dent my image before the people I appointed them to visit, until the people couldn't bear it, and I was told of their nefarious attitudes. They would tell them lies of how they had received miracles when they visited other churches. Some of them were agents to some prophets around, and they were there to get customers for those prophets and at the end would receive commission out of the money they were able to collect by trick from their prey. But the Bible was my hope – Isaiah 59:19: *When the enemy shall come in like a flood, the Spirit of the Lord shall lift up a standard against*

CHAPTER TEN

him. And indeed, the spirit of the Lord's wrath wanders among them – many are in pains right now as I write this book. The Lord has spoken to me – *they are not trying to pull you down, it is my work they are destroying.*

- Abraham showed allegiance to Melchizedek, which implies that he also showed allegiance to his subjects. Servants of God are subjects of Christ and deserve to be respected – Matthew 10:42: *And whosoever shall give to drink unto one of these little ones a cup of cold water only in the name of a disciple, verily I say unto you, he shall in no wise lose his reward.*

- When the disciples went to collect the donkey, they acted as Jesus commanded them. The King has need of it was all they said, and the donkey was released to them – Matthew 21:2-3. The servant of God cannot be denied anything, but this does not mean he should be covetous.

- Abraham was to inherit the land of Canaan; but there was a Melchizedek who was in charge of Salem. For him to enjoy the good of the land, he gave a tithe to the spiritual ruler in the land. The servant of God is in a covenant with God – tithes link those paying it to the covenant upon him. God blesses you in a kingdom as He promised Abraham – Genesis 12:3: *And I will bless them that bless thee, and curse him that curseth thee: and in thee shall all families of the earth be blessed.* Blessing the servant of God attracts the blessings of God likewise – this is the life in the Kingdom. Awareness of a kingdom life is the reason people have christened their children with names such as King, Queen, Prince, Princess etc., and the obvious fact is that many of these have never learned to live a royal life pleasing unto God. Most of those bearing these names have also been involved in crimes that can't be imagined of one bearing a royal name. In the same way I have seen people bearing names such as Mercy, yet find it difficult to forgive others, and some answering the name Grace who have no idea who Christ is. An irony of life, indeed! Every one of us must belong to one of His kingdoms and not to the rebel camps that are not connected. When you don't belong to any kingdom but your acts please the King of kings, he connects you to one of His kingdoms (Peter and Cornelius). We are greater than Abraham, having been begotten after Jesus Christ in the Order of Melchizedek.

CHAPTER TEN

Prayer connects you to the throne of God, as someone knocking and hitting the gate of a wealthy man would receive the attention of whoever dwells in the house.

❖

Obeying The Rules of the Kingdom

❖

It is advisable to obey your pastor, whoever the Lord has set to lead you to Him, as it is pleasing unto to the Lord. For the purpose of peace, unity and tranquillity, the king makes some promulgation to ensure no one is hurt in the Kingdom. Here, wise counsellors also help him. This is how it is in heaven. People have asked if God can be advised. 'Yes' is the answer, but we cannot force Him to take the advice. Satan indeed advised Him in Job 1:6. And we are also told that Satan is the accuser of the brethren – Revelation 12:10. If the devil's advice wasn't causing pandemonium in that Revelation 12:10, as it did to Job, the angels who favour the course of Jesus Christ and His salvation wouldn't have thrown him out. This is what we call reasoning with God – Isaiah 1:18. What we do mostly in prayers is to argue our case with Him – Micah 6:3. Is this not advising someone? Well, we would see that Jesus once sought the opinion of Peter about who people said He was, and then whom Peter said He was. If what Jesus does is what God does, as He said – John 5:19, then we would say that God can also want us to confirm events before He can take a decision, as He sent the angels to do in the case of Sodom and Gomorrah.

What am I driving at? The fact that the rules sets in place by a servant of God in the Kingdom may have been agreed with God, and anyone who would break the rules in the church, as established by the servant of God, and those who would fail to respond to his announcement may be in like manner disobeying God.

CHAPTER ELEVEN

THE VISIT OF THE KING OF KINGS

On the 10th day of August 2014, as I was preparing for the Sunday service, most of what I will be discussing here was handed down to me from the realm of glory above. And as you read, you will be convinced that flesh and blood did not reveal this – Matthew 16:17. The Lord inhabits Heaven, but from time to time, He comes to dwell amongst us, as a Father would occasionally visit his children wherever they may be, in a cloud – Revelation 14:14: *And I looked, and behold a white cloud, and upon the cloud one sat like unto the Son of man.* The process is somewhat similar to what we do as humans – when we are having a special celebration, we would invite our parents to come visiting. In the same way we have also called on the Lord to intervene in our affairs. Jesus says – Matthew 7:11: *If ye then, being evil, know how to give good gifts unto your children, how much more shall your Father which is in heaven give good things to them that ask him?* This statement also extends to the fact that if we can invite our parents to visit us, we can also invite the presence of God and He will in no wise reject the invitation. We are informed in the book of Zechariah 2:13 - *Be silent, O all flesh, before the Lord: for he is raised up out of his holy habitation.* The Lord has *raised up out of his holy habitation;* ready to visit anyone who invites Him. The children of Israel longed to see God in the Old Testament, and He came down – Exodus 24:16-17: *And the glory of the Lord abode upon mount Sinai, and the cloud covered it six days: and the seventh day he called unto Moses out of the midst of the cloud. And the sight of the glory of the Lord was like devouring fire on the top of the mount in the eyes of the children of Israel.* This glory is what is referred to in Hebrew as Shekinah. His presence in the sea calmed the storm – Mark 4:35-41. This is the Immanuel Cloud of His Presence. This cloud sets everything in motion when present. It is my advice that until this cloud is present and felt, worship should not be stopped. I am not happy when we time worship sessions and hurriedly run through the service. The presence of this cloud allows people to yield to God when they are under the influence. Even in our present dispensation we now have software developed on the popular Cloud computing platform, such as iCloud, Google Cloud, etc. Cloud computing, according to the U.S National Institute of Science and Technology, is 'the delivery of computing as a service rather than a product, whereby shared resources, software, and information are provided to computers and other devices as a utility (like the electricity grid) over a network (typically the Internet). Clouds can be classified as public, private or hybrid.[1]'

From the above definition, since this phenomenon will help me to explain what the presence of the Lord is like, I will be borrowing the cloud computing concept to explain what happens when the Shekinah comes down. In cloud computing concept, we have three main classifications – Public, Private and Hybrid. Let us explore this further:

---

1. http://csrc.nist.gov/publications/nistpubs/800-145/SP800-145.pdf – correct as retrieved on the 2nd September 2014.

CHAPTER ELEVEN

■ **Congregational Immanuel Cloud of His Presence** – Psalms 42:4: *When I remember these things, I pour out my soul in me: for I had gone with the multitude, I went with them to the house of God, with the voice of joy and praise, with a multitude that kept holyday.* This is the cloud that is created often during a worship session, either in crusades, or in church service. Wherever the children of God gather in a multitude, a tabernacle is set in place. The environment becomes so misty that cameras could hardly capture clear images. When this cloud rests on people who are there present, they are seen praising God at the tops of their voices; some are weeping and repenting, others speaking in other tongues, and there is a feeling of a 'lifting' effect. Believers focus their mind on the things of God. There is joy in everyone's heart – Psalm 16:11. We see this phenomenon happening in Acts 2. It generates internal boldness to stand for the Lord, and to profess His good works. Revelations are heard, and this is the cloud that sets public prophecy in place – 1 Samuel 10:10-11. This is the time the Lord will usually pour His spirit upon all flesh, there present – Joel 2:28. Everyone within the vicinity would eventually know that God is indeed in the midst of His children. Praise, worship and prayer are instruments that can set this in place – but all present must do this in one accord and expectation, else He would not come down. This can also happen the moment an anointed servant of God mounts the pulpit, or he is in the same environment where people are gathered. Often, this cloud accompanies the Lord, when He wants to reveal Himself to those around and we would see a multiplication of miracles, signs and wonders. Moses wasn't ready to go further to chase the Canaanites out until the Lord promised to go with him – Exodus 23:20-21. It is a cloud that makes impossibilities become possible. Those who miss this cloud struggle in life more than those who are always having this encounter. This is the reason servants of God ensure they attend a program where another servant of God will be present and would minister. The presence of the cloud already set by other prophets enables Saul to prophesy as we saw earlier. A very significant purpose of the cloud is seen in Numbers 9:17: *And when the cloud was taken up from the tabernacle, then after that the children of Israel journeyed: and in the place where the cloud abode, there the children of Israel pitched their tents.* The cloud is for spiritual guardianship in all we do in life. The dew-like deep penetrating nature of the cloud allows the human soul to absorb His presence. The human soul acts as a spiritual absorbent once in contact with a spiritual environment. The soul acts as the female of the human spirit, while the mind acts as the male. The purpose of the human heart is to give life to the physical body. The human soul and mind cannot work to please God until the *Immanuel Cloud* is present, and had been sucked in by the soul. And once the human soul is saturated with the Immanuel Cloud, the human mind is then sucked into the soul, and then enveloped with the thought of God; this is when we become subtracted from the physical environment. This is a phenomenon explained by David in Psalms 42:7 as, *... all thy waves and thy billows are gone over me.* Once the mind is sucked into the soul and both are now carrying the presence of the Lord, a new being is formed, known as the 'human thought.' And with time, we would see the person behaving in manner dictated by the spiritual cloud.

The soul is a reservoir of spiritual clouds, and all it does from time to time is feed the human mind by sucking it in, in an enveloping or wrapping manner – similar to a magnetic coupling. This is why we should be careful where we spend our quiet times, because this is mostly when the soul is sucking in whichever spiritual cloud is presence. It is this understanding that makes the priests of old burn incense, so as to envelop the soul, and saturate it with the incantations fused into the burning incense, which would then produce the expected result and response in line with the coded spiritual message. Then, the person now goes home to his/her abode to set the individual cloud with the residual cloud he/she is carrying in his/her soul.

- **Individual Immanuel Cloud of His Presence** – Matthew 6:6: *But thou, when thou prayest, enter into thy closet, and when thou hast shut thy door, pray to thy Father which is in secret; and thy Father which seeth in secret shall reward thee openly.* This is the presence of the Lord which an individual can create through living a righteous life, a life of praise and worship, and a life of studying the word of God. Jesus says that when we begin to manifest His glory among men, as we teach them to observe His commands, this

Shekinah will be with us always – Matthew 28:20: ... *lo, I am with you always, even unto the end of the world.* This is often impossible until such a person had being in the environment described above, it is the residual cloud that his/her soul carries from the public encounter that now becomes the foundation for rekindling the Shekinah. But the effect is not as intense as the one created in the public Immanuel Cloud. As discussed earlier, the Praise, worship and prayer life of the individual is very important for this to happen. When this cloud is present; often seen as a spiritual halo or circle of lights, there is warmth created around the carrier. Even when everyone seems to be mourning, his/her presence immediately begins to radiate warm lights, transcending layers of spiritual depths, and bringing life to many. Such people look attractive without any artificial beauty enhancement. Their smile is charming, and they are very courageous. They naturally take the lead to confront evil. The purpose of this is to connect the individual to a resident altar – Mount Zion, which is a receptor of the Shekinah. This is why Saint Paul told them to treat the body as a temple. This is often hard; hence there is the need for a receptor – like the Ark of the Covenant.

Wherever an Altar is set in place for the Lord, His angels also takes charge, and the Shekinah circumscribes their abode. Where a servant of God abodes is also circumscribed with the Shekinah, because the presence of the Lord is present.

- **Relational Immanuel Cloud of His Presence** - Matthew 18:20:*For where two or three are gathered together in my name, there am I in the midst of them.* This can be created by two or three persons who had been filled with the cloud as discussed above, and now come together to agree in prayer, praise or worship of the Lord, often referred to as 'in one accord.' Whenever they gather, there is a spiritual multiplicity of the power inherent in their soul, and because the soul is already linked to God, and the mind had been sucked into the soul, these will generate a spiritual pulsating wave, which then forms a cloud. This spiritual cloud could be dense or light, depending on the intensity of their spiritual agreement or unity. Once any of them is distracted, the cloud shifts its tip, like a flame going down because of the reduction of fuel supply.

A clue relating to the presence of the cloud was given in

CHAPTER ELEVEN

Psalms 48:1-3: *Great is the Lord, and greatly to be praised in the city of our God, in* **the mountain of his holiness**. *Beautiful for situation, the joy of the whole earth, is mount Zion, on the sides of the north, the city of the great King. God is known in her palaces for a refuge.* The Receptor is here called the mountain of His holiness and is preferably known as Mount Zion. This is where the Ark rested in the time of David. The power that accompanies the cloud can be harnessed using a mantle. The receptor was Moses' rod. It was also Elijah's mantle. The body of Jesus was the receptor, as would be seen when the Holy Spirit descended on Him, etc. Our body can receive it if it is kept holy. When Obededom opened his house to house the Ark of God, because the ark was a receptor of the cloud of His presence, God practically inhabited his house, and he was favoured. Many have argued that there is no need for a physical altar because the Lord now dwells in the heart of men. This is well said - there is an altar in heaven, as shown in the book of Revelation 8:3. All we do on earth here is replicate the vision of what exists in heaven, to enable us to have a perfect walk with God. The house of worship should house an altar, a consecrated place dedicated to God. Just as the Shunammite woman kept a place of rest for Elisha, it is advisable to keep a sacred place where you would meet the Lord. Wherever you give to Him is where He will be waiting for you.

From time to time, the King of kings visits each kingdom upon the request of the king, which usually happens during Sunday services, crusades or periodically as fixed by the King of Kings.

❖

The Immanuel Cloud Receptor

❖

We talked briefly about the cloud receptor earlier on, but here I want us to dwell a little deeper. We read a story of how Jesus went into the temple to chase out those who had turned the house into a business centre - Matthew 21:12-14. Why would Jesus drive out people who turned the temple into a place for preaching the sermon of how to make wealth - money changers, selling of doves? How will you compare this character with modern day selling of holy water, holy oil, holy mantles, etc.? The dove was a spiritual symbol for the Holy Spirit, which they would have thought Christ should be happy with. But He threw them out even at that. He told them why He did what He did in verse 13: *It is written, My house shall be called the house of prayer…* In heaven, prayers are seen as the burning of incense, which would make the environment cloudy, telling us that prayers brings His presence also. Why would we pray there? It is the house of God. What makes it the house of God? The Ark is there. That Ark needed to be honoured as the receptor of God's presence. It is like the high table where we usually invite our special guest to sit. So when God comes in, He manifests from His altar.

Let's take a look at Haggai 1:5-11, and we will see that God was angry because He said His house was left in a state of devastation and unkempt, why everyone goes to their beautiful homes after coming to worship at the altar. Why was God so interested in the renovation of His house? One of the problems of many who claim to be Christians is that they don't see the importance of the house of God to their spiritual safety, security and provision. And they certainly don't know that this was where Jesus completed His last days of ministry - Luke 19:47: *And he taught daily in the temple*, which is why we also gather, believing that He will be present through His servants to teach us. Then we would offer songs of praise and worship, then prayers as His servant teaches us. John the Baptist taught his disciples how to pray, and this prompted the disciples of Jesus to ask to be taught by Jesus also. Who is a servant of God? He is one who hears the voice of Heaven. We have a confirmation in Revelation 15:1,3: *And I saw another sign in heaven, great and marvellous, seven angels ... And they sing the song of Moses the servant of God.* Was it coincidence that the Angels sang Moses' song? No! The song Moses sang was the song he heard from heaven. I have heard voices singing to me and when I sing the same songs, the environment becomes filled with the presence of God. We know that God would not pay attention to anything that does not catch His fancy. If it were not important to His course for His children - He won't be interested.

We would also see people crying before the Lord in His house because of the oppression of the enemy - asking why, repenting, pleading for His assistance - Judges 21:2: *And the people came to the house of God, and abode there till even before God, and lifted up their voices, and wept sore.*

Why then is there a House of God in our midst? If we look around, we see them all over the places.

CHAPTER ELEVEN

Why Come to the House of God? - Isaiah 56:7: *Even them will I bring to my holy mountain, and make them joyful in my house of prayer: their burnt offerings and their sacrifices shall be accepted upon mine altar; for mine house shall be called an house of prayer for all people.* From here we would see what the House of God is:

- A gathering place where God uses the testimonies to strengthen believers.
- A place where sacrifices, vows, and prayers are offered and accepted.
- A place to make a joyful noise unto the Lord.
- A place where people gather for a united purpose.
- It gives identity to people.
- A place to celebrate weddings.
- A home of refuge for all - in times of war, natural disasters etc.
- A place where the dead lie in state, etc.

These are what would quickly come to our mind when we think about the House of God and its purpose in our lives. But the House of God is more than these. As we dig further, we won't want to miss any gathering in this place, call the House of God.

The visitation of the King of kings in the Immanuel Cloud of His Presence is what we earlier called, 'Shekinah.' This is His presence, and we know what this means: healing, deliverance, prophecy, revelations, restoration, etc. Wherever the Shekinah is Present, we also know the chariot of the Lord is there. This is when the King of kings is on our midst.

The Shekinah is found in the Throne of God

Now let's see what happens in His throne - Revelation 5:11-12: *And I beheld, and I heard the voice of many angels round about the throne and the beasts and the elders: and the number of them was ten thousand times ten thousand, and thousands of thousands; Saying with a loud voice, Worthy is the Lamb that was slain to receive power, and riches, and wisdom, and strength, and honour, and glory, and blessing.* Matthew 25:31 also says - *When the Son of man shall come in his glory, and all the holy angels with him, then shall he sit upon the throne of his glory.* From these two Bible portions we just read, we would see that:

- If we want His presence we must create something similar to His throne in heaven. This is very important so that the Immanuel Cloud can rest among us.

- If the Kingdom of God must rest among us (Immanuel), there must be a place which would become a replica of His throne - where He would sit. This is the understanding that made David desire to build God a house - and God saw this understanding as a demonstration that shows that David was 'after his heart.'

- To create this throne, someone must be appointed to oversee the throne, and ensure it remains in the spiritual state that pleases God, Jesus drove thieves out of the Temple, before He started ministering. If there was an overseer there, there wouldn't be any need to drive out thieves first because the place would have been kept sanctified and consecrated. This person is the Servant of God in our midst.

CHAPTER ELEVEN

- For the presence of God to continually be in the midst of the Israelites while they were sojourning, God told Moses to make a Tabernacle (House of God) after a pattern as revealed in a vision to him - Exodus 25:9,20,21,22,40. In verse 22 we would see that God only spoke with Moses all this while, and until the pattern was set in place - there was no meeting between God and the people – Numbers 11:16-25. They started gathering to meet with the Lord after the Tabernacle was in place (Numbers 2). It was after the Tabernacle was instituted that God took from the spirit upon Moses and gave to the seventy elders who prophesied and worked with Moses.

- Honestly, this pattern referred to here, is not meant for personal use, it is for a congregation of worshippers - Revelation 5:11

- Any mistake in the pattern would make Him angry and will see human as taking Him for granted, as He did to Moses when he struck the rock instead of speaking to it.

- When David went to bring the Ark the first time, he hadn't built a house yet for the Ark - and we would see that the Ark didn't get to the City of David.

CHAPTER ELEVEN

The House of God is where God feeds His flocks. It is a home of restoration; of strength and renewal of our mind, to be in our right senses, after been battered by the confusions sets in place for His children. The Lord said concerning His flocks to His prophet – Ezekiel 34:14-15: *I will feed them in a good pasture, and upon the high mountains of Israel shall their fold be: there shall they lie in a good fold, and in a fat pasture shall they feed upon the mountains of Israel. I will feed my flock, and I will cause them to lie down, saith the Lord God.* This is what He does in His house.

The Shekinah is the spiritual atmosphere that makes things happen. It carries the glory of His presence - this is the ultimate event every servant God waits for: e.g., at the upper room, and in Solomon's temple. It was this glory that was missing when Jesus went into the temple that made Him to chase out the things that prevents God's glory from resting. The Shekinah cloud creates a heavenly traffic for angels to easily move to and fro - between heaven and earth (Genesis 28:12, John 1:51, Matthew 16:7). It is hard to bring down the Shekinah - the Cloud of His Presence outside the house of God. Why?

The Shekinah is brought down when the following happens:

- Multitudes praying and crying in need - this brings forth the compassion of God towards mankind - Matthew 15:31.

- High Praise of thanksgiving - from a multitude - Psalm 42:4, Revelation 5:11. We would see the Hosanna by the crowd as Jesus was carrying the Shekinah, and when the people wanted Him to stop the multitude from singing, His answer – Luke 19:40: *I tell you that, if these should hold their peace, the stones would immediately cry out,* tells us that the Shekinah is made manifest in the midst of high praise of worship and adoration onto the King of kings.

- But the house of God was not ready to receive the Shekinah as Jesus approached the temple, and His actions shows that the resting place have to be sanitised first - hence he wept over Jerusalem who killed the servants of God who would have help to sustain the Shekinah – Matthew 23:37.

The Shekinah rests in a Holy Place - hence their sin offerings and sacrifices were offered at the door of the tabernacle (the Brazen Altar) so that the Lord would see it first and forgive them before coming into the Mercy seat - He sees their repentance first, before approaching the mercy seat to sit down. The cloud does not pass through the ceiling; He comes through the main entrance door. This is why we must have repented before we can see Him attending to us. Sin causes the vexation of His Spirit. It is also not a good practice to lock the main entrance door to the church during service. Once the Lord takes His seat, we will see that more people start running into the service – because they heard Him calling from the altar. I have noticed that the moment I appear at the church auditorium, there is always a change in the atmosphere in the church. Sometimes it becomes cloudy. The Shekinah often follows the anointing bearer, the servant of God, into the worship arena. Now we will see the roles of everyone as they prepare to receive the Shekinah – the presence of the King of kings:

The Servant of God sets the House of God in place, in wait for the Shekinah - 2 Samuel 6:17, because he is the king hosting and reporting to the King of Kings. His main duty is to reveal the heart of God to the people at that material time. So He needs all the 'spiritual focus' to hear and see beyond the physical. He must be helped to get into that spiritual realm for this.

CHAPTER ELEVEN

The Role of the choir is to bring down the Shekinah - Revelation 5:11, 2 Chronicles 20:21-22.

The Role of the usher is to maintain order in His presence. There must be no noise and no loitering – Ecclesiastes 5:1: *Keep thy foot when thou goest to the house of God, and be more ready to hear, than to give the sacrifice of fools.* So that God would not be angry and start flogging people in the spirit, and chasing them out as Jesus did. When there is disorder, the Shekinah can depart. The presence of the Shekinah sets the pace for the service and the message from the altar. If there are people who will foment trouble, they should not be allowed to sit within where the Servant of God can see them, so that they don't distract him - any woman or girl who wears a revealing dress would be taken away from the sight of the servant of God, so that he can maintain spiritual focus.

The role of the sanctuary keepers is to make the place habitable for humans, God and His hosts of heaven - cleanliness is next to godliness.

On the congregation, we would see Leviticus 16:2-4, and Matthew 22:11. Everyone, including the women and young girls, must not be naked and not look too attractive and seductive, so that the angels can concentrate. The Lord walks in the midst of the churches (Revelation 1), and we won't want the Lord to be seeing our nudeness. We shouldn't forget that angels have emotions and sexual passions too - Genesis 6:2. The role of the congregation is to be attentive - Ecclesiastes 5:1-2. Ecclesiastes 8:3, Psalm 33:8.

All this said so far explains the pattern God wants to see in our service days. Until we set the pattern shown in place there will be no meeting with God - Exodus 25:22.

This is what Christ has done for all - Hebrew 9:11: *But Christ being come an high priest of good things to come, by a greater and more perfect tabernacle, not made with hands, that is to say, not of this building.*

When you have received Him as your Lord, you must prove to the world that you are in Christ through your character, attitude and way of life. Then He will present whoever represents Him to God and the Holy angels when the Shekinah is in place - Matthew 10:32, Luke 12:8. When this happens, there is a lifting in our souls, and we are connected with the realm there present - Psalm 42:7

CHAPTER ELEVEN

(this verse transformed my life, as it has done to great men of God in the past and now) to enable us to offer sacrifices of praise. The court of God is also set in place, and the enemy of His children is judged right away – with evidence of healing, breaking of ancestral curses, promotion, you name it. A well of opportunities is created therein.

CHAPTER TWELVE

ENLARGING THE KINGDOM

I have always likened the church to a commuter bus. The driver is the servant of God, the owner of the commuter service is Jesus and the passengers are the called, who heard the voice of Jesus and responded. However, not everyone inside the bus will get to the driver's final destination. As the passengers are dropped off, so more passengers will be joining from each of the bus stops until the driver gets to his terminal. His calling has ended, and God will raise another to continue where he stopped.

One day in February 2009, I sat down on a sofa, having just landed from a helicopter in Nembe flowstation, in a

CHAPTER TWELVE

shell oilfield. As I closed my eyes to take a rest, I saw an old man standing at my front. He had the air of a prophet, and he said to me – 'you have been given from so and so to so and so area to evangelise and take control over, and don't fail to catch the churches around,' and he disappeared. This startled me. I was barely five months into the ministry. I was young to many things relating to the running of a church, yet my spiritual understanding was attested to by people as a display of spiritual maturity. I had lots of challenges to cope with – lots of people didn't believe I had been 'called' by God. So much advice was popping in, even from those I had not asked. I was in a world of my own. Then on the 6th of February 2011, I received a word of wisdom while I was preparing for the Sunday service – 'The easiest and best way to success is Knowing people, Investing in them and Retaining their loyalty.' This finally became my 'KIR', the principle of reaching out to people. Still in 2011, in the month of August, on Sunday the 21st night in the month, I was in a dream, and I arrived in a dream town called Eberthy. I saw myself and my wife trying to unite the people and bridging the gap between the rich and the poor. After a long discussion of our intention, and making

CHAPTER TWELVE

the rich to help the poor in their midst, to our amazement, the rich were really very glad and ready to assist and they offered to train the daughter of one of the poor amongst them, but the poor man refused out of pride. We tried to persuade him to receive the assistance; he only apologised and then went away with his daughter. I woke up from the sleep and pondered over the meaning of the dream. And I received a word of knowledge – that most poor people really hate the rich as if they are the reason for their situation. Then my mind went to the Bible – Jesus had performed so many miracles for the poor, they had eaten bread and fish from His hand, but soon they were amongst those who said He should be crucified. I learnt also that the best way to help the poor is to change their mind-set, and to make them see the brighter side of life. This way, they will be useful for the work of the Kingdom, and then will appreciate the help of God. One other insight that came to my mind, which I see to be a reflection of the dream, is that God represents the rich, my wife and I bearing the gospel of unity represents what Jesus Christ came to do for mankind, and the poor represent humans. Christ came so that we can be united with the Father, so as to merit

His help, but often, though we recognise this fact, we are not willing to accept the Lord. Enlarging the Kingdom has to do with accepting the arm of the Kingdom. God is happy with soul winners. To Him they are winners always. Nobody celebrate failure; this I know from experience. This is why when we are failing, we should find ways to ensure we rise again, and one of such ways is by standing to defend the Kingdom of God by yielding to serve.

One of the problem servants of God face is the loyalty of those working with them, to the vision they are bearing for the Lord. For instance, Elijah running to God in 1 Kings 19 wouldn't have been necessary if the seven thousand who were in the land had supported him. The solution God proffered at the end shows that his problem was the lack of workers driving the vision with him. Let's see the conversation that transpired between God and Elijah:

- **Elijah's complain:** *And he said, I have been very jealous for the Lord God of hosts: because the children of Israel have forsaken thy covenant, thrown down thine altars, and slain thy prophets with the sword; and I, even I only, am left; and they seek my life, to take it away*

CHAPTER TWELVE

■ **God's response and solution:** *And the Lord said unto him, Go, return on thy way to the wilderness of Damascus: and when thou comest, anoint Hazael to be king over Syria: And Jehu the son of Nimshi shalt thou anoint to be king over Israel: and Elisha the son of Shaphat of Abelmeholah shalt thou anoint to be prophet in thy room. And it shall come to pass, that him that escapeth the sword of Hazael shall Jehu slay:and him that escapeth from the sword of Jehu shall Elisha slay. Yet I have left me seven thousand in Israel, all the knees which have not bowed unto Baal, and every mouth which hath not kissed him.*

After his encounter with God, he had the plan to:

- Anoint Hazel to be king over Syria

- Anoint Jehu to be king over Israel

- Anoint Elisha as a prophet after his stead – meaning the Lord was already satisfied with his work, and making him to know that he would soon be taken to heaven. A meritorious reward indeed!

- Recognise that there are yet seven thousand in Israel who are holy unto Him, which, if Elijah so wanted, can still appoint into various positions of trust.

CHAPTER TWELVE

Many of us are not willing to win souls unto God and add to His Kingdom. The more we preach the gospel, the more the Lord reveals Himself to us – Romans 1:17: *For therein is the righteousness of God revealed from faith to faith: as it is written, The just shall live by faith.* The strength of a kingdom is measured by the number of faithful adherents. We often forget where we were coming from, and when we see others experiencing the life we used to experience before, instead of offering them the message of Christ, we end up complaining and unnecessarily condemning them as people who have been dogmatised. This is not how a kingdom is enlarged. When I remember the story of the Ethiopian eunuch who was baptised by Philip – and knowing that he was reading the book of Isaiah before he encountered Philip, told of the love of the Ethiopians for the God of Israel. Now the eunuch was not just an ordinary person but a wealthy man in charge of the treasures of the Kingdom, yet undermining his status, still considered it a necessity to worship God in Jerusalem, when he now encountered Jesus – Acts 8:27: … *a man of Ethiopia, an eunuch of great authority under Candace queen of the Ethiopians, who had the charge of all her treasure, and had come to*

CHAPTER TWELVE

Jerusalem for to worship. And we shouldn't forget that the Ethiopians were Moses' in-law because his wife Zipporah was an Ethiopian woman – Numbers 12:1. It shows that the life Moses lived in Ethiopia was worth emulating, hence his in-law would even lead his family to him in the wilderness and even offer to give him leadership advice. Let's see what God says in Deuteronomy 24:18: *But thou shalt remember that thou wast a bondman in Egypt, and the Lord thy God redeemed thee thence: therefore I command thee to do this thing.* We should never forget where we are coming from in a hurry. Let's use our testimonies of the Lord's deliverance to help others, and bring them to the fountain of living waters so that they too can have a drink of life and live. The Kingdom of God is enlarged through the working evidence of the move of God, as Paul will confirm in Romans 15:19: *Through mighty signs and wonders, by the power of the Spirit of God...* It is a necessity that we must work to earn the reward from God by contributing our own quota to spread the gospel of Christ, and His salvation unto the end of the world so that Christ would be glorified in our lives – spiritually, as we pray, and physically through the works of evangelism in deeds and welfare, and financial support. The kingdom must break fallow ground; this is why Jesus said we must put our hands to the plough. We have heard of assistant pastors leaving with members of the congregation that the founder of the church had laboured to grow – this is not how to enlarge the Kingdom. Saint Paul explained that such act is building on another's foundation – Romans 15:20: *Yea, so have I strived to preach the gospel, not where Christ was named, lest I should build upon another man's foundation.* It is a thing of joy to watch the seed you have sown grow into a giant tree that begins to bear fruit. However, the health and size of the fruit is dependent on how well the tree was tendered by the owner and other factors such as weather, nutrients in the soil and species of the seed. If we want to grow a healthy kingdom, we first of all know whom the Kingdom is targeted at, which represents the seed we are sowing. Paul was sent to the Gentiles, and God worked miracles through him to convince the gentiles of the working power of Jesus Christ, and as a proof of what they stand to gain if they yield to follow the gospel – Romans 15:16: *That I should be the minister of Jesus Christ to the Gentiles, ministering the gospel of God, that the offering up of the Gentiles might be acceptable, being sanctified by the Holy Ghost.*

CHAPTER TWELVE

The foundational doctrine is very important. This represents the land where the seed will be sown. If the land is fertile and well positioned to receive rains in due season, then the seed will germinate to yield increase. The rains represent the favour of God. We have had many farmers having wonderful farms with good crops yet inaccessible due to bad roads, and as such the farmer ends up as a poor peasant farmer. Even with sound doctrine, accessibility is key – people must be able to access the doctrine through evangelism and mass publicity. Thanks to God for increasing IT awareness. The Bible says of Jesus in Matthew 4:13: *And leaving Nazareth, he came and dwelt in Capernaum, which is upon the sea coast, in the borders of Zabulon and Nephthalim.* Jesus came to the sea coast, in the borders, which are accessible to a large number of people coming to trade, and as such He had the traffic to minister to, hence His message of repentance drew large crowd and interest; he recruited a handful of disciples and set out, and the result is - *And there followed him great multitudes of people from Galilee, and from Decapolis, and from Jerusalem, and from Judaea, and from beyond Jordan –* Matthew 4:25.

CHAPTER TWELVE

Again, very few farmers have what it takes to keep their customers. So also is the ministry; many first timers find it difficult to come back after the first encounter. Many factors may be responsible for this – it could be the doctrine is not suited for them; they haven't made up their mind yet to accept the doctrine, distance from their residence, attitude of the ushers or security at the gate, etc. but our overall concern is preparing the fruits for the harvest of the Lord when He shall send His angels to gather all abiding fruits into His everlasting kingdom.

Every servant of God is endowed with a doctrine to enable him lead some set of people to God. Often times, this doctrine is watered down to bring in some other sets of people who have the finance or social image that will make the servant of God become popular, and with time, the servant of God will stop consulting God, but will be consulting men who will now give him advice that would lead the new kingdom astray, and there God will look for another to do His work, while these now self-acclaimed servants of God will pursue the mission of deceit and bringing glory to the Kingdom of the devil. They are deceived that they are still with God as a result of the miracles that happen in their gatherings – they forget so easily that the Jews in Jesus' days made reference to Beelzebub as the agent behind Jesus' healing, implying that some miracles did happen in the past, done by the priests of Beelzebub, and that there was a Simon Magus, in Acts 8:9-24, who was also performing miracles in the Bible with the power of the devil.

Jabez prayed for enlargement, so also Solomon. Prosperity enlarges the Kingdom no doubt, and this is quite possible when the people follow the ways of the Lord. As the good tidings of the king are spread abroad from how many people are delivered from all manner of problems, people submit to the Kingdom. But often, when they come in, they would want to change the doctrine to suit their life styles. Crusades are also avenues to enlarge the Kingdom. As the Kingdom grows and more branches are set up around the world, the king visits his other kingdoms for progress reports and the citizens honour their king because of the good tidings and the peace they are experiencing. And this has also made many of the citizens disregard the headship of Christ over them. They would believe their king to a fault, and would pay lip service to the message of holiness and righteousness. With time, Jesus would have no man to use in the whole of the vineyard. Other nations submit unto him the more. Governments want him to bless them.

In the discussion session that follows, we will be discussing how we can enlarge the Kingdom, with power and wisdom from the Lord, and to ensure that the Kingdom will really grow to the glory of His holy name. These people who make the Kingdom are what I refer to as Extreme Christians.

Extreme Christianity

When we do the extraordinary, we grow spiritually and our glory is a clear testimony that helps to enlarge the Kingdom.

How can we take Christianity to the extreme? The problem in the world today demands that believers should employ all the powers within the Kingdom that Christ has given us (Matthew 28:18) to proffer solutions that can restore this world, rather than using worldly wisdom to lead people away from God.

CHAPTER TWELVE

This starts with knowing who we are and what we stand for. We will be taking learning from Psalm 8:5-6: *For thou hast made him a little lower than the angels, and hast crowned him with glory and honour. Thou madest him to have dominion over the works of thy hands; thou hast put all things under his feet.* Why are we a little lower than angels? It is because we have the human corruptible body – but when we are in the spirit, and fully in the power and wisdom of Christ, angels will minister unto us as heirs of the Kingdom – in regard and respect. Now the real beauty of what God expects from us is reflected in verse 6 above – we are given the authority to rule over the creations of God, and the works of the devil are under our feet. Again, in Psalm 82:6: *I have said, Ye are gods; and all of you are children of the most High.* Any who were children of the old covenant were referred to as gods, not to talk of those operating with the rights imputed on Christ – John 10:34. Now gods have adherents who serve them for protection and provision. If we, as heirs of a heavenly kingdom, truly operate with the rights of sonship in Christ, then those in the synagogue of Satan have no choice but to come over to the holy mountain of God to bow down before us, to lead them to Christ –Revelation 3:9: *Behold, I will make them of the synagogue of Satan, … to come and worship before thy feet, and to know that I have loved thee.* Then the testimonies of the works of God in the Kingdom will bring the much anticipated increase – Zachariah 8:23: *Thus saith the Lord of hosts; In those days it shall come to pass, that ten men shall take hold out of all languages of the nations, even shall take hold of the skirt of him that is a Jew, saying, We will go with you: for we have heard that God is with you.* Ten is to One (10:1) is the ratio for a Jewish man who did the will of God under the old testimony. Those of us in the new testimony ought to have more people holding our garments and begging us to lead them to Christ – the Acts of the Apostles point to this fact – in a single event, about three thousand were added to the church. Originally they were 120. So if we divide through, this ratio would be 3000 to 120, or succinctly put, 25 to 1 (25:1). This is a better ratio, which shows that the new testimony has greater power to enlarge the Kingdom than the old testimony. There the power of the Lord was held up in an Ark; here the Power of God is manifested in our speech. So we have greater power now to do exploits for the Kingdom.

We are therefore settling for nothing less until we renounce the works of the enemy in our midst, even as Moses stood for the righteousness of God and forsook his Egyptian royal treat to suffer for Christ - *By faith Moses, when he was come to years, refused to be called the son of Pharaoh's daughter; Choosing rather to suffer affliction with the people of God, than to enjoy the pleasures of sin for a season; Esteeming the reproach of Christ greater riches than the treasures in Egypt: for he had respect unto the recompence of the reward* – Hebrews 11:24-26.

Yet the Bible says that we are greater than all these people for whom Moses sacrificed his life. Our body is a temple and there is an altar of God in us, meaning that we are sacred because of the altar of God we bear. Definitely people are going to worship us as a result of this, but we must always point them to God. People worship great people, meaning we can be great when we do all we do God's way.

For us to exercise our faith to the extent that we would win more adherents to the Kingdom, as the strength of a kingdom is measured by the number of people and nations who show allegiance, each one of us in the Kingdom must desire gifts of kingdom establishment, implying that we must live the culture and life of heaven here on earth. This was said of Daniel - Daniel 5:12,14: *...an excellent spirit, and knowledge, and understanding, interpreting of dreams, and shewing of hard sentences, and dissolving of doubts, and light and understanding and excellent wisdom were found in the same Daniel* (re-arranged to suit context). We could see Daniel's reward in Daniel 6:3: *Then this Daniel was preferred above the presidents and princes, because an excellent spirit was in him; and the king thought to set him over the whole realm.* Aren't we greater than Daniel? Yes of course, because Jesus tells us so - Luke 7:28: *For I say unto you, Among those that are born of women there is not a greater prophet than John the Baptist: but he that is least in the Kingdom of God is greater than he.* Even if we, as heirs of the Kingdom, can do what Daniel did, we would not be intimidated by the politics and economies of this world – Daniel was preferred, we just read. Why are we not preferred in our work places? Why are we hiding the light of God upon our forehead under the bushel? Ignorance may just be the right answer – and all we do is to seek miracles rather than go after the power and wisdom the Kingdom has to offer for anyone who will diligently seek it. Why are we living a life of fear and still afraid even of animals? We have fasted, we have prayed, we have cried, yet it seems as if we are not getting any results.

Christianity is about the exercising of power, and the Bible tells us so - Matthew 28:18, Acts 1:8. Have we adopted another doctrine aside from what the Bible preaches and defends? Machines have rated and maximum powers. The use of power depends on the demand load. In reality anything that gives comfort requires extra power - for example, our air conditioner requires twice its rated power to start and so does the refrigerator and television set. We also see that water pumps, fluorescent lights, halogen lights etc demand high power to operate. These phenomena explain why if we want extra success in life we have to do the extraordinary for the Kingdom – winning and keeping souls. What Jesus did while on earth could therefore be seen as 'Rated Power'– this is what gave the believers in Antioch the name 'Christians.' But Jesus wants us to do greater things with the greater power he has acquired for us, as explained in Matthew 28:18: ... *All power is given unto me in heaven and in earth.* These greater things (John 14:12) are possible when we take Christianity to the extreme, then we would be operating at 'Maximum Power'. But the condition to achieving this is spelt out here - *If ye shall ask any thing in my name, I will do it. If ye love me, keep my commandments* - John 14:14,15.

I hear preachers keep on telling people what God is going to do for them without telling the people what they have to do for God. Now, let's see Jesus' declaration in Matthew 11:12 *…And from the days of John the Baptist until now the Kingdom of heaven suffereth violence, and the violent take it by force.* I need not remind us that 'violent people' are extremists, utilizing the power in them for the glory of the Kingdom, not in war and religious fighting, but in the application of power and wisdom over the Kingdom of darkness. It is also not in ruthless acquisition of wealth as many preachers have connived with the devil to preach the same message the devil preached to Jesus in Matthew 4:8-9: *Again, the devil taketh him up into an exceeding high mountain, and sheweth him all the Kingdoms of the world, and the glory of them; And saith unto him, All these things will I give thee, if thou wilt fall down and worship me.* This power

CHAPTER TWELVE

and wisdom of God is what we need to reach out to many, so that they would repent and follow the Lord; leaving all they have ever treasured on earth – Matthew 19:21: *Jesus said unto him, If thou wilt be perfect, go and sell that thou hast, and give to the poor, and thou shalt have treasure in heaven: and come and follow me.* This implies here that nothing should be more important than the gospel of Christ. Let's see what Christ expects – Acts 18:9-10: *Then spake the Lord to Paul in the night by a vision, Be not afraid, but speak, and hold not thy peace: For I am with thee, and no man shall set on thee to hurt thee: for I have much people in this city.* What was Paul expected to speak about? Here is it in verse 11: *And he continued there a year and six months, teaching the word of God among them.* It is the word of the Lord that purifies and edifies the body and soul.

If we look closely into Matthew 11:11, we see that Jesus meant that before John the Baptist none was actually great – Not even King Solomon. Aren't we luck to have a better testimony of greatness right before us? Why then travel with the devil on the sea of illusion by joining him to derail the world? Jesus said that the elected could also be deceived (Matthew 24:24). Is this not happening now?

CHAPTER TWELVE

Is the Kingdom enlarging or shrinking? Have we not fallen asleep so that the tares are now more than the wheat (Matthew 13:25)?

Let's take a look at what those we are greater than did in the name of the Lord, judging from what Jesus said in Matthew 11:11:

1. Noah built an ark in the midst of opposition and a morally decaying society.

2. Abraham had an army in his house that joined him to rescue his nephew successfully, showing that he wasn't intimidated. He met obstacles no doubt, but he never gave up; he won the battle and came back to appreciate God.

3. Moses became a leader at age eighty. He spent eighty years in idolatry homes – forty in Egypt, much of the time in the house of Pharaoh with all its magical practices, and another forty in his in-law's home, yet he wasn't an idol worshipper, making Zipporah, his wife circumcise his son on their way to Egypt, showing that he indeed preached about his God while in the in-laws' house. We may have read how while in Egypt he defended the Jew against the

Egyptian. He led the Israelites out of the dungeon after meeting with God. We have all met with God and given our lives to His service – where is the evidence of our work in His vineyard?

4. Elijah and Elisha did great works. Elijah wiped out idolatry by challenging the powers that be in the land. He dared the king and his queen against all odds. Elisha continued in his stead and the Lord wrought wonders and miracles through him. Where is our faith if all we do is to fill the altar of the Lord with tears of needs and wants? Is it that Elijah and Elisha never had needs and wants? To them, it was about the Kingdom of God. It was about purity and sanctity. Elijah said – 1 Kings 19:10: ... *I have been very jealous for the Lord God of hosts: for the children of Israel have forsaken thy covenant, thrown down thine altars, and slain thy prophets with the sword...* Is this our desire for the Lord too? We also may have read how Isaiah even went abroad naked in the land of Egypt and Ethiopia without fearing being killed for three years, to proclaim the word of the Lord to these nations.

We are greater than these people. We have all come unto Mount Zion and received deliverance from the

CHAPTER TWELVE

oppression of the Kingdom of darkness - what are we doing for the Lord? Are we still begging God to save us when He has done it at Golgotha? Romans 13:11-14 says - *And that, knowing the time, that now it is high time to awake out of sleep: for now is our salvation nearer than when we believed. The night is far spent, the day is at hand: let us therefore cast off the works of darkness, and let us put on the armour of light. Let us walk honestly, as in the day; not in rioting and drunkenness, not in chambering and wantonness, not in strife and envying. But put ye on the Lord Jesus Christ, and make not provision for the flesh, to fulfil the lusts thereof.*

The night is far spent. We have wasted precious time on all-night prayers, rather than the physical work of reaching out to the people with the word of repentance. We must be honest with the truth. Our desire for material wealth must give way now to the truth. Coining the Bible verses to suit our message of wealth-seeking must change now for salvation. Severally many have had encounters that took them into heaven, and their pathetic story of souls languishing in torment of hell should awaken everyone call of God. Saint Paul once cried out in bitterness - *How shall we escape, if we neglect so great salvation* (Hebrews 2:3). We have the opportunity, now that it is day, to save souls for the Kingdom. Let's leave the pursuit of material wealth behind now – Mark 8:36,37: *For what shall it profit a man, if he shall gain the whole world, and lose his own soul? Or what shall a man give in exchange for his soul.* We have the power to cause a change all around our world – let's go for the change. The era of righteousness and holiness is here – let's go for it and stand to defend the Kingdom against devourers.

After the apostles encountered power in Acts 2, things began to change in their lives - *And by the hands of the apostles were many signs and wonders wrought among the people* (Acts 5:12). And the result in verse 14 showed that - *…believers were the more added to the Lord, multitudes both of men and women.* Below is some of the evidence of what the working power of Christ can do to enlarge the Kingdom.

- Philip vanished and appeared in Azotus after converting the Eunuch - Acts 8:39-40: *And when they were come up out of the water, the Spirit of the Lord caught away Philip, that the eunuch saw him no more: and he went on his way rejoicing. But Philip was found at Azotus: and passing through he preached in all the cities, till he came to Caesarea.* By the hand of Philip, the Lord brought the Church into Africa.

- The people trust Peter's shadow to heal the sick - Acts 5:15: *Insomuch that they brought forth the sick into the streets, and laid them on beds and couches, that at the least the shadow of Peter passing by might overshadow some of them.*

We can have all these and even more, if we truly do the work of the Lord; if we truly hold Him in high esteem. I encourage you to seek this power and be free, rather than running from one prophet to another. The Lord said to me some time ago – stay where you are and I will take you through a training that will last for six years. I am really better now. The answer to your predicament is not in the hands of any man – God has the answer. Many of us wait until our enemies have make a mockery of us that we would almost want to end of lives before coming to God. This was the case of Hannah – 1 Samuel 1:6,10: *And her adversary also provoked her sore, for to make her fret, because the Lord had shut up her womb. And she was in bitterness of soul, and prayed unto the Lord, and wept sore. And she vowed a vow…* My question had been, why didn't Hannah seek the face of the Lord on time? Where did she finally get the wisdom that she had not applied from? I guess it was her ignorance of the ways of the Lord that kept her barren for so long until she knew what to do. He uses men to connect you to Him, and thereafter takes charge over you. But He also expects you to function in one of His kingdoms on earth, which He has entrusted into the hands of His servants, so that you have a home and a family, with whom you can grow in the things of the Lord. When you receive the power of the Lord, you will operate as Jesus and would be able to do the following:

1. Read other people's thoughts so you can never be deceived –This is a character of the Lord, and He has also allowed us to have same Psalm 139:2: *O Lord, thou hast searched me, and known me. Thou knowest my downsitting and mine uprising, thou understandest my thought afar off.* You will know whoever is talking with you – their intentions will be laid down for you to see, and you can predict their actions with precision. The Lord did it also in Matthew 12:25: *And Jesus knew their thoughts…* This gift is more than wealth you can seek. Get this first, and I bet you men will come to worship at your feet, for you to lead them to Christ, and they would

be willing to bring their wealth to you. Hence the Lord said in Matthew 6:33: *But seek ye first the Kingdom of God, and his righteousness; and all these things shall be added unto you.* I read once an article on the Internet that claimed that scientists had developed a machine that can read people's thoughts. If this is the case, why can't we use the free gift available for us when we truly submit to Christ? With this gift, you can win more people to Christ and the Kingdom will be enlarged, as they would have no doubt over the working power of God in your life.

2. See into your tomorrow: This is a special gift that is also related to what we just talked about above. Jesus knew when He was going to die, who would betray Him and Peter's denial of Him.

3. Know the minutes of a meeting without being there physically.

4. Unpredictable because you can seal your thoughts from being accessed by people – you can be judged by no man.

5. You can come into an environment and hear all that was said there without being there physically.

CHAPTER TWELVE

6. Help you to project your prayers with high precision as you watch it ascend towards heaven against every barrier.

7. Get whatever you want, as you would go ahead to put things in order spiritually while watching it happen physically.

8. Students with the gift of the Lord can predict examination questions correctly. Because you can read the thoughts of the lecturer as he is teaching and also receive the questions as you study the night before the exam, except that the questions have not being set. In such cases what I do is to get into a calm environment 30 minutes before the exam. And all I would do is to flip through the lecture material.

9. Pass employment interview the night before the interview in your dreams. Many of us have had dreams where we attended an interview. If you know how to use the power in you, it would be as you saw it.

The book of Joel 2:28 is for you to know what you may have been missing: *And it shall come to pass afterward, that I will pour out my spirit upon all flesh; and your sons*

CHAPTER TWELVE

and your daughters shall prophesy, your old men shall dream dreams, your young men shall see visions.

All we have said points to the fact that our exploits will make many envy the gift in our lives and then when they yield to the gospel, we will have an enlarged kingdom where the Lord will continually perform wonders, rather than the emptiness we are having today in our churches so that even many pastors now run down to witch doctors and Buddhist temples for powers.

Desiring the power in the Kingdom

There are keys to receiving power, for instance:

- Moses stayed on the mountain summit and after 40 days he came back with authority.
- Elijah went to Mount Horeb and came back with power.
- Elisha followed Elijah closely in what I will consider the most risky endeavour, and he was endowed with power.
- Jesus went into 40 days' fasting and the power was there to heal the sick.

CHAPTER TWELVE

■ The disciples stayed in the upper room in obedience to the Lord's command and power came down to meet them.

Power is about desire. We have desired material things rather than the spiritual. The Bible says that bodily exercise profits little and that we should seek godliness - 1 Timothy 4:8. Godliness is endeavouring to be as perfect as God (Matthew 5:48). The more we become spiritually conscious, the more our breakthrough will come, because we will be able to overcome barriers to the physical, as we now have to deal with these in our spiritual form. Don't forget that spirits have no physical boundaries. Hence the Bible says that we should set our hearts on things above - Colossians 3:1. What are these things from above? Philippians 4:8 tells us what they are: ... *whatsoever things are true, whatsoever things are honest, whatsoever things are just, whatsoever things are pure, whatsoever things are lovely, whatsoever things are of good report; if there be any virtue, and if there be any praise, think on these things.* The last qualification says, ***if there be any virtue, and if there be any praise.*** Virtue means righteousness, and Praise is the dwelling place of God. So we are brought back to the first point, which is to seek the Kingdom of God and His righteousness first.

Explaining further, 2 Peter 1:5-8 has this secret to reveal: *And beside this, giving all diligence, add to your faith virtue; and to virtue knowledge; And to knowledge temperance; and to temperance patience; and to patience godliness; And to godliness brotherly kindness; and to brotherly kindness charity. For if these things be in you, and abound, they make you that ye shall neither be barren nor unfruitful in the knowledge of our Lord Jesus Christ.*

Then the spirit will come to make us perfect. So, from above we have all it takes now to seek the Lord perfectly: *Praise, Diligence, Faith, Virtue, Knowledge, Temperament, Patience, Godliness, Brotherly kindness, and Charity.*

Who is God looking for? A clue is given in Psalm 15. God wants those who have the attributes of selfless service unto Him.

How can we merit Paradise? It starts from our lives here on earth. This is why God calls and choses people to lead people to Him so that His Kingdom will manifest here on earth, having people who would be able to please Him. This thus far will now enable us to understand what it takes to obtain Kingdom membership.

Kingdom membership

There will be no increase if there is no established way to account for the souls that are attracted and won daily into the Kingdom. This is what gives rise to kingdom citizenry, or what we usually call church membership. As we go further, we will see the importance of being a member, what is required to be a member, and how to sustain our membership in the midst of tribulations.

What is God's ultimate concern for you and me? Let's see it this way:

1. God is willing to help us so that we can live a wonderful life without sorrow, and also make heaven - Isaiah 9:2-3: *The people that walked in darkness have seen a great light: they that dwell in the land of the shadow of death, upon them hath the light shined. Thou hast multiplied the nation, and not increased the joy: they joy*

before thee according to the joy in harvest, and as men rejoice when they divide the spoil. Verse 3 says that our joy is possible when there is a harvest and how many battles we have won. It is expected of us that we must then labour to sow and overcome temptations.

2. God's earnest desire is that we become workers in His vineyard - Matthew 9:37.

The Church is a gathering of believers for the purpose of the harvest and preservation of souls for onward ascension to heaven - Ephesians 5:27: *That he might present it to himself a glorious church, not having spot, or wrinkle, or any such thing; but that it should be holy and without blemish.*

The Old and New Testament Church – Their Confluence and their Divide

The Old Testament church started with the purpose espoused in Exodus 3:7-12, and it can be said to be a gathering of God's children for the purpose of liberation from the shackles of slavery and disinheritance. Jesus started the New Testament church by telling the disciples to gather in the upper room for a blessing of the Holy Ghost. Prior to this time He had prayed for them to receive the glory of the Lord - John 17:10:*And all mine are thine, and thine are mine; and I am glorified in them.* From here we would see that we could not receive this glory by our own merit, but by imputation. Jesus received a direct glory from God, but we are qualified through Jesus to receive this glory, hence our glory is imputed glory as a result of our work with Jesus. Who God sees is Jesus in the glorified form, while we are covered within this glory upon Jesus. So the difference between the two is that while one was centred on physical well-being, which became the centre message, the other is centred on our spiritual well-being. Saint Paul explained this in Ephesians 6:12:*For we wrestle not against flesh and blood, but against principalities, against powers, against the rulers of the darkness of this world, against spiritual wickedness in high places.* So, while the Israelites fought physical wars, we fight spiritual wars. This was why when Jesus came, the Jews didn't believe in His Messianic mission, because they expected a man of physical war like David. Jesus' claim of the pattern of the New

Testament church is seen in John 18:36: *Jesus answered, My kingdom is not of this world: if my kingdom were of this world, then would my servants fight, that I should not be delivered to the Jews: but now is my kingdom not from hence.* With this statement from Christ, the purpose of the New Testament church is defined as the gathering of God's children unto an eternal kingdom. This being the case, the onus is on the king in the earthly kingdom, under the service and employment of the King of kings, to teach adherents the culture of heaven. It is important to note that people live with the predominant thoughts in their lives. Now the idea of an everlasting rest in God's kingdom in heaven is the reason for the Church. During the Old Testament era, there was no plan to start admitting souls into heaven yet, but all departed souls were kept in the bosom of people who walked with God. The coming of Jesus disbanded such realm of existence, hence all departed souls will either transcend into the realm of light or that of darkness. So it is a must-do duty for all of us to ensure we emphasise the salvation prosperity of the soul more than material prosperity. But the reverse has always been the case, and many are attracted to God with the mind-set of the Old Testament church. Then the Ark of the testimony was physical, but now the Ark of the testimony lies in our hearts – as a result of our belief in eternal redemption in the blood of Jesus Christ. Even as the Israelites carried the Ark wherever they were, so also the consciousness of the life we live in Christ must follow us wherever we are. While the Israelites fought physical wars, we fight spiritual wars. The reason why they couldn't fight spiritually then was simply because the power to overcome the devil hadn't been released until the death of Jesus Christ.

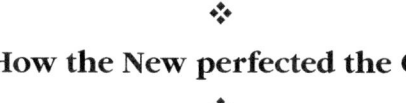

How the New perfected the Old

In line with what I said earlier, the New Testament church is for the perfection of souls so that they could ascend unto heaven. In the Old Testament church, the dead faithful were only gathered to Abraham's bosom. King David, after attaining a height of spiritual awareness, wanted to be glorified when he died. The time for that wasn't at hand; but he prayed a prayer – Psalm 16:10:*For thou wilt not leave my soul in hell; neither wilt thou suffer thine Holy One to see corruption.* He went further to ask of the Lord in verse 11 of this same Psalm - *Thou wilt shew me the path of life: in thy presence is fulness of joy; at thy right hand there are pleasures for evermore.* First he wished to be glorified at the end of the day, to walk the path of life (John 6:35, 8:12), and to be in the presence of the Lord. He saw the right hand of God, full with everlasting pleasures – Matthew 26:64, Ephesians 1:20, Colossians 3:1). Jesus referred to this expectation of the dead faithful, who slept in the Lord, when He said – John 8:56: *Your father Abraham rejoiced to see my day: and he saw it, and was glad.* Again He reiterated this fact when He encouraged His disciples to toe this path of eternal life when He also said –Matthew 13:16,17: *But blessed are your eyes, for they see: and your ears, for they hear. For verily I say unto you, That many prophets and righteous men have desired to see those things which ye see, and have not seen them; and to hear those things which ye hear, and have not heard them.*

The New Testament church perfected the Old by taking away laws and human wisdom that offend God, and teaching whoever wishes to hear those things which please God, which if practised would pave the way for the departing soul to be imputed with the glory upon

Jesus. However, this purpose was misinterpreted by the majority of the early New Testament Kingdom adherents, as they sold all they had, having being tired of the imperial reigns of hardship from both Judean Herod and the Roman empire, and gross misinterpretation of the purpose of God in the Torah, leading to deprivation and dispossession. Saint John finally advised that the New Testament church is a kingdom of glorification in body and soul –3 John 1:2: *Beloved, I wish above all things that thou mayest prosper and be in health, even as thy soul prospereth.* He maintained that the reason he expects this to happen to them is because they are already walking the path of light, and as such this ought to have been imputed also as a reward and a manifestation of the glory they have in Jesus – 3 John 1:3-4: *For I rejoiced greatly, when the brethren came and testified of the truth that is in thee, even as thou walkest in the truth. I have no greater joy than to hear that my children walk in truth.* After this, we would see that in the preceding verses, he explained their acts, which resulted to their walking in truth, as the act of charity to the brethren and the church. So the New Testament Church (NTC) equals the Old Testament Church (OTC) minus the things that offend God, such as the multitude of the things that offend God, including the Levitical laws and ordinances (TToG) plus the wisdom of God (WoG) plus the Power of God (PoG) plus the imputed glorification of the soul after death (IGS).

Hence,

NTC = OTC − TToG + WoG + PoG + IGoS

Where, as stated above:

NTC = New Testament Church

OTC = Old Testament Church

TToG = Things That offend God

WoG = Wisdom of God

PoG = Power of God

IGoS = Imputed Glorification of Souls

The Wisdom of God (WoG) and the Power of God (PoG) are both present in the Holy Spirit (HS). Hence we would say that:

HS = WoG + PoG

CHAPTER TWELVE

Therefore:

NTC = OTC − TToG + HS + IGoS

Instances of TToG were explained in Jesus' statements in Luke 11:42-52. For example, in verse 42 &52 He says: *But woe unto you, Pharisees! for ye tithe mint and rue and all manner of herbs, and pass over judgment and the love of God: these ought ye to have done, and not to leave the other undone. Woe unto you, lawyers! for ye have taken away the key of knowledge: ye entered not in yourselves, and them that were entering in ye hindered.* So the real problem with the OTC was that it lacked an important requirement for the glorification of souls - *the key of knowledge*. If we now say that the OTC approximates to TToG, judging from the statement of Jesus in John 8:9-10: *All that ever came before me are thieves and robbers:...* we would say that this statement renders the OTC practice unholy and unhealthy.

Hence,

OTC = TToG

Therefore,

NTC = HS + IGoS

This leaves us with the Holy Spirit's purpose in our lives and the glory of our souls imputed in us through Jesus Christ, so that we would receive double glorification – joy on earth in place of His suffering, and the ascension into heaven to partake in the great wedding feast He is preparing for the faithful in His kingdom in heaven. The NTC is the Kingdom of God on earth, which boasts of the presence and the working power and wisdom of the Holy Spirit in their midst. Jesus Christ walks in the midst of their midst and as such they are not frightened by the threats of the enemy – Revelation 1:13,20: *And in the midst of the seven candlesticks one like unto the Son of man... The mystery of ...the seven candlesticks which thou sawest are the seven churches.*

The NTC promises a two-stage reward – John 10:10: *I am come that they might have life (here on earth), and that they might have it more abundantly (eternal life)* (emphasis mine). Hence the NTC boasts of keys which would be handed over to all kingdom adherents, so that they may have life and have it more abundantly, as Jesus says – Matthew 16:19: *And I will give unto thee the keys of the Kingdom of heaven: and whatsoever thou shalt bind on earth shall be bound in heaven: and whatsoever thou shalt loose on earth shall be loosed in heaven.* So we are back again to the main reason why souls were not transcending immortal realms of powers into heaven – impurity through worshipping of idols, falsity from lies, ignorance due to lack of the true knowledge of God, and the negligence of the values of heaven as a result of these.

So, from these perspectives, we would agree with Paul that Jesus *'...hath made us able ministers of the new testament; not of the letter, but of the spirit: for the letter killeth, but the spirit giveth life (*2 Corinthians 3:6)'. I will then say that the church in our dispensation involves every one of us taking an Oath of Allegiance to the Messianic Order of Spiritual Consciousness. This oath is what we often refer to as confession of faith in Christ. This well explained, we would now proceed to know why people do gather as one in the church and bears a name. The units of spiritual consciousness we call Church today exist for the following reasons:

- It is for the purpose of preservation of our identity in Christ in line with the calling upon the bearer of the anointing – the servant of God.

CHAPTER TWELVE

- God makes this easy by appointing leaders who we now call servants of God. Then He fills them with gifts to enable them function. This enables single-point accountability.

The Church cannot function adequately without a calling. The church usually starts with one person, who is the bearer of the anointing, and then he announces to everyone about the anointing character he bears, and others are led to join him. We can see this in the life of Jesus which is our model - Matthew 4:17-18: *From that time Jesus began to preach, and to say, Repent: for the Kingdom of heaven is at hand.*

Today we have a lot of breakouts because of disloyalty in the church due to doctrinal immaturity, the quest for money, and control. If we are not sure God is calling us, we shouldn't start a church. But if He is the one calling, then we have His support and presence. Many of us have advertised for companies unknowingly when we recommend their products to friends and relatives, with no reward from them. But these same companies pay for media adverts. This is how it is with God. The Bible tells of someone who was healing in Jesus' name, yet was not counted among Jesus' Disciples. This is why we must

CHAPTER TWELVE

belong to a calling or commission and not just a gathering of people clapping hands and blind to spiritual matters. We don't need to beg to God; He already knows what is good for us. All He requires from us is to obey and follow His instruction so that we can receive Him and the glory and splendour of His kingdom here on earth. If Elisha didn't follow Elijah, there is no way he would have received his ministry. He would have died a farmer with no heavenly reward.

As we conclude this chapter on enlarging the Kingdom of God, we would take some additional Bible resource to press down the fact that God requires us to gather unto Him in units we call churches, under the care of one of His servants.

Against the belief of most people that they don't need to gather with other brethren, this is what the Bible says:

- Hebrews 10:25: *'Not forsaking the assembling of ourselves together, as the manner of some is; but exhorting one another: and so much the more, as ye see the day approaching.'*

- *Exodus 3:12: 'And he said, Certainly I will be with thee; and this shall be a token unto thee, that I have sent thee:*

CHAPTER TWELVE

When thou hast brought forth the people out of Egypt, ye shall serve God upon this mountain.'

- Numbers 2:1-2: *'And the Lord spake unto Moses and unto Aaron, saying, Every man of the children of Israel shall pitch by his own standard, with the ensign of their father's house: far off about the tabernacle of the congregation shall they pitch.'* This particular portion talks about identity, *'with the ensign of their father's house.'* Every gathering of the church of Christ is recognised by an 'ensign' which establishes the covenant between the servant and the work he will do, and the Lord. The ensign is in spoken words and symbols. The servant of God understands the ensign given to him, and from time to time he would repeat the words and raise the ensign towards heaven. Just as the tribes pitched around the tabernacle, which was a pattern after that in heaven, so also all the churches on earth pitch around the heavenly altar. And as they lift up their voices towards heaven and call upon the name of the Lord, the Shekinah is released into each of the gatherings. God ordered that His children should gather around His tabernacle as a focus of worship, and in the midst of those, He instructed Moses to cast out the lepers in Numbers 5:1 from among the people so that they don't infect the people with the contagious disease. Today there are people the Lord has inform the servant of God not to be in the midst of the gathering, but these servants have often disobeyed, or maybe they didn't hear, as they continually seek counsel from men and water down the doctrine of the Kingdom. Many souls are heading for hell today, as a result of being infected by people who are not willing to repent but rather ready to infect everybody with their spiritual leprosy.

The wisdom in Revelation 2 shows that we are a church under an umbrella name. Why must one become a member of the Royal Diamonds International Church?

1. To build a family:

- That we can learn to live, and tolerate one another in love because you will always see those who are supposed to be your enemies often, hence we must be ready to imbibe the spirit of forgiveness, which is a prerequisite for you to be in heaven - Ephesians 4:32

- So that you can grow together in faith - Proverbs 27:17

2. To work in a commission and be more focused because the servant of God tells you the Mission Statement and Vision he is pursuing, meaning there is a purpose and you won't walk like someone without a leader and direction. So the church is like a compass to you and it helps you to become more faithful to receive a reward of the Lord - Matthew 25:21: *His Lord said unto him, Well done, thou good and faithful servant: thou hast been faithful over a few things, I will make thee ruler over many things: enter thou into the joy of thy Lord.* Those who support the servant of God enjoy the terms of the covenant upon him, provided they obey the terms of the covenant; for instance, Abraham had to circumcise every male in his household the same day he entered into the covenant with God. To Abraham, God says, *I will bless those who bless you.* To me He says, *'I will bless those who support you in this work.'*

3. To have a strong voice in the affairs of the government - as we witness with one voice - Acts 1:8

4. To ensure the continuity of the Vision. Jesus raised the disciples and then Paul and even today He is raising all of us.

5. For spiritual blessings - hence they gathered in the upper room to receive the Holy Ghost. It paves ways for miracles of material blessings and healing - the water to wine, the five loaves of bread.

6. For a head count, to take responsibility. I know whom I should bother about in this commission. This is why I take attendance every Wednesday. John 10:27 - I know my sheep and they know me. They won't gossip about me or say no to what I tell them to do. They will not argue. They will read my books. So I take responsibility for their lives.

The standard of working with God is, 'Fear and Trembling – Philippians 2:12.' If we must pray for people, we should be sure first that God will hear us because we are right standing with Him – Matthew 7:3-5. We would see that because we speak in tongues or claim to be Christians it doesn't really mean that we are doing what God requests of us. Many of us have more prayers of mercy to pray for ourselves first before thinking of others. Let's learn the word of God with understanding, and then preach for the Lord to empower us to teach and preach with understanding also. Our works are in these folds:

CHAPTER TWELVE

- We are to testify about Jesus to others – Acts 10:42.

- But before we can be successful, the people must need us – Acts 16:9.

- The Lord too must back us – Acts 18:7 and,

- We must please the Lord – Acts 23:11.

The kingdom cannot be enlarged if we are not willing to do the work of the Kingdom the Holy Spirit way. We would remember that after Jesus had healed so many, and when He went back and saw that they were not repented yet to follow God, He had no other choice but to curse them with an eternal curse of destruction – Matthew 11:21. We should pray for the Holy Spirit filling us because it is the spirit that quickens the body - John 6:63. May the Lord give you the zeal to become part of this great commission and reap the fruit of your service in God's vineyard. This church is God's investment for the purpose of profit making - Hebrews 11:6. If you will yield to this call to enlarge the Kingdom, your reward is now. Because you have read this, you will not beg to eat nor know sorrows, in the name of Jesus – amen!

CHAPTER THIRTEEN

LOSING THE KINGDOM

A key word spoken by the Lord is very important here – *what shall it profit a man to gain the whole world and lose his soul?* We lose the Kingdom when we chase after the world. What has made many servants of God backslide is the chase after material things. People miss the Kingdom of God in this Messianic era when they begin to judge with the values in the Old Testament. As I explained earlier, the New Testament focuses on the restoration of the lost man in the Garden of Eden. It focuses on those who will worship the Lord in spirit and in truth, as the angels do in heaven. The central message is on reuniting the soul and spirit of man back to its original source. We would remember that God breathed upon man to live. Over the years, the dead could not ascend unto God because they were cast out into outer darkness because their spirits were not made perfect, and imperfection cannot ascend unto God. What takes every soul to God is the Glory of God upon the soul, and this is what we lost as humans when we were yet in sin (Romans 3:23). The Glory of God is likened to a high concentration of light rays that will make the substance it is falling on glow with a halo. This is what covers every soul going to heaven, and it is the ensign used to recognise the souls whose spirit have been made perfect while on earth because of their righteous did and the holy life they lived while on earth. To ascend back from earth into heaven, Jesus requested God to clothe Him with His Glory – John 17:5: *And now, O Father, glorify thou me with thine own self with the glory which I had with thee before the world was*; this was the form Jesus left behind to become human, and now that He was going back, to be able to ascend across the layers of spiritual realms present along the pathway to heaven, the glory has to come upon Him like a white glowing linen. To ensure souls make heaven, God decided to come in human form, growing and living with humans, so that He would understand from personal experience what is needed to restore mankind back to Him. The result of that was the Golgotha sacrifice. A simple way to unite souls back to Him was instituted therewith; every soul while still living on earth would have to be united to the soul bearer – the vine (John 15:1-5), by believing in the soul bearer - Jesus, baptised, confessing Jesus to others, receiving the Holy Spirit, and participating in the communion. The final sacrament of wine and bread binds earthly souls to the spring of life, preparing the soul for its onward journey when it expires on earth. Hence the Lord said that whoever did not partake in the communion was not worthy of Him – John 6:56: *He that eateth my flesh, and drinketh my blood, dwelleth in me, and I in him.* This logically implies that the soul will not become one with the Lord in purpose and thoughts, thus making it difficult for its ascension, except the sacraments that would aid its admission into the realm of light are performed by us while our souls are still connected to our earthly bodies. The practice of communion has its spiritual significance and there are rules to be followed. The first time I took the communion was in a Pentecostal church. Right from

CHAPTER THIRTEEN

the moment I took it, because of my earlier knowledge about the communion as an Anglican, I felt so guilty that I couldn't forgive myself. This has made me now, as a minister of the gospel, delve into the scripture to bring out facts that will help me understand what it stands for. We would see that the first time Jesus made mention of the communion, those around Him did leave Him, showing the sacredness they perceived of the communion. The life of the soul depends more on the efficacy of the communion. I recall here, Malachi 4:7: *Ye offer polluted bread upon mine altar; and ye say, Wherein have we polluted thee? In that ye say, The table of the Lord is contemptible.* And Matthew 9:17 says - *Neither do men put new wine into old bottles.* The above verses explain the fact that the communion, which is simply dining with the Lord, cannot be taken into a body that is not holy and dedicated unto God. It is not to be given to people who have not truly accepted Christ. Many have taken the communion under duress because they are sick, and the minister has told them that the communion is the last solution to heal them, and then they will quickly profess Jesus as their Lord and saviour. Though many do get healed, they hardly remain in the faith thereafter.

CHAPTER THIRTEEN

This much said, we would now discuss why a shepherd, or rightly put, the servant of God, will lose the Kingdom put under his care by the King of kings. I came across Revelation 2:5: *Remember therefore from whence thou art fallen, and repent, and do the first works; or else I will come unto thee quickly, and will remove thy candlestick out of his place, except thou repent,* and I became terrified. Many servants of God have lost their relationship with heaven, and are also leading many astray. Once the candlestick is out of its position in heaven, the church, or the Kingdom of God thereto, will have no shower of wisdom and power of God; such church is like a sinking ship at sea with no rescue opportunity available. And what many have done is to cajole their congregation into long hours and days of prayers for the Lord to look upon their affliction, whereas the environment to enable God to move is never created. In these churches all the servant does is to organise money-making seminars and workshops, and gradually the hearts of the brethren are turned away from the fear of God. Bible verses are always quoted out of context, only to drive home the point the servant of God is trying to push forward, waiting for someone in the congregation who will nod in acceptance, then he throws in another lie. The word of the Lord says again - *Awake, O sword, against my shepherd, ... smite the shepherd, and the sheep shall be scattered: ...* – Zechariah 13:7. Did God care about His sheep? Yes of course, but His care for the sheep is somewhat connected to His relationship with His shepherd. Severally, we may have read in the Bible that when the head errs, God punishes the subjects with him. When the Lord sent His warning to the church in Revelation 2&3, it was addressed to the shepherds, there referred to as the angels of the church.

From what we have read above, when a king loses his kingdom after falling out of favour with the King of kings, he receives a blow from the Lord and as he falls down, his kingdom crashes with him, and often he becomes a celebrated king only living on past glory, which he earned when the Lord was yet his Shepherd, before he started taking counsel from men of the world. The implication of this is likened to court-martialling and imprisonment - Matthew 13:49,50: *So shall it be at the end of the world: the angels shall come forth, and sever the wicked from among the just, And shall cast them into the furnace of fire: there shall be wailing and gnashing of teeth*. The fire will only be used at the end of the world, then those who have been cast into outer darkness (Matthew 8:12), will now be cast into the fire with all the evil spirits, ancestral fathers and the devil and his angels.

How will the Lord know those who haven't done His will? When faithful souls depart the earth they will ascend unto heaven like angels clothed with glowing spiritual linen – some are golden, others are silver; thus, implying that any soul not clothed in glory cannot make it to the Kingdom of God in heaven -Matthew 22:11 -*And when the king came in to see the guests, he saw there a man which had not on a wedding garment: And he saith unto him, Friend, how camest thou in hither not having a wedding garment? And he was speechless. Then said the king to the servants, Bind him hand and foot, and take him away, and cast him into outer darkness; there shall be weeping and gnashing of teeth. For many are called, but few are chosen.*

Before now, there are some who have been with the Lord but because they were sown in by the devil, and have manifested evil in his kingdom, they shall also be cast into everlasting torment. They have been enjoying the light but refused to repent because they were the tares of the devil – (Matthew 13:24-43). The good seeds represent the mind of God, the vision of the church handed down by God, the tares are the corrupt visions sown into the church by the devil, to fill the church – it therefore includes doctrines, and wisdom of men that are brought in to increase the church. The tares increased the number of plants growing in the field. But the ultimate judgement of God is seen in verse 42: *And shall cast them into a furnace of fire: there shall be wailing and gnashing of teeth.*

Why are we replaying all these? Many don't believe that they can lose the Kingdom. How do we lose the Kingdom? When we waver in our love for the things of God – Jesus said the sin of the devil is not savouring the things of God. If that is the sin of the devil, the truth is that many of us are worse than the devil already.

Any unproductive believer will lose the Kingdom rights and privileges, Matthew 25:30 - *And cast ye the unprofitable servant into outer darkness: there shall be weeping and gnashing of teeth.*

We are brought into a reality of what the Kingdom duties

CHAPTER THIRTEEN

entail in Matthew 25:37-40: *Then shall the righteous answer him, saying, Lord, when saw we thee an hungred, and fed thee? or thirsty, and gave thee drink? When saw we thee a stranger, and took thee in? or naked, and clothed thee? Or when saw we thee sick, or in prison, and came unto thee? And the King shall answer and say unto them, Verily I say unto you, Inasmuch as ye have done it unto one of the least of these my brethren, ye have done it unto me.*

Three persons have been mentioned in the verses above that function in the Kingdom of God on earth; the Righteous, the King and My Brethren. Who are these? The King is the Lord Jesus; those He referred to as His brethren are the disciples and the 'righteous' are those who supported the disciples (the kings) to succeed in their duty unto the Lord. So, we would see where the title 'King of kings' is coming from. One thing is common with both the righteous and the brethren; they all did the will of God as apportioned unto them by the Lord. The brethren of a king are those with royal hearts who had been cultured in the values of the Kingdom, and therefore potential kings. Jesus referred to these disciples, here referred to as brethren, as kings when He said He

CHAPTER THIRTEEN

will appoint unto them kingdoms, which they will rule over -Luke 22:28,29: *Ye are they which have continued with me in my temptations. And I appoint unto you a kingdom...* They bore the burden of the gospel wherever they go. The pastor of a flock, who has been appointed by the Lord to take care of His flocks, needs to be taken care of by those they minister to as explained above as an act of righteousness (also see Joshua 19:49-50).The book of 1st Timothy chapter 5 verse number 17 says: *Let the elders that rule well be counted worthy of double honour, especially they who labour in the word and doctrine.* The double honour refers to the manner of the expected reward – physical respect as those representing Jesus in your midst, and care for the physical needs. Saint Paul went further to say – 1 Corinthians 9:11-12: *If we have sown unto you spiritual things, is it a great thing if we shall reap your carnal things? If others be partakers of this power over you, are not we rather.*

Having said all this, we would now investigate the characteristics that would make a believer lose the Kingdom, or be cast out of the Kingdom. The very first thing that should come into our hearts as we recognise the possibility of being cast out of the Kingdom is that the Kingdom of God is set in place with an ensign of royalty. This being the case, those who would inherit this kingdom must have a royal mind-set. Hence Saint Peter, who was so close to Jesus, once explained that before we surrendered under the authority and rulership of Christ, we were nobodies; and that now, because of the relationship between us and God through the covenant upon Christ, we have been admitted into a Royal order – 1 Peter 2:9: *But ye are a chosen generation, a royal priesthood, an holy nation, a peculiar people; that ye should shew forth the praises of him who hath called you out of darkness into his marvellous light: Which in time past were not a people, but are now the people of God: which had not obtained mercy, but now have obtained mercy.* To explain further, we would see that outside this royal order, the mercy of God stops working for us. It is widely misunderstood by many that once we are born again, then we are admitted without a recourse, quoting the Bible portion which says: *For the gifts and calling of God are without repentance* – Romans 11:29. This verse only explains the faithfulness of God towards mankind. The qualifying behaviour, which we ought to show to be able to enjoy this, is contained in James 4:8: *Draw nigh to God, and he will draw nigh to you. Cleanse your hands, ye sinners; and purify your hearts, ye double minded.*

Now let's see something that beats my imagination in Songs of Songs 1:4: *Draw me, we will run after thee: the king hath brought me into his chambers: we will be glad and rejoice in thee, we will remember thy love more than wine: the upright love thee.* And I will want us to also quickly take a look at John 6:44, 12:32: *No man can come to me, except the Father which hath sent me draw him: and I will raise him up at the last day. And I, if I be lifted up from the earth, will draw all men unto me.* We would now bring the hidden facts out of these verses – God draws people to Christ here on earth, and the spirit of Christ shall cry in their heart (Galatians 4:6), as a river of living waters – full of open doors, or rightly put, streams of opportunities that will enable them to showcase the gift of God in their lives to such an extent that others would glorify God, and will be also attracted into the Kingdom. These faithful of the Lord are then supposed to value the work of the Lord more than wine. The King's chamber referred in Songs 1:4 above simply refers to the Kingdom of God. The chamber is the innermost court of the King, where He only takes His closest associates. It is

CHAPTER THIRTEEN

also the home of secrets. So we would say that those drawn to Christ are admitted into His inner court where He reveals secrets to them that will bring them honour before men. When this is not the case, it simply shows that one is only seeing the Kingdom of God (John 3:3), and hasn't yet entered into the inner chamber (John 3:5).

Now let's go back to Songs 1:4: ... *we will be glad and rejoice in thee, we will remember thy love more than wine: the upright love thee.* Once we are saved and drawn unto the Lord, and are now in His chamber, we are expected to:

- Be glad and rejoice in Him; ensuring that our lives bring Him glory. We no longer have names of our own, but have inherited upon our forehead the name of Christ – a royal name that is above every other name. This implies that when we frown before His presence or unbelievers, we are on our way out of His chamber, and that automatically means we won't have the privilege accorded those who are with Him in His Royal chamber. No wonder the Bible admonishes us to rejoice evermore (1 Thessalonians 5:16), as an evidence of our light shining before the world (Matthew 5:16), and we are also told not to publish

CHAPTER THIRTEEN

our shame before unbelievers (2 Samuel 1:20, Micah 1:10). This will further show that a believer who is yet to receive the spirit of perseverance is not yet in the King's chamber. We should note that we lose the Kingdom, and all the benefits that would have been appointed unto us after we might have successfully rejoiced in the Lord when we are unhappy. Common sense should teach us that no one who is with the king is ever sorrowful, except a big calamity befalls such a kingdom; this we know cannot be the case with the Kingdom of God – He has all powers under His feet. If we are the reason why heaven will rejoice, why can't we be part of that celebration? – Revelation 18:20: *Rejoice over her, thou heaven, and ye holy apostles and prophets; for God hath avenged you on her.*

- Songs 1:4 also says that those in the Kingdom are supposed to remember the King's love more than wine. Sincerely, this is where many have missed it. They want to still have all the fun they used to have when they were nobody, when the King hadn't brought them into His chamber, and as such have complained as the Israelites did in the wilderness – to enjoy all the goods in the whole world. They have also been framed up by prosperity preachers in what I will term spiritual wickedness in high places, that being born again is a licence to make quick wealth, and to reap where they did not sow. Jesus loves us, and this fact should occupy our minds more than every other thing. If we would live to remember His unfailing love towards us, we will definitely not do things that will offend Him, thus paving the way for our early triumph in life when we have absorbed the character of the Kingdom and its righteousness. This path has taken me six years now. I still remember when I wanted to step out and imbibe cheap prosperity doctrine when I heard one morning as I drove in my car, 'you can't jump the gun.'

- The very last part of that song says – *the upright love thee*. And here is the truth that must be told, that we show love to those we believe in their dreams. This is what uprightness means. To be upright with someone is to maintain a long-standing relationship of trust and mutual dependence. Many a believer has a parasitic relationship mindset and because of their avaricious nature, would hardly follow the Lord's leading. How can one say he/she has surrendered to Jesus and is still controlled by emotions and human authority? Many have also decided to become visitors who only expect goods from their hosts daily, and have also forgotten that a time comes when the host will no longer treat them as a guest, and therefore will not entertain them again, such that the host may no longer give in to their requests. Ordinary human wisdom teaches us this too. What the host will expect now is that a mutual relationship of trust and interdependency can be built with clearly defined objectives of association and commitment. This is what we refer to as a vow of covenant.

It is a popular adage of old, reflected in Proverbs 16:18, that *'Pride goeth before destruction, and an haughty spirit before a fall.'* Does this imply to why people lose the Kingdom of God? Yes of course!

And to conclude this chapter, we would see some more Bible verses:

- Romans 8:38-39: *For I am persuaded, that neither death, nor life, nor angels, nor principalities, nor powers, nor things present, nor things to come, Nor height, nor depth, nor any other creature, shall be able to separate us from the love of God, which is in Christ Jesus our Lord.* Our hope is hinged on Christ Jesus. We are nothing without the redemptive work He does. As long as the servant of God is there, hope will surely come. He is already in the war front, so if he is safe, you will be safe. We can take learning from 2 Kings 4:40-41: *So they poured out for the men to eat. And it came to pass, as they were eating of the pottage, that they cried out, and said, O thou man of God, there is death in the pot. And they could not eat thereof. But he said, Then bring meal. And he cast it into the pot; and he said, Pour out for the people, that they may eat. And there was no harm in the pot.*

CHAPTER FOURTEEN

COUNTDOWN TO JUDGEMENT DAY

Finally, before the final day of judgement, the Lord will withdraw His Holy Spirit from the earth. If we love the Kingdom of God, we will do all it takes to merit heaven. What we hate is what we disregard. As believers, we need to live a life that shows that we belong to a royal kingdom. The Kingdom of God on earth is likened to an airport where everyone waits for his or her own schedule to fly. In this case, our journey unto eternal glory is more of an international flight, and as such we need to get all our particulars in place – here on earth, we are given a heavenly passport, which is the mark of the Lord, and this passport has to be stamped by the Lord, representing

CHAPTER FOURTEEN

the visa, and our flight ticket to get on board the flight to heaven. Who are the pilots? The angels of course! There are some international airports from which international flights don't take off because of infrastructural decay. The same could be adjudged of many kingdoms of God here on earth, which we call churches, where at the end, the Lord will have no souls to harvest, meaning the Lord won't bother to send His heavenly chariots there. The environment is unholy and filthy, and unprepared for the Shekinah that accompanies every heavenly flight. In these churches, their radar systems may even no longer be functioning – the angels sent to them may have decided to follow daughters of men, because of their seductive dress. We have been in this discussion with special focus on what the Kingdom of God represents here on earth, and how each of us contributes to the propagation of the Kingdom values as we live. In this chapter, we will be discussing some general character that we ought to exhibit that will help and strengthen us here on earth. We shouldn't forget that the flesh is weak but the spirit is willing. The flesh is made of material substances that depreciate in value naturally, and as such the body also experiences depreciation. We have often seen many people trying to fight the ageing process. Many lie about their age, pointing to the fact that humans don't want to get old. However, ageing is inevitable. But we have a being in us that grows mature, and yet never grows old. The following discussion will talk about how this inner being in us can be matured in the way of the Lord, so that when our flesh fails us, the spirit can keep on giving us hope.

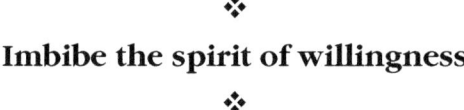

Imbibe the spirit of willingness

We need to be willing to follow the teachings of the Lord and His revelations, which the Holy Spirit has brought from Him to us in the form of Rhema. We would see that until Samuel answered the call of God the night he slept, God didn't stop calling. Many of us have neglected the voice of God for so long that all we now hear is the voice of the devil. The devil now runs the Kingdom that our Lord kept under our care. King David once lamented – *…how are the mighty falling?* - 2 Samuel 1:19. Why did Saul go down? He lost the Kingdom to his self-indulgence and disobedience. We have seen all over the world the rate at which many servants of God are amassing personal wealth, through the message of deceit which they have employed as weapon to defraud God's children. Is their evil more than that of Saul? The path of the Lord is narrow and often difficult to endure - Matthew 7:14, by human standards, but His spirit is with us to lead us through. This is why we must be willing to follow through rather than inventing a path for ourselves – Proverbs 14:12: *There is a way which seemeth right unto a man, but the end thereof are the ways of death.* Many servants of God have used the kingship authority they have to undermine the authority of the King of kings who they are to report to, and have therefore build castles of disobedience within their own empire of lust. Paul lamented this act in 1 Thessalonians 4:5: *not in the passion of lust like the Gentiles who do not know God* (ESV). Our relationship with God has a lot to do with our zealousness for His works. Our zealousness for the work of God brings establishment to us. As we enter into our days of consolidation, brought about by our service to the Lord, to be able to reap the fruit of our service we must be zealous - Numbers 25:10-13. We need to also be firm and willing. Those who wander about in their service to the Lord, who are not planted in any of His kingdom here on earth are like birds wandering from their nest - Proverbs 27:8: *As a bird that wandereth from her nest, so is a man that wandereth from his place.* Such birds will have to cope with adverse weather, and be hunted by a predator.

We need to create the atmosphere that would bring down the Shekinah of God always, and not only in our crusade grounds. Our abode should be filled with the power of God, as a means to winning the willingness of the world to follow the ways of God. This was David's candid prayer and expectation - Psalm 110:3: *Thy people shall be willing in the day of thy power, in the beauties of holiness…*

In doing this, we should encourage every adherent of the Kingdom to receive the Holy Spirit - Acts 1:8, and be filled with the power to make things happen - Matthew 28:18. I have come to realise in my six years of walk with the Lord, that:

- *There is no Zealousness without Willingness*
- *There is no Willingness without Power*
- *There is no Power without the Holy Spirit*

CHAPTER FOURTEEN

And this gives the order: **Holy Spirit – Power – Willingness –Zealousness**.

Power is time dependent. Its result is beautiful when it is supplied as and when needed. So also are willingness and zealousness. Since these elements are time dependent, the earlier we receive the Holy Spirit, the better, so that we can begin to reflect the beauty of the glory of God. We can see the culmination of the Power of God in Hebrews 1:3: *Who being the brightness of his glory, and the express image of his person, and upholding all things by the word of his power…* everything depends on the power of God, and how this power works for us goes a long a way to determining what we will become in life. We must learn to build our tomorrow on the word of God. Whatsoever is not founded on the word of God cannot stand the test of the harsh weather of our times – spiritually, socially, politically and otherwise.

We need the spirit of willingness to excel in life; continue with our academic studies, stay in our marriages, do the work of God, stay continually on our job, carry on with life after a series of disappointments, forgive people who offend us, remain focused on our drive for success, etc.

CHAPTER FOURTEEN

Sometimes we wake up in the morning and feel so tired about life, and then we need to be encouraged. This is what the spirit of willingness does to us. We are injected with power from on high, and we become stronger than before. In effect, the Bearer of the Kingdom values is the Holy Spirit – He is the Kingdom of God in our midst – Mark 9:1: *And he said unto them, Verily I say unto you, That there be some of them that stand here, which shall not taste of death, till they have seen the Kingdom of God come with power.*

Do you want the spirit of willingness? Pray for it now. In case you have not received the Holy Spirit, ask God now. There is a voice speaking to you now. As long as you are focused on receiving Him and have given your life to Christ, there is no other voice that can speak to you now. You should stop reading and take about five minutes to communicate with the Holy Spirit as you wish – just be quiet, and you will hear a voice deep in your spirit. If you have not received Him, pray for the Holy Spirit now, in your closet, let nothing distract you. Now do it.

Now you know you have the Holy Spirit – this is the knowledge of the Kingdom. With the power of the Holy

CHAPTER FOURTEEN

Spirit in you now, you will succeed in life as it pleases the Lord – this is what is termed 'understanding.' Then the physical application of the power in you- when, where and how to apply it is 'wisdom.'

Do you need power to excel in life? Receive the power of the Lord, even as you read now. Every yoke standing as a barrier to your receiving the Lord in your life, is destroyed right now with the anointing of the Lord. When we yield to the Lord, this is what He does – Ezekiel 16:9: *Then washed I thee with water; yea, I thoroughly washed away thy blood from thee, and I anointed thee with oil.* What was this oil supposed to achieve? Psalm 89:20-23 tells us - *I have found David my servant; with my holy oil have I anointed him: With whom my hand shall be established: mine arm also shall strengthen him. The enemy shall not exact upon him; nor the son of wickedness afflict him. And I will beat down his foes before his face, and plague them that hate him.* And so, you would see that the anointing of the Lord is all you have been looking for all this while – and that anointing is what attracts the Holy Spirit. This is why the oil is called the 'oil of gladness' – because when the anointing oil comes upon your forehead, it earmarks you for the possession of the spirit of God. There would be no David without a Samuel. And there would be no seventy prophesying elders without Moses. The oil of your announcement is in the hand of the servant of God – go after it, and obey the rules that set the anointing in place. You may want to see my book *Gifted and Anointed* to understand the anointing better.

The crown we will wear later when we ascend unto eternal glory depends on how far we were able to learn the ways of the Kingdom of God, and also apply them while we were on earth. A pastor's duty is to show the congregation the ways of the Kingdom – Jeremiah 3:15, and to stand in the gap for the children of God – 1 Samuel 7:8: *And the children of Israel said to Samuel, Cease not to cry unto the Lord our God for us ...*

Understanding The Calling of God

A calling is simply an extension of the arm of God to assist mankind so that we can learn to live the character of God as seen in heaven, so that as time goes on, we are turned into citizens of heaven while on earth, so that when we depart the earth, we can easily fit into heaven, and carry out our duties unto the Lord. *All those called of the Lord shall be with the Lord Jesus* - Matthew 6:10, Matthew 22:30, John 12:26.

We now understand what a calling is. For those still looking for God, the moment He raises a servant to lead us, we are already with Him. The Kingdom of God is His court – here on earth or in heaven. When we enter into the court, we would see the position for the Judge sited, facing the people and the testifying platform between the people and the judge. From time to time the people in the courtroom look at the judge, then the testifying counsel, to perceive how the judge is reacting to what the testifiers are saying. The prosecuting counsel asks questions and the testifiers answer. What the court wants to know is how well the truth is presented and how morally justified is the truth. This shows the knowledge the testifiers have of the case at hand. Now let us take it to the Church.

1. The Judge is Jesus - John 5:30:*I can of mine own self do nothing: as I hear, I judge: and my judgment is just; because I seek not mine own will, but the will of the Father which hath sent me.*

2. The Testifiers are the Servants of God who He called to do this on His behalf - Revelation 22:6,16: *These sayings are faithful and true: and the Lord God of the holy prophets sent his angel to shew unto his servants the things which must shortly be done. I Jesus have sent mine angel to testify unto you these things in the churches.*

3. The Persecuting Counsel is the Devil, accusing the Lord and His brethren before Him - Revelation 12:10,12: *And I heard a loud voice saying in heaven, Now is come salvation, and strength, and the Kingdom of our God, and the power of his Christ: for the accuser of our brethren is cast down, which accused them before our God day and night. … for the devil is come down unto you, …* We would see Satan accusing God directly In the book of Job 1:9-11: *Then Satan answered the Lord, and said, Doth Job fear God for nought? Hast not thou made an hedge about him, and about his house, and about all that he hath on every side? thou hast blessed the work of his hands, and his substance is increased in the land. But put forth thine hand now, and touch all that he hath, and he will curse thee to thy face.* So, at every church service and gathering of God's

children, the pastor stands to present the word of the Lord, as it is, according to the standard of heaven before the Lord in the Altar, His hosts of angels, the congregation there present, and the devil. Unlike in the case of Job, we have Jesus, seated as the Judge who is also our mediator, and as such our case ends with Him. Whoever persecutes believers persecutes Jesus also, and this is true of the character of the devil. The devil, through Judas and the teachers of the law, persecuted Jesus until He was crucified. The Lord said, if he was called Beelzebub, then every believer should expect his or her own share of the accusation (Matthew 10:25). Jesus says in Matthew 5:11-12: *Blessed are ye, when men shall revile you, and persecute you, and shall say all manner of evil against you falsely, for my sake. Rejoice, and be exceeding glad: for great is your reward in heaven: for so persecuted they the prophets which were before you.*

4. The people in the courtroom, sitting to hear the judgement, are sympathisers of both 'the accused' by the devil (the Lord and all believers) and 'the accuser' (the devil), who now makes up the congregation - Matthew 13:25-26: *But while men slept, his enemy came*

and sowed tares among the wheat, and went his way. But when the blade was sprung up, and brought forth fruit, then appeared the tares also.

This is why the work of the servant of God is dangerous. He is testifying on behalf of the judge, who is right seated at the court. So his testimony of the Lord before the people and the accuser must be righteous before the Lord, seated as the judge. Whatever he says before the people will be taken against him by the Lord - Luke 19:22: ... *And he saith unto him, Out of thine own mouth will I judge thee* ...

To ensure I don't make mistakes, the Lord is holding my hand and leading me - Isaiah 42:16. Sometimes I do things just to confirm the things I receive of the Lord, like an inquisitive child in training and trying to learn more by having a practical experience. If God is holding my hand and leading me, where is the arm of God? You need not look elsewhere once there is Servant of God in your midst – this is 'understanding.' You must regard Him to the extent that you should be ready to give your life to preserve the calling. Paul gave accounts of those who stood by him as he did minister the word of the Lord before them - Romans 16:3-4: *Greet Priscilla and Aquila my helpers in Christ Jesus: Who have for my life laid down their own necks: unto whom not only I give thanks, but also all the churches of the Gentiles.*

What people usually do is to fight and destroy the Servant of God so that the purpose of God for His people will not be achieved. This has also happened severally to me as I carry out my humble service in the Lord's vineyard. The Lord said in - Matthew 23:35: *That upon you may come all the righteous blood shed upon the earth, from the blood of righteous Abel unto the blood of Zacharias son of Barachias, whom ye slew between the temple and the altar.* People don't know that when they try to pull down servants of God, that they are invariably trying to blackmail the Lord. It is only gluttony that will make people not seek after truth. Those who fall into the hands of deceitful pastors are often materialistic people. And the Bible says that the blind cannot lead the blind. So for those seeking the Lord, and wanting to know who is a genuine pastor, the acid test is simply in their hands. They should desire only the Kingdom and the righteousness of the Lord as the main reason for their coming to the service of the Lord – Matthew 6:33-34: *But seek ye first the Kingdom of God, and his righteousness; and all these things shall be added unto you. Take therefore no thought for the morrow: for the morrow shall take thought for the things of itself. Sufficient unto the day is the evil thereof.* This is the acid test. Anything outside this quest is the root of deceit. If they seek after material things, then there is every tendency that the pastor they will meet will be positioned by the devil to deceive them. And this yardstick is what we would also use to weigh the messages and sermons of supposed servants of God before you can draw your conclusion. The message of Jesus was centred on the Kingdom of God, and so will anyone representing Him. Jesus was not a man of too many words – most preaching of deceit is laborious, saying the same thing in different ways, so as to buy the acceptance of the congregation into believing their message. Then it is concluded with a request to sow money into the Kingdom they are building for themselves.

Why does God call people; the Servant of God sets the standard he received from heaven in place so that the people can please God, and live a life of unity. This can be seen in the 10 commandments. Sometimes the servant of God errs before the Lord while trying to please the people - Matthew 19:8: *He saith unto them, Moses because of the hardness of your hearts suffered you to put away your wives: but from the beginning it was not so.* The proviso here clearly says that the law in this case contravenes the purpose of God. How often has the church erred while trying to satisfy its innate desires? This is because the church often wants a doctrine that pleases the crowd and undermines the long-standing precepts of God. When the man of God resorts to preaching and teaching in public places in what I would call an 'open air cathedral,' he has few disciples, without a church he oversees. This helps him to retain focus, as the number of people attending services does not bother him. All that bothers him is how he would preach the truth. This was Jesus' pattern.

A call is to answer a need of the people - when people pray, God sends help. The first call was in Eve, who was to help Adam. God raises your help from among you, as the creation of Eve shows. God called Noah to preserve a generation of humans and animals. Nimrod was doing a job of unity and announcement, but he called himself and God stopped their plan, establishing the fact that except the Lord builds a city, those that build labour in vain. In our case, it would be the reward we earn from the Lord at the end of the day that would show if we have built in vain or not. Abraham's call took him from his home into a new land, as a crusader of Faith. When the people complained against Eli and his children, God raised Samuel. When Saul failed God, David was raised.

When we pray for God to answer us, He raises people. Jesus confirmed this when He said the disciples should pray for more labourers, because despite the presence of the teachers of the law, the people were living as though they had no shepherd. So when the people become so many, the servant of God prays that Jesus, the Lord of the Harvest, should recruit more hands. The one called receives the Holy Spirit and the spirit speaks through him to glorify Jesus. The message of the servant of God must be within these premises and other secrets that defines his authority. His teachings must:

- Reprove people of sin

- Teach on righteousness and judgement

- Reveal secrets, which he asks from the Lord, only meant for those who have attained that level of spiritual maturity, and these secrets are what distinguish them from the ordinary flocks. There is a special warning on the dissemination of spiritual information - Matthew 7:6: *Give not that which is holy unto the dogs, neither cast ye your pearls before swine, lest they trample them under their feet, and turn again and rend you.* The servant of God is also, in line with this, warned not to be quick in laying of hands on people for the service of the Kingdom – 1 Timothy 5:22: *Lay hands suddenly on no man, neither be partaker of other men's sins: keep thyself pure*

- A servant of God operates with deep spiritual insights and revelations - John 16:13-14, Isaiah 42:9.

This is how he leads people to Christ. These people have varied character and experiences.

- Some have lived a prodigal life; these need to be taught prudence. Jesus says – Matthew 16:11: *If therefore ye have not been faithful in the unrighteous mammon, who will commit to your trust the true riches.* Our ability to manage the physical riches God has given unto us shows how far we would also manage the spiritual gifts He is giving to us, as Jesus admonishes - *And if ye have not been faithful in that which is another man's, who shall give you that which is your own* – Matthew 16:12.

CHAPTER FOURTEEN

- Some have being denied life by those who oppressed them, either physically or spiritually - Isaiah 42:22.

- The servant of God does what God wants for the people, but in some cases, like the doctrine of many churches, the servant may want to do things just to please the congregation, while displeasing God and Himself - Because he wants to keep his flocks, believing that overtime, he would preach a message that will make them have a re-think and now be ready to accept the message of Restoration.

- Sometimes the actions of rebels will not allow the work to stand, and for such people, they are taken out with the word, as the truth kept on being preached. One day the burning fire of the word will push them out.

- The only reason Mary the mother of Jesus followed through was because she was a bearer of the testimony of Christ.

What should be our attitudes now? We should forget about every other worry of life and follow Jesus, as shown by the following verse of the Bible –

CHAPTER FOURTEEN

- Matthew 4:19:*And he saith unto them, Follow me, and I will make you fishers of men*

- Matthew 8:22:*But Jesus said unto him, Follow me; and let the dead bury their dead*

- Matthew 9:9:*And as Jesus passed forth from thence, he saw a man, named Matthew, sitting at the receipt of custom: and he saith unto him, Follow me. And he arose, and followed him*

- Matthew 16:24:*Then said Jesus unto his disciples, If any man will come after me, let him deny himself, and take up his cross, and follow me*

- Matthew 19:21:*Jesus said unto him, If thou wilt be perfect, go and sell that thou hast, and give to the poor, and thou shalt have treasure in heaven: and come and follow me*

- Luke 9:23: *And he said to them all, If any man will come after me, let him deny himself, and take up his cross daily, and follow me*

- Luke 9:61: *And another also said, Lord, I will follow thee; but let me first go bid them farewell, which are at home at my house. And Jesus said unto him, No man,*

CHAPTER FOURTEEN

having put his hand to the plough, and looking back, is fit for the Kingdom of God

- John 10:27:*My sheep hear my voice, and I know them, and they follow me*

- John 21:22:*Jesus saith unto him, If I will that he tarry till I come, what is that to thee? follow thou me*

All we have read so far shows that Christ want us to follow Him and do what He has asked us to do in His name.

❖

Learning to give Testimonies

❖

You slept and woke up to see another new day. This is enough to say thank you to God. But before I continue, I would want you to testify of the goodness of the Lord in your life to your neighbour. You can just give a phone call to someone and tell him/her that you want to share a testimony with them. Today we would be having knowledge and the understanding of giving testimonies, so that by wisdom we may do it wherever we go. The Book of Psalms is a book on how to give testimonies. Our prayers should have an element of testimony of God's faithfulness.

CHAPTER FOURTEEN

What is a Testimony? Let's see what makes up a testimony as shown in 1 John 1:1-4: *That which was from the beginning, which we have heard, which we have seen with our eyes, which we have looked upon, and our hands have handled, of the Word of life; (For the life was manifested, and we have seen it, and bear witness, and shew unto you that eternal life, which was with the Father, and was manifested unto us;) That which we have seen and heard declare we unto you, that ye also may have fellowship with us: and truly our fellowship is with the Father, and with his Son Jesus Christ. And these things write we unto you, that your joy may be full.*

From 1 John 1:1-4 we just read we would learn the following:

Testifying means declaring unto people what you believe and hold to be true, which you have experienced or seen in the life of others as a result of what the Lord did as a manifestation of His faithfulness to men on Earth, so that these people would believe and join in fellowship with you. It is about saying good things - for instance declaring the mercy of the Lord. Therefore we would say that testifying is a strong tool of evangelism.

CHAPTER FOURTEEN

1. God testifies - that is how He announces His presence in the life of whom He uses: these testimonies have become what we call miracles. He also testified of Jesus as His only begotten son. He has revealed me to many as a confirmation of His calling.

2. Jesus testified that the works He did was what God does in heaven, giving us a clue about what goes on in the throne of God.

3. The Holy Spirit testifies of the beauty of God when He manifests the presence of God in our midst.

Anyone who walks with God lives a life of testimony. Testimonies are what have kept Christianity alive till this day. Testifying is the act of righteousness before God. The increase from God is hinged on our testimonies. God rewards us when our testimonies can win Him souls. This is why He said that if we can confess Him before men, then He would confess us before His Father and the Holy Angels.

Who are testifiers?

- Free thinkers - unbelievers testify more than believers of the goodness of God in some cases. In most cases

CHAPTER FOURTEEN

believers are unable to declare the testimonies of others because they are waiting for their own to manifest.

- Faithful to God: They see testifying as a covenant they must keep with God, as a way of shaming the devil and helping to loose others from his grip of deceit.

- Values posterity: They want God to perfect that which they have received.

- In need of increase: They know that when they testify of what God has done, they will move His heart to do more for them.

Why is it that in the midst of all these benefits, people don't still give testimonies?

- Ignorance: Some don't know that they must give testimony to all that God does for them.

- Spirit of ingratitude: This is the character of the devil. How many of us would want to give to people who don't say thank you?

- Pride: This is mostly found in the church where many feel giving the testimony may mean they are submitting to the pastor as being more gifted than they are.

- Secrets: Many of us are too secretive. We feel people will know our secrets - People have given testimonies of HIV, what is more shameful than that?

- Greed: Fear of paying their vows and tithes.

- Shyness: Some people are too shy to speak in public. If you are one, receive the spirit of boldness in Jesus' name.

- Afraid of authorities they submit to: For instance many women have eaten the Lord's testimonies in our church because they were afraid of their husbands. Those of other religious faiths may also be afraid to give their testimonies of what the Lord did for them to anyone.

How to give a testimony

- Before the crowd, not to the pastor only.

- Continuously - in the presence of another set of people who hadn't heard your testimony before. Any soul won here to Christ and added to the church is counted for you.

- In your prayers: Any time you are praying, mention them before God. This act is seen as gratitude before

CHAPTER FOURTEEN

His face. And the angel who He used to deliver that answer is always willing to do more and would want to take your next prayer point to God.

- Link the pastor to the testimony: He is the physical arm of God - If the breakthrough came after hearing a message, a prophecy, prayer from his mouth or after reading His books. Watching a video of the message, make sure you mention it. This increases the faith of others in his calling.

- Link the church - This increases the membership in the church, especially when you come in to pray secretly and God intervened. This way many people will love the house of God and not depend on the servant of God. Which means, whether he is there or not, people can still experience the hand of God. Don't forget that iron sharpened iron. No man is an island. No single tree makes a forest.

- Link any other person God used in the church, but such persons must be seen to be loyal to the pastor, else you would grow more rebels in the church. And you have scattered the house of God. Mentioning rebels in church as someone God used to answer your prayers is like praising the devil in the house of God.

CHAPTER FOURTEEN

Be careful in the following instance:

- When you are in a particular church be careful not to mention a pastor of another church, because you may abuse people's minds and then empty the church.

- Servants of God can sometimes be jealous and be careful how you mention the names of other pastors in their presence.

Testimony goes with thanksgiving:

- You can give to support the work of God.

- You can give a gift to the servant and any other person God used.

- You can invite people to celebrate with you and you enthusiastically share the testimony again.

After testifying:

- Portray the character of Christ wherever you go.

- Continually join in fellowship with the brethren and any time you see more new additions that have not heard the testimony, it is an opportunity to cast your net again – your testimony is your net as a fisher of men. It is your investment tool, and who know, God may just favour you again.

- Mind your mouth. Don't curse the links - the pastor, the church or any other person God uses as a link. If you curse the link, the reward of the testimony ceases. This is actually where the devil is smarter than many of us.

My prayer for you today is that the Lord should give you a testifying spirit. Anything eating your testimony is cast out of your life by this understanding in the name of Jesus.

❖

Be Impactful on Earth, Be Rewarded in Heaven

❖

Now that we have discussed given testimonies, the next thing I want us to look into is how we can really make an impact here on earth to the glory of the Lord. One thing that has eluded many believers is that because they have not received spiritual insights into what the plan of the Lord is for them, they continually fall into the hands of people claiming to be servants of God, who actually mean to dupe them of their hard-earned money. The

CHAPTER FOURTEEN

question now is - what kind of impact is required of us as Christians? We are all here on earth to affect lives positively, and to bring glory and honour unto God.

We are created for Dominion - Genesis 1:26 – 28. Here we are told that God commanded the first humans to be fruitful, multiply, replenish, and subdue the earth.

What then is our stake on this earth?. We can get a clue from Revelation 5:10-12:

- Power
- Riches
- Wisdom
- Strength
- Honour
- Glory
- Blessings

These are the indicators of how successful we have been here on Earth. And the character to achieve this is meekness - Matthew 5:5: *Blessed are the meek: for they shall inherit the earth.*

CHAPTER FOURTEEN

We all have a destination on Earth. But we need our destiny to guide us to our destination. John 12:27-28 says that Jesus fulfilled His purpose on earth. Paul also says in 2 Timothy 4:7-8 that he finished his course.

How impactful are you?

We become impactful by doing the will of God. And this comes through understanding the heart of God. Isaiah 28:5 say: *In that day shall the Lord of hosts be for a crown of glory, and for a diadem of beauty, unto the residue of his people.* This is what God is expecting from all of us. He wants to be our crown of glory because we were created to be successful. This is why Christ came, so that the glory of the Lord which now resides with us will pave way for us to have life, and have it more abundantly - John 10:10. But for this to happen, we have to listen to the teaching of the Lord. We saw the manifestation of this when those thousands listened to Him for a good three days without complaining, hearing Him talk about the Kingdom. We often see people running out of church when teaching is going on. Many love preachers, but hate teachers. Preachers energize people with the promises of

God, while teachers open your understanding to what is required to get the promises working for you, and how to keep them to last for eternity. Preachers make you forget about your sorrows, while teachers often make you have a rethink, and to see that one really needs to put in some effort to make God move for them. A wise believer would need both. This is what Isaiah 28:9-10 is saying: *Whom shall he teach knowledge? and whom shall he make to understand doctrine? them that are weaned from the milk, and drawn from the breasts. For precept must be upon precept, precept upon precept; line upon line, line upon line; here a little, and there a little.* Anyone desiring the teaching of the Lord must learn to be humble, and willing to endure the 'slow tick of the clock.' They are born again - *weaned from the milk and drawn from the breast.* This is what Peter referred to - 1 Peter 1:23: *Being born again, not of corruptible seed, but of incorruptible, by the word of God, which liveth and abideth forever.* Anyone who is born again has thrown away every prior knowledge they have gained in the world about God and the meaning of life, and is willing to be trained in the precepts of the Kingdom of God. *No one puts a new wine in an old wine skin* – this is what our Saviour said. King

CHAPTER FOURTEEN

David knew that he needed to be purged with hyssop, then a clean heart has to be created in him which would now house the spirit of the Lord – Psalm 51:7, 10. For this to happen, we must know His ways, learn them, and live in them - Isaiah 1:17, 19: *Learn to do well; seek judgment, relieve the oppressed, judge the fatherless, plead for the widow. If ye be willing and obedient, ye shall eat the good of the land.* Humans, knowing that the standard of God is hard to live through human wisdom, and that until one is in Christ it cannot be attained, and since many have decided to follow all manner of antichrist religions, often resorting to trying every means possible to empower them to eat the good of the land, by submitting to the devil, and then losing their souls.

The danger many of us will eventually face is reflected in - Hebrews 3:12: *Take heed, brethren, lest there be in any of you an evil heart of unbelief, in departing from the living God.* In Hebrews 3:11, we were told that God swore that they would not enter into His rest because they erred, hence the advice of Paul in verse 12. Only when we know His ways can we receive 'rest.' To enter 'His rest,' we must labour to earn it - Hebrews 4:10-12: *For he that is entered into his rest, he also hath ceased from his own works, as God did from his. Let us labour therefore to enter into that rest, lest any man fall after the same example of unbelief. For the word of God is quick, and powerful, and sharper than any two edged sword, piercing even to the dividing asunder of soul and spirit, and of the joints and marrow, and is a discerner of the thoughts and intents of the heart.*

God expects a level of dedication from us, as seen in verse 10 above. Why are we unable to learn the ways of the Lord, for He said – Matthew 11:29-30: *Take my yoke upon you, and learn of me; for I am meek and lowly in heart: and ye shall find rest unto your souls. For my yoke is easy, and my burden is light.*

These are the facts below:

- ✓ The devil knows that God speaks in due season - not every time - Proverbs 15:23
- ✓ The devil also know that if we don't please God then his protection over us, His Shekinah, will depart from us.

So he makes many of us become:

- ▇ Impatient
- ▇ Unwilling

CHAPTER FOURTEEN

- Rebellious
- Murmurers
- Gossips

And all these are targeted against the work of God.

But there are forces that are making it difficult for us to achieve much and they are those forces that have ganged up against your destiny, and the destiny of the Church of God. They operate by impregnating people's hearts with a rebellious and murmuring spirit so that they are cast out of God's presence. They curse everything that concerns God and as such the goodness of God in the land is far away from them.

❖

Overcome the Spirit of Rejection

❖

When the Lord gave me this message, it was difficult for me to comprehend it, but now I understand. As I lay on my bed that early morning, which happened to be the 1st day of September 2013, I heard the following words:

- It is difficult to please people who reject you.

CHAPTER FOURTEEN

- It is difficult to grow in a polluted environment.
- It is difficult to work with rejected people.

Throughout my growth in the work of the Lord, these sayings have come to play a major role in my route to spiritual maturity. September is the period that marks the onset of flooding and it has a spiritual significance with blessings and curses.

Flood carries refuses and faeces around and leaves them behind in many places to deface the beauty of the landscape. At the end of the day, it is difficult to appreciate the places where the flood visited. Even so, it is the month when the Lord opens also the floodgates of heaven to beautify our lives.

What causes rejection?

We can get a clue from the book of Hebrews 6:8:*But that which beareth thorns and briars is rejected, and is nigh unto cursing; whose end is to be burned*. People are rejected when they have nothing good to offer. This is why the devil will always want to deface all the good works we are doing by recruiting lying tongues to condemn us in high places.

CHAPTER FOURTEEN

Consequences of Rejection

Apostle Peter says of this in his letter - 2 Peter 2:5 - 6: *And spared not the old world, but saved Noah the eighth person, a preacher of righteousness, bringing in the flood upon the world of the ungodly; And turning the cities of Sodom and Gomorrah into ashes condemned them with an overthrow, making them an ensample unto those that after should live ungodly.* The flood came and swallowed the first set of evil doers in the days of Noah, and the fire of God consumed those in Sodom and Gomorrah. The acceptable character which saved Noah is also explained here as a preacher of righteousness. Many of us are happy with those who clap hands for us when we are going astray and dancing to the gallery. We should rather abhor such and concentrate in loving the works of righteousness.

How does rejection come?

- We can receive rejection through our own actions.
- We can also receive rejection through the actions of others.

When we are rejected we cannot exercise the gift of God

in our life and as such we cannot make news. Many of such people have gone into hiding.

I am led to pray for you:

Today, because of this knowledge, every spirit of rejection in your life is cast out in the name of Jesus. Today is a day of acceptance. The Lord almighty is following you home to put things right and to give you the spirit of acceptance.

Every spirit of rejection hovering in your vicinity - even in your church, we come against you in the name of Jesus – Amen, and Amen.

What causes rejection?

1. Mutilation: God beautifies, but the devil mutilates what God has glorified when we fall for his tricks. Mutilation brings condemnation.

Examples of mutilation can be seen in the following examples –

- Someone scandalises your person - character assassination.

CHAPTER FOURTEEN

- Someone hates you because of your outstanding performance and as such condemns you before others, like some persons have gone out to meet prophets and prophetesses who told them I belong to cult.

- Let us look at some scandalous remarks in the Bible:

  - Genesis 37:19: *And they said one to another, Behold, this dreamer cometh*

  - Numbers 12:1-2: *And Miriam and Aaron spake against Moses because of the Ethiopian woman whom he had married: for he had married an Ethiopian woman. And they said, Hath the Lord indeed spoken only by Moses? hath he not spoken also by us? And the Lord heard it.*

  - Mark 6:3: *Is not this the carpenter, the son of Mary, the brother of James, and Joses, and of Juda, and Simon? and are not his sisters here with us? And they were offended at him.*

2. Pollution: Jesus knew that some of His disciples were already polluted by the old doctrine and would hardly receive Him - John 6:64: *But there are some of you that believe not. For Jesus knew from the beginning who they were that believed not, and who should betray*

him. Surviving in a polluted environment with the doctrine of purity is a hard task. Here our rejection is for the Lord's glory, rather than to please men. To receive the new wine, the wineskin must be new, hence we are admonished to be born again, by renewing our minds, to accept what the Lord is offering to us, rather than go after cheap doctrines fused with materialism. What happens in a polluted environment? - Mark 13:12-13, says: *Now the brother shall betray the brother to death, and the father the son; and children shall rise up against their parents, and shall cause them to be put to death. And ye shall be hated of all men for my name's sake: but he that shall endure unto the end, the same shall be saved.*

3. Rejection can only happen when you find yourself in the following scenarios:

- Associating with a polluted person - so you must know who you are associating with. Evil communication corrupts good manners, the Bible tells us - 1 Corinthians 15:33.
- When you live in a polluted environment - e.g. the moment you say you are from some parts of the world, everyone thinks you are a trickster.

We would see that though Noah was saved, he still got himself drunk, because of his earlier relationship with such drunkards in the world that the Lord destroyed.

Rejection brings avoidance

Many people try to avoid those rejected, except those who have a bold heart to stand against the decision of the crowd, but over time, they may become worn out.

For instance:

- A city of armed robbery and war is often deserted.
- A quarrelsome person is often avoided.

If we are of the Kingdom of light, no matter how much people bring down our name, the Bible says that the light will so shine as we continue to do God's work that men will glorify His name for our sake.

Rejection brings desolation

Jesus warns - when we see desolation coming, we should take precautions - Mark 13:14-15. Some will be saved even in the midst of this desolation - Mark 13:20: ... *but for the elect's sake, whom he hath chosen, he hath shortened the days.*

If we must overcome the spirit of rejection, then:

- ▪ Embrace life through Jesus Christ so that we can enter into the Kingdom of Light. Let us repent wholeheartedly.
- ▪ Be Unique with your service to God.
- ▪ For anyone who has gone astray - Return to God - John 6:37. If God accepts you, you will be accepted by everyone - Luke 2:52.

Developing unrelenting faith in God

Before we move on, we shall figure out what makes up FAITH:

F = Fear not, for God is with you always, even to the end of time.

A = Accept all that happen to you in good faith, as a test of your love for God.

I = Intercept the challenges of life with the fear of God.

T = Take the work of God seriously.

CHAPTER FOURTEEN

H = Hope continually in God.

So Faith from above is about the ability to become:

- As fearless as a lion.
- Unmoved by the challenges of life.
- One who intercept the situations of life with the word of God.
- Totally dependent on God.
- Hopeful of victory daily.

Now we shall take a look at Psalm 98 and get out the elements of someone with an unrelenting Faith in God:

1 O sing unto the Lord a new song; for he hath done marvellous things: his right hand, and his holy arm, hath gotten him the victory.

2 The Lord hath made known his salvation: his righteousness hath he openly shewed in the sight of the heathen.

3 He hath remembered his mercy and his truth toward the house of Israel: all the ends of the earth have seen the salvation of our God.

CHAPTER FOURTEEN

4 Make a joyful noise unto the Lord, all the earth: make a loud noise, and rejoice, and sing praise.

5 Sing unto the Lord with the harp; with the harp, and the voice of a psalm.

6 With trumpets and sound of cornet make a joyful noise before the Lord, the King.

7 Let the sea roar, and the fulness thereof; the world, and they that dwell therein.

8 Let the floods clap their hands: let the hills be joyful together

9 Before the Lord; for he cometh to judge the earth: with righteousness shall he judge the world, and the people with equity

Now let's discuss the verses in turn:

- Recognise the strength of God and how He uses this mighty strength to cause deliverance - verse 1. His right and holy arm talks about Jesus seated at the right hand of God. And everyone begotten of God through Christ stands at His right hand; His holy arm. This means that, if we don't tend to become like Christ, we cannot maintain our position with Him. Our faith matures from a mustard seed faith level to a tree level when we grow in Christ – through Justification, Sanctification and Consecration.

- Faith comes by Observation - verse 2. You must observe the times and the seasons and know when to seek the wisdom of God to breakthrough.
- Faith is about covenant - verse 3.
- Faith is about appreciation and praise in the midst of the heathen nation. Not washing your dirty linen in the public for others to mock your God. It means you must learn to trust God and wait on Him - Verse 4-8.
- Faith is knowing that there is a day of reckoning when you shall present your works before the Lord - verse 9.

The beauty of Faith is summarised in Proverbs 3:5 -12:

5 Trust in the Lord with all thine heart; and lean not unto thine own understanding.
6 In all thy ways acknowledge him, and he shall direct thy paths.

7 Be not wise in thine own eyes: fear the Lord, and depart from evil.

8 It shall be health to thy navel, and marrow to thy bones.

9 Honour the Lord with thy substance, and with the firstfruits of all thine increase:

10 So shall thy barns be filled with plenty, and thy presses shall burst out with new wine.

11 My son, despise not the chastening of the Lord; neither be weary of his correction:

12 For whom the Lord loveth he correcteth; even as a father the son in whom he delighteth

It is a yielding effort. We yield our weakness to God and receive His strength in return. And this can only happen when we trust in Him as one who would see us through. To achieve this, we need to allow God to overhaul our thoughts, and take pride away from us so that we would have a serving heart.
We therefore need to:

- Overhaul our thoughts - Psalm 51:10
- Renew our thinking with the promises of God - Romans 12:23.

CHAPTER FOURTEEN

- Trust in the Lord - Isaiah 40:31, 1 Peter 1:13-17
- Know that there is a price for betrayal - Hebrews 6:4-6

We have seen now that faith is two ways –'give and receive.' What most of us know is the 'receive' part of faith, which is expecting the Lord to meet our needs. But frankly speaking, God wants to have faith in us too – He is continually hoping that one day we would bear Him first-fruits. Our faith in the Lord has a lot to do with fruit bearing and our ability to preserve the fruits so that we could present them to God one by one to God. Faith means we have yielded our entire life to God.

Pray that the Lord gives you an unrelenting spirit to serve Him, even in the midst of adversity. May the Lord preserve you and guide you with His strength, in the name of Jesus.

❖

Becoming a Tree of righteousness

❖

It is the desire of the Lord that we represent Him wherever we are as trees of righteousness. Before we continue I am led to pray with you – 'The Lord God Almighty whom I serve, who calls me to stand before Him this day shall make you a tree of righteousness, that you may bear fruits of righteousness all the days of your life, in the name of His Son Jesus, we pray - Amen.'

Let's see Isaiah 61:3:*To appoint unto them that mourn in Zion, to give unto them beauty for ashes, the oil of joy for mourning, the garment of praise for the spirit of heaviness; that they might* **be called trees of righteousness**, *the planting of the Lord, that he might be glorified.*

From today the Lord is giving you the enablement to succeed beyond human measure and you shall be served and respected, because the anointing of the Lord is beautifying your life. The moment we read verse 3, where the Lord spoke of making us – trees of righteousness, we come across promises of what this status can bestow on us from Isaiah 61:4-6. If becoming a tree of righteousness is what will lead to all these blessings from the Lord, the subject is therefore, worth investigating.

We would see some scriptures now to understand the acceptable characters that will make us trees of righteousness:

CHAPTER FOURTEEN

- Psalm 32:8-9: *I will instruct thee and teach thee in the way which thou shalt go: I will guide thee with mine eye. Be ye not as the horse, or as the mule, which have no understanding: whose mouth must be held in with bit and bridle, lest they come near unto thee.* The Lord is saying be careful of those who you mingle with - those who don't have understanding.

- Psalm 71:7: *I am as a wonder unto many; but thou art my strong refuge* - this is the evidence of the Lord working in your life. David became a wonder in the eyes of many, but hardly did they know the Lord was his strong refuge.

- Romans 8:11: *But if the Spirit of him that raised up Jesus from the dead dwell in you, he that raised up Christ from the dead shall also quicken your mortal bodies by his Spirit that dwelleth in you*- the spirit of the Lord is the one that doth all this.

- Revelation 22:14-15: *Blessed are they that do his commandments, that they may have right to the tree of life, and may enter in through the gates into the city. For without are dogs, and sorcerers, and whoremongers, and murderers, and idolaters, and whosoever loveth and maketh a lie.* Sustaining the beauty of God is when we are in His kingdom. Outside His kingdom are sorcerers, whoremongers, murderers, those who love lies and do lie.

What we need to become trees of righteousness - Ecclesiastes 9:8: *Let thy garments be always white; and let thy head lack no ointment.*

- We must watch our desires - Philippians 4:8: We should set our hearts to follow the Lord.
- We must be careful to love whatever we see. Not all that glitters is gold. Many have turned to the devil by belonging to all manner of cults because of the quest for wealth. Follow the Lord all through and your increase will come in His own time. The devil has a way of making us forget who we are when He tries to show us things that we would want to achieve in a hurry, and when we succumb to him we are led out of the path of beauty.

Many of us who have been saved before are waxing cold and those we preached to are waxing strong in the things of God. Why? We are becoming too religious and not following the ways of the spirit of the Lord and so we have denied newness and are finding it difficult to follow the Lord in what He is doing in our lives. Let us pray that the Lord should create in us new spirit that would desire Him all the days of our lives.

Bearing the fruit of righteousness

Now that we are growing our Faith in the Lord, and have become trees of righteousness, I want us to recite Psalm 73:28 three times so that the words can take root in our hearts: *But it is good for me to draw near to God: I have put my trust in the Lord God, that I may declare all thy works.* The Lord shall give you the heart to draw near to Him in Jesus name – Amen. Why is it good for us to draw near unto the Lord? In the Psalm we just read we have these facts about bearing righteous fruits for the Lord:

- Draw near to the Lord.
- Trust in the Lord God.
- Declare all His works.

How can we achieve all these tasks?

- You draw near the Lord with everything in your life. Isaiah 29:13,24: *Wherefore the Lord said, Forasmuch as*

CHAPTER FOURTEEN

this people draw near me with their mouth, and with their lips do honour me, but have removed their heart far from me, and their fear toward me is taught by the precept of men. God's expectation of us, when we repent is contained in verse 24 - *They also that erred in spirit shall come to understanding, and they that murmured shall learn doctrine.*

Now we would see from above that;

- People err because they don't understand.
- They murmur because they don't have doctrine. The doctrine is what we discussed earlier in this book as the culture and precepts of the Kingdom of God.

This explains the fact that we must understand to overcome and that we must be patient and observant to learn doctrine.

- We must Trust in the Lord God: - 2 Samuel 22:3: *The God of my rock; in him will I trust: he is my shield, and the horn of my salvation, my high tower, and my refuge, my saviour; thou savest me from violence.*

    What makes up trust? We shall see this from the verse we just read:

- He is my Shield - Protection from the arrows of the enemy.
- The Horn of my salvation - Horn is for strength, defence and emblem of maturity.
- My high tower - where you can see the enemies approaching.
- My Refuge - A hiding place.
- My Saviour - deliverer, and rescuer. Trust brings about Deliverance.

We must declare His works as the reason we are alive. What works are we declaring?

- Psalm 22:22 - His name
- Psalm 22:31 – His Righteousness
- Isaiah 12:4 - His doings
- Jeremiah 31:10 - His word and prophecies.

Preserving our fruits of righteousness

Every tree bears fruits of its kind. Once we start bearing fruits, we need to also preserve our fruits. Physically, agricultural produce is stored in barns, silos and modern storage facilities, with the right temperature, pest management chemicals, etc. All these are aimed at preserving the fruits, to ensure that they are available when needed. Societies with poor preservation techniques often suffer from hunger and deprivation. So also it is when we are unable to provide abiding fruits unto the Lord when He needs them. Jesus gave us a clue of what fruit preservation is all about when He said that His disciples should pray for labourers – Matthew 9:38: *Then saith he unto his disciples, The harvest truly is plenteous, but the labourers are few.* We would see that apart from us becoming saved, we have a responsibility to pray for God to send in labourers. We also have the responsibility to teach people the manner of the Kingdom, so that labourers will be readily available. You are a labourer, I am one – there are many souls out there we also need to bring into the fold, so that they too can become labourers. For this to happen, these souls want to see us living the life of the Kingdom. They will hear us teach sound doctrine, and then they will follow us to meet the Lord, so that one after the other, the Lord will teach everyone His ways – then, even as we are living within the precept of God, so that we are found worthy of being in His chamber, so also these would work out their salvation, with fear and trembling, and receive the recommendation of the King of kings – Philippians 2:12. There are verses in the Bible that gives us a clue on how we can preserve our fruits of righteousness, so that they will stand the test of time:

Matthew 3:10: *And now also the axe is laid unto the root of the trees: therefore every tree which bringeth not forth good fruit is hewn down, and cast into the fire.*

Luke 3:8: *Bring forth therefore fruits worthy of repentance, and begin …*

John 15:5: *I am the vine, ye are the branches: He that abideth in me, and I in him, the same bringeth forth much fruit: for without me ye can do nothing.*

Now let's try to explain the key words in what we are discussing.

- The first one is preserve – what is to preserve? It means to protect or safeguard. It means to ensure that we are able to stand through for Christ no matter the trials and temptations that may come our way. How many of us can take what a child is holding and playing with? The child will cry until you give it back to him. That is how our walk with God is. We should not allow the things of the world to take away the joy we have in the Lord. Protect your salvation by getting busy for the Lord.

- The second word there is fruit. No one wants to keep a tree or plant that does not bear fruit. Usually fruits come after a plant has produced flowers. Everyone loves flowers because they are beautiful and unique. When we become born again, we begin to produce flowers that make people appreciate us and want to come near to us. If you look at flowers, in the evening they die and then the plant will start to produce fruit where the flowers were. It is the fruit from which many would know the kind of tree that produced it. The fruits have to ripe, and then will be delicious. This is how our works are before the Lord. When the Lord comes today, is there any evidence of the fruit you have grown? Don't also forget that we have both good and bad fruit – make sure to bear good fruit only. Let the life we are living not bring shame to our loved ones and us.

- And thirdly we would talk of righteousness – which simply means doing what is right and acceptable to God in such a way that we would promote His kingdom here on earth.

CHAPTER FOURTEEN

What can affect our fruits of righteousness and prevent them from being preserved? We see a clue from what Jesus says in Matthew 16:11-12: *… ye should beware of the leaven of the Pharisees and of the Sadducees? Then understood they how that he bade them not beware of the leaven of bread, but of the doctrine of the Pharisees and of the Sadducees.* We must beware of doctrines that will make it difficult for the fruits we bear to stand the test of time. One key cankerworm that eats up our fruit and reduces its value is false doctrines. What was the main language and tone of the doctrine of the Pharisees and the Sadducees? We may found out from the Bible, and then we will relate it to our present day, and advise ourselves what manner of teachings we must adhere to as adherents of the Kingdom of God here on earth.

We find it difficult to preserve our fruits of righteousness for a number of reasons, some of which are discussed below:

- ■ The number one factor is the fear of the unknown. Let us see what Moses, the servant of God, told the children of Israel when they were about entering their promised land in Deuteronomy31:5-6: *And the Lord shall give them up before your face, that ye may down*

CHAPTER FOURTEEN

to them according unto all the commandments which I have commanded you. Be strong and of a good courage, fear not, nor be afraid of them: for the LORD thy God, he it is that doth go with thee; he will not fail thee, nor forsake thee.

To face the challenges of life because nothing comes easy, we would see the facts above:

- Be strong – Jesus is the Lion of the tribe of Judah. If the spirit of Christ cries in your heart, you will be as bold as a lion – Proverbs 28:1: … *the righteous are bold as a lion.*
- Good Courage – Jesus carried on with the work of God with all zeal and dedication.
- Fear Not – Jesus challenged the Pharisees several times in order to put things right.

In verse 5 above, Moses told them to do according to what he had commanded. God speaks to us always in this altar; if we follow, we will not be disappointed in life.

As we are all here, it is only when we obey the commandment of God above concerning His commission that our fruits will stand the test of time. We cannot compare ourselves with any other standard – we have a commission, a calling and a commandment from the Lord to fulfil.

Pray this prayer before the Lord. Ask the Lord to give you strength, courage and a fearless spirit to enable you to execute His will here on earth. Also ask of the Lord to raise men, women, youths and children in this end time that are ready to listen to His voice and are ready to be trained so that they can grow spiritually to champion the work of God rather than their selfish desires.

If you are reading this and haven't given your life to Christ, you don't have a place in heaven yet – you can right that now by just opening the confession page of this book and repeating the words there, and thereafter following the instructions therein.

The Necessity for Deliverance

❖

What is deliverance? Why do we need deliverance? We can get some clues from the following Bible verses:

- Matthew 6:13: 'And lead us not into temptation, but **deliver** us from evil: For thine is the Kingdom, and the power, and the glory, for ever. Amen'

- Luke 4:18: 'The Spirit of the Lord is upon me, because he hath anointed me to preach the gospel to the poor;

CHAPTER FOURTEEN

he hath sent me to heal the broken-hearted, to preach **deliverance** to the captives, …'

- Psalm 97:11-12:'Light is sown for the **righteous**, and gladness for the **upright in heart**. Rejoice in the Lord, ye righteous; and give thanks at the remembrance of his **holiness.'**

- Psalm 107:1-2: 'O give thanks unto the Lord, for he is good: for his **mercy endureth forever**. Let **the redeemed** of the Lord say so, whom he hath redeemed from the hand of the enemy.'

- Hebrews 3:13: 'But exhort one another daily, while it is called 'today'; lest any of you be hardened **through the deceitfulness of sin**.'

Form the verses we have just read, starting from the last one, we would find out that what leads us into sin is deceit. And deceit brings about hardness of the heart. When the heart becomes hardened, we find it difficult to love, and then we sink into greater condemnation. When this happens, our righteousness before the Lord becomes like a filthy garment. As we wear this look daily, we will also become unfaithful to the purpose of the Kingdom. This is the basis for deliverance. Before the devil would possess anybody, he must present an environment that will entice us; this is done in a deceitful manner. Now we should answer the following questions:

Q. When can we be deceived?

A. When we are still within the devil's circle of influence.

Q. How do we become delivered?

A. Through the restoration of our Souls - Psalm 23:3, Isaiah 42:22.

Q. How does Restoration come?

A. Through deliverance and then your walk with God - Psalm 23:4.

Once we are delivered, we will enjoy the beauty of repentance and salvation. This should be the number one desire of every child of God. Without deliverance, our days in the Kingdom of God here on earth are numbered, and we will be flung to and fro and become perturbed by the worries of life, which the devil always puts across before us.

We get delivered through prayers, sincerely asking for God's intervention. Prayer is to help the flesh to be conditioned in such a manner that it would abhor sin and flee from the appreciation of worldliness, so that the willing spirit within can become established in our body. The more we pray for deliverance, the more we would become focused on heavenly values, and hence, God is seeking those who will worship in truth and in spirit – many have claimed they worship God; of course anyone can worship God, all His creations does this. The Samaritan woman said that the Samarians worshipped God on the mountain, but the Lord told her that they really didn't know what they were doing, they didn't know who they were worshipping – John 4:21-24. We cannot claim to worship the Lord in truth and spirit when our prayers are mostly geared towards the need for bread and clothing. The provision of bread, raiments and protection from wickedness can be achieved by employing the grace in the anointing to do the works of God.

'Touch not, do no harm,' is what God says. Jesus also says that we should not bother about raiments or food because we are of more value than birds in the sight of God. So if the birds would survive, why are we so bothered? We are delivered from worries already, and let this fact remain in us.

CHAPTER FOURTEEN

Bear a burden for the Lord

❖

Our reward in the Kingdom is tied to the level of burden we bear for the Lord. Let's take a look at 1 John 3:16-17: *Hereby perceive we the love of God, because he laid down his life for us: and we ought to lay down our lives for the brethren. But whoso hath this world's good, and seeth his brother have need, and shutteth up his bowels of compassion from him, how dwelleth the love of God in him.* What burden are we bearing for the Lord? It is when we begin to do those things He did while on earth. The book of Ephesians 4:24 says that we can do this when we: *'put on the new man, which after God is created in righteousness and true holiness.'* Once we are delivered from the devil and his antics and we put on the form of Christ, then we would begin to live a life that glorifies Christ through the indwelling of the spirit of Christ (Galatians 4:6), and for us to continually be in this form, which is acceptable to the Lord, we also ought not to grieve the Holy Spirit – Ephesians 4:30: *And grieve not the holy Spirit of God, whereby ye are sealed unto the day of redemption.* Our final redemption is made possible by the presence of the Holy Spirit in our lives throughout our stay on earth, and that will help us to do the following, which are the evidence of the seal of the Lord upon our forehead – Ephesians 4:31-32: *Let all bitterness, and wrath, and anger, and clamour, and evil speaking, be put away from you, with all malice: And be ye kind one to another, tender-hearted, forgiving one another, even as God for Christ's sake hath forgiven you.*

This character will establish us as heirs of the Lord's kingdom. Our lives should show that we are adherents when we do what the Lord commands us to do:

- Participating in the communion service. An opportunity to share in the love of Christ. This is because the communion helps us to bear the burden of the Lord. It strengthens us to stand firm and unshaken.

- Win souls. The problem with many of us is the claim of self-holiness - Isaiah 65:5; many of us are too holy for God to use. When we walk before God unto righteousness, we are brought into a covenant with Him, and then He teaches us the way of holiness.

CHAPTER FOURTEEN

Foundations of Faith

And finally, we will discuss how we may live in the Kingdom. Earlier we said that we needed to develop unrelenting faith in God. I would have discussed the foundations of faith then, but since without faith, we are told no one can please God – Hebrews 11:6, it would be right in place to discuss the foundations of faith last. A centurion once demonstrated the Faith that Jesus recommended. What was it he did that made the King of kings recommend his servant for angelic intervention? Let's see Matthew 8:9-10: *For I am a man under authority, having soldiers under me: and I say to this man, Go, and he goeth; and to another, Come, and he cometh; and to my servant, Do this, and he doeth it. When Jesus heard it, he marvelled, and said to them that followed, Verily I say unto you, I have not found so great faith, no, not in Israel.* And Jesus referred to this utterance as 'so great faith.' If this were what it entails to live a life of 'so great faith,' we will now discuss the requirements below:

CHAPTER FOURTEEN

What then are the foundations from what we have read?

- Faith has to do with authority.
- It has to do with belief and trust.
- It has to do with total dependence on the power of God.

How can we talk faith into action? It is through the use of words -Matthew 8:8: *…but speak the word only, and my servant shall be healed.* Faith is manifested in what we say. This fact takes us to the power of the tongue. What we say carries our faith. So, if our sayings are not yielding fruit, then something is wrong. The reward of prayers is tied to the strength of our faith. Our faith bears fruit only when the spirit of the Lord is upon our tongue, as seen in - 2 Samuel 23:2: *The Spirit of the Lord spake by me, and his word was in my tongue.* The book of Zephaniah 3:7-9 gives us a clue to what we need to build and grow our faith in the Lord, to enable us receive His reward:

7 I said, Surely thou wilt fear me, thou wilt receive instruction; so their dwelling should not be cut off, howsoever I punished them: but they rose early, and corrupted all their doings.

8 Therefore wait ye upon me, saith the Lord, until the day that I rise up to the prey: for my determination is to gather the nations, that I may assemble the Kingdoms, to pour upon them mine indignation, even all my fierce anger: for all the earth shall be devoured with the fire of my jealousy.

9 For then will I turn to the people a pure language, that they may all call upon the name of the Lord, to serve him with one consent

- Foundation no 1 - verse 7: *Fear of God* - Proverbs 9:10. No one can live without wisdom from God. Without God we can't get to our individual destinations in life because we are all blind spiritually - Isaiah 42:16. If you were blind, it would take you years of untold hardship to grope your way to your destination. But God knows the end from the beginning, and when He leads us, we will be able to plan our lives on time. This is why we need God in order to avoid stagnation.

- Foundation no 2 - verse 7: *Receive Instructions* - We need humility to receive instructions on what we ought to do to please God.

- Foundation no 3 - verse 7: *Be steadfast.* Keep on doing what pleases God - don't join others to corrupt the image and person of God.

- Foundation no 4 - verse 8: *Wait upon the Lord always* - He is never late. Don't be in a hurry. In most cases the first voice you hear when you are about to perform an action is that of the devil - Ecclesiastes 5:1-2. God is in heaven. We need to be deeply silent enough, in the spirit to hear Him - 1 Kings 19:11-12. The commonplace voice on earth is that of the devil - he speaks so fast, always contradicting himself. Waiting requires calmness - Isaiah 30:15.

- Foundation 6 - Verse 8: *God is jealous,* know it. So you must give Him thanks, always. Appreciate everything He does for you. Appreciate the servant of God whom God has raised for you - 1 Corinthians 9:11-14.

Let's take a look at the word 'then,' in verse 9; It is only when we do the above, that God can give us a new tongue and a new voice that can please Him. This way our faith can move mountains.

Thank you for spending this precious time with me in this discussion. I pray that the Lord, who held my hand while I wrote this book, should uphold you all the days of your life – Amen!

EPILOGUE

We have read what this book has to offer. Am I trying to convince you? I don't really think so – it is my belief that the Lord has spoken to you severally as you read across the pages that makes up this treatise, the way He spoke to me. Severally you have read some areas with the voice of the Lord speaking in your mind and this is the beauty of our communication with God. To conclude this piece of writing, we would now add an epilogue to our initial discussion.

The message of amassing wealth, aka 'prosperity message', is not a message simply acting as an enticement used to attract people by servants of God, so that along the line, as they preach and teach, they will fuse in the message of salvation. It is a mind manipulation act aimed at using the predominant situation people are in to minister to them, and many have used this to rob people of their hard-earned money. Some prosperity preachers have suffered great want, and the devil has also presented the world to them the way he did to Jesus, but rather than reject it, they have followed the advice of the devil, and have also searched for Bible verses to support their unholy advancement – that today we have all manner of prophets who now romance those in the corridors of power, and help them to loot national treasuries worldwide. These categories falls into what the Lord said – Matthew 24:24: *For there shall arise false Christs, and false prophets, and shall shew great signs and wonders; insomuch that, if it were possible, they shall deceive the very elect.* Many of these have been involved in various money laundering schemes as their members have looted funds kept in their custody, or which they have powers to manipulate. And the question keeps coming – 'what did Christ die for?' I heard the Lord speak on the 28th of August 2014, as I wrote this book, 'so and so pastor has deceived those I kept in his custody and has lost the kingdom to the control of the devil. The Kingdom is now filled with immorality and corruption.' And I understand what He is saying – the message of sanctity, which He came to establish here on earth, has to be preached.

EPILOGUE

This book is not an attack on the integrity of people who have yielded to the call of God, heretofore called the 'servants of God, or the 'kings' in the Kingdom, but a book that calls for a reconsideration of our faith and the message of the faith we proclaim. We are either for the Lord or we are for the devil, who many of us have held responsible for all the ills that have happened to us. Someone has to be bold to condemn every unholy act in the house of God, the way Jesus cast out all those who turned the temple into a place of business. While many servants of God have twisted the scriptures to suit their unhealthy quest for wealth, many others have travelled through the sea of demonic, diabolic and idolatry illusion, with charms now buried in their churches, and at every junction that leads to their place of worship. The preaching of integrity and dedication, holiness and righteousness has been pushed aside to tell the people only what they want to hear, and not what God wishes them to hear. These sets of preachers are skilled at masturbating the minds of their prey with seductive and mouth-watering promises, that their wealth will come when they make some releases for the work of the Lord, and that these releases have to be done not as free will donations, but as a mandatory seed, that will provoke the invisible realm to bless them.

In 1 Chronicles 20, we were told how David took the crown of the enemy. This is what the Kingdom of God does on earth; to take over the control of affairs from the hand of the unbelieving folks. It is dethroning for enthronement. The enemies' kingdom is dethroned, the leadership authority of the Pharisees was dethroned in three days, and a new temple was raised instead. Our journey to spiritual purity is likened to the journey of the Israelites from the Land of Egypt into Canaan. First they had to cross the hurdles of the Red Sea, about 300km wide, which is the first stage of repenting and getting baptised. Then they were in the wilderness where they ought to learn and serve God. Then the river Jordan has to be crossed. In all these hurdles you need the servant of God who will lead you through, showing you the pillar of fire and of cloud, interceding for you, even when you already have the Holy Spirit, until you attain maturity and begin to separate other voices from the voice of God.

Exigencies and determination are the climax of human intellectual proliferation. People want to enjoy the life they see without restriction and want to commit all the energy in them to see that their desires are met. Yet we all live a life where we either hurt others or ourselves, knowingly or unknowingly. As we live daily we have in some ways tried to figure out why we aren't getting the kind of peace we expect and why it seems as though we are having misgivings.

The ninth verse of the first chapter of the gospel of John explained this mystery thus: *That was the true Light, which lighteth every man that cometh into the world.* This light is the glory of God, which was taken away from mankind as a result of sin (Romans 3:23). And so, all Jesus is doing is: *giving us this glory back so that we would become born again to have life - enter into life, and be born of water and spirit to have life more abundantly as we become as perfect as God* (John 3:3-6, John 17:14, John 10:10, Matthew 5:48). This process involves training and indoctrination so that our minds would become renewed and beating with the pulse of heaven in a three-fold process of *Justification, Sanctification and Consecration.* Jesus recruited His disciples, trained them for three years, spiritually empowered them and then sent them out to touch lives to the extent that He saw the devil fall down like lightning.

The light of God represents the wisdom of God and we know from elementary science that light comes from a power-generating source. So we would say that the light of God is the wisdom of God and the power that energises our inner consciousness to enable us see and appreciate God so that one by one, we all can start acting like God as though we are acting in a movie where we take up the role of replicating Godly characters wherever we go. This is the beauty of the Kingdom of God, which Christ prayed we should long for on earth, so that eventually, all the chaos of bitterness in our lives will give way to everlasting joy, and the triumph of victory over the plots of the devil in our lives.

The Kingdom of God is full of mysteries and we cannot afford to belong to a place of worship that is not a commission. We would end up like one gathering for the winds if we were not positioned in one of His commissioned kingdom on Earth. The way and manner we go about getting to our destination is what brings commendation or condemnation to us. Saint Paul confirms that he kept the faith – 2 Timothy 4:7. What do we labour for daily? Food, clothing, shelter, personal fame – and all self-aggrandizement pursuits? Are these worth dying for? When we visit any kingdom on earth and wish to stay and live there, the best place to visit is the king's palace, so that you will receive the protection of the king.

Why go to the palace?

- For recognition, so as to gain the king's favour.
- To learn the culture.
- To pay homage and show allegiance and support for the progress of the Kingdom.
- For the purpose of being abreast with historical facts as they concern the Kingdom.

In totality our discussion with the King explains how we can understand his heart, and we can only live and progress in the Kingdom when we abide by the laid-down rules of the Kingdom - in other words, when we are friends of the Kingdom. We cannot change the rules, we only need to abide and be changed to conform to the rules that exist.

This book has presented the fact that:

- The Kingdom of God exists in Heaven - Genesis 1, Matthew 6.

- This Kingdom has a culture which represents the will of the King.
- There is a manner of worship in the Kingdom – He demands that He be worshipped in truth and in spirit.
- He is a God of order sublimed in authority and leadership hierarchy.
- The Kingdom boasts of heavenly cuisines and delicacies – Psalm 78:25, Matthew 26:29.
- There is a way of dressing acceptable to the King - Angels wore linen – Revelation 15:6. The priests also dress in linen - Exodus 28:42. And we are Royal Priesthood; we should look even more royal and adorable.
- Jesus says that this same Kingdom has come to earth and we must become heirs of the Kingdom, on earth and in heaven. Are you in the Kingdom?

Shalom – Always!

EPILOGUE

COVENANT CONFESSION

If you are not born again, you may have read this book as literary material and will not receive the spirit it carries. You can make a decision to correct that now by saying this covenant confession: Lord Jesus, I know now that you died for my sins. I believe and confess you as my Lord and Saviour. Please come into my life and dwell inside of me. If you just said this confession, you should locate a spirit filled church to fellowship with them – let the pastor know you just gave your life to Christ and you will be directed on what to do next. Salvation is a personal race and you must be serious with it.

You can also call us through the numbers below: +234-8076190064, +234-8086737791 or send us an email at:

christmovementinternational@gmail.com

info@christmovementinternational.org

BOOKS BY THE SAME AUTHOR

1. Existing In The Supernatural
2. The Altar In Golgotha
3. How Good and Large is your Land?
4. Born To Blossom
5. Battles Beyond The Physical
6. The Path To Absolute Freedom
7. The Man God Made
8. Aspects of Marriage
9. Leadership – An Eagle-Eye Perspective
10. Gifted and Anointed
11. The Subject of Love – A Discourse
12. Mystery of the Kingdom of God on Earth

ABOUT THE AUTHOR

Pastor Oghenethoja Umuteme encountered God the day he was baptised at the St Stephen's Anglican Church, Owhelogbo Delta State, when he received a warm feeling in his heart as he confessed the Lord Jesus as His lord and personal saviour. His birth was surrounded with mysteries – he was born to a mother who had been barren for 8 years.

There was hardly anything he said that did not come to pass as he was growing. In 1994 he had a dream in which he received an orange which contained a bible with a red cover. Events continued dramatically until he started hearing voices telling him to go for rescue, as many souls were heading for destruction. Then it became clear to him that he was being called to carry out the task of restoring mankind back to Jesus.

In January 2006, he heard a voice telling him to read Isaiah 42. On reading to verse 6, he felt a deep force within him and started trembling and a voice said - 'I have called you'. As he read further he was getting immersed in the spirit of God and when he read verse 22, the voice said, 'this is your task'. Then on the 13th of October 2008, he heard a voice while driving:

'Service starts in your house on Sunday.' Events happened that were beyond his understanding and on Sunday 19th October 2008, the first public worship service came to pass.

Pastor Oghenethoja Umuteme is a prolific writer and oversees a leadership foundation, Umuteme Leadership Foundation, which he uses to teach good leadership and a School of Ministry to empower church leaders. A member of the Nigerian Society of Engineers, he has eleven years work experience in the oil and gas industry in different pipeline engineering functions – design, procurement, fabrication, construction, integrity management, maintenance and operation. A gospel musician with a recorded album, Breaking Through, he is also the Founder and Senior Pastor at Royal Diamonds International Church, Port Harcourt, Nigeria. He is an established teacher of the word of God and a prophet to the nation, as shown by his books. Using his crusade ministry – Giant Strides World Outreach Crusade - Pst. Oghenethoja reaches people with the undiluted word of salvation. And as a prophet to the nations, he has declared prophecies that have been fulfilled – the latest one being the famine that will visit the earth for ten years starting from the year 2017 and ending in 2027. He is also a man of miracles with testimonies said by those who have benefited from the gift of God in his life. As a motivational preacher, he has encouraged many to become successful in their chosen careers. The books God has used him to write has brought healing and encouraged many all over the world with testimonies. Many, including pastors, have also used these books as teaching and counselling materials. A time with him is a time filled with wisdom, joy and humour. He is often referred to as *'primus inter pares.'* His wife, Mrs. Umuteme Adokiye Obele, who supports him in this call of God upon his life, has borne him children.

BV - #0012 - 230326 - C0 - 210/148/29 - PB - 9781909874695 - Gloss Lamination